AUGENER'S EDITION, No. 9188.

APPLIED FORMS

A SEQUEL TO 'MUSICAL FORM'

BY

EBENEZER PROUT, B.A. (London)

Hon. Mus. Doc. Trin. Coll. Dublin and Edinburgh and
Professor of Music in the University of Dublin.

AMS PRESS
NEW YORK

Reprinted from the edition of 1895, London

First AMS EDITION published 1971

Manufactured in the United States of America

International Standard Book Number: 0-404-05138-3

Library of Congress Catalog Number: 71-155615

AMS PRESS INC.
NEW YORK, N.Y. 10003

PREFACE.

WITH the present volume the treatment of Musical Forms, begun in the preceding volume of this series, is completed. So many enquiries for the book have been addressed both to the author and to the publishers during the time of its preparation, that a few words of explanation seem due to readers, to account for the delay in its appearance.

In the preface to *Musical Form* it was said that that work had involved more labour than any of its predecessors. But the compilation of that volume proved to be mere child's play in comparison with the research necessary for the present one, which has required more than eighteen months' hard work to complete it. This has been the inevitable result of the system on which the author has worked. Though he has consulted numerous theoretical treatises, he has in no case taken either his statements or his illustrations at second hand; in every single instance he has gone direct to the works of the great masters, both for his rules and for his examples. What this involves may be judged from one or two illustrations. Before writing the three paragraphs on the Minuet (§§ 71–73), the author examined every minuet in the complete works of Handel, Bach, Couperin, Corelli, Mozart, Beethoven, and Schubert, the whole of Haydn's 83 Quartetts, all the symphonies (about fifty) which he possesses by the same composer, and a number of miscellaneous specimens by other writers. The result of all this work occupies less than three pages. Even more laborious were the preliminary investigations for the sonata form (Chapters VII. and VIII.). About 1,200 movements were carefully examined before a line of the text was written; and this task occupied the whole of the author's spare time for nearly a month. When it is added that every separate form has been dealt with on the same plan, it is hoped that no further apology for the tardy publication of the volume will be needed.

The greater part of the present work is devoted to the evolution of the larger forms from the two typical forms, the simple Binary and simple Ternary, treated of in the ninth and tenth chapters of *Musical Form.* In order to assist beginners in composition with practical hints on matters not often touched upon in theoretical treatises, the study of these forms is preceded by a chapter on Pianoforte Writing. Students, even though they may themselves play the piano well, often write uncomfortably or incorrectly for the instrument; and it is hoped that the directions here given will assist them in various points on which the author's experience has shown him that they are apt to go wrong.

As being the simplest, the Dance Forms (Chapter III.) are the first dealt with. It has been impossible to describe all the existing varieties; it would, besides, have been of little practical utility. But all the more important dances to be met with either in older Suites, or in the compositions of the great masters, are treated of, and the student who understands these will have little difficulty with the analysis of others. The smaller instrumental forms, nearly all of which are simple binary or ternary, and the different variation forms occupy Chapters IV. and V.

In treating of the older Rondo form (Chapter VI.) the author found himself upon more debateable ground. Here the various theorists differ widely; in fact, hardly two are in complete agreement. Instead, therefore, of following any preceding writer, the author thought it best to try to evolve some system for himself by the study of the best models. The plan here adopted will probably not commend itself to all readers; but it is at least a logical carrying out of the general principles laid down in *Musical Form.* By regarding the older Rondo as an extension of the ternary form, in precisely the same manner in which that form is an extension of the binary, a clear line of demarcation between the two is established, and the analysis becomes simplified.

The Sonata Form, the most important, and in some respects the most perfect of the instrumental forms, fills the two following chapters. Many writers consider this form to be binary; and this view was long held and taught by the author himself. Closer investigation, however, convinced him that it was more accurate to regard this form as ternary; the reasons for adopting this view are given in the seventh chapter of this volume. The term "second subject" is employed in a larger sense than that generally given to it, because the form of the movement thus becomes much easier to analyze than if such expressions as "auxiliary," "subsidiary," &c., are employed. In treating of the 'Free

Fantasia' it has been found impossible to give more than general directions to the composer, because of the infinite variety to be met with in this part of the movement. It is hoped that the examples selected and analyzed will sufficiently show the principles underlying thematic development in general. The recapitulation of a sonata movement has been dealt with at some length, because there is far more irregularity to be found here than is generally supposed. The various modifications of Sonata form, including the modern Rondo, naturally occupy the next place in the volume.

The student is often much troubled in his attempts at analysis by meeting with movements which he is unable to explain as belonging to any of the categories described in the earlier chapters of this volume. An effort to assist him is made in Chapter XI. The mixed and irregular forms there spoken of are so Protean in their disguises that any attempt at classification was more than ordinarily difficult. The author dares not flatter himself that he has exhausted the subject. All that has been possible for him here has been to select and analyze some representative examples. The student who is thoroughly familiar with the normal forms will soon learn to recognize the variations when he meets with them, and must try to do for himself with other movements what is done for him here with those selected for analysis.

After dealing with the separate forms of the different movements, their combination into larger works naturally follows as the next step. This subject is treated in the chapter on Cyclic Forms. A chapter on Organ Music, in which some practical directions are given as to writing for the 'king of instruments,' concludes the portion of the volume which deals with instrumental music.

It was the author's original intention to have treated vocal music at much greater length than he has done in the final chapter. His first idea has been modified, partly because the instrumental forms had required much more space than he had expected, but chiefly because, on going carefully into the subject, he found that such a method of treatment as he at first designed would have necessitated writing a complete history of the rise and progress of vocal music. This would not only have increased the size of the volume inordinately, but it would have been beyond the scope of the present series, which is intended to be educational rather than historical. The vocal forms differ from the instrumental chiefly in their greater freedom, resulting from their association with words. It is hoped that enough has been said to guide the student in his examination of the works of the great masters for himself.

It cannot be too strongly impressed upon the learner that mastery of form cannot be acquired merely by reading this or any other book. A thorough knowledge of it can only be obtained by carefully studying and analyzing the works of the great composers. It is in this way that the author has learned whatever he knows about the subject; and just as the works of other theorists have been of use to him in showing him what to look for, he hopes that the present volume may assist students in investigating for themselves the glorious heritage bequeathed to us by the immortal masters of the past and present centuries. Without a knowledge of their principal compositions no musician can be said to be fully equipped for his work.

Though, as already said, nothing in the present volume has been taken at second hand, it would be disingenuous of the author not to acknowledge the help he has obtained in preparing this book from the labours of others who have preceded him. He would especially mention Dr. Marx's 'Composition,' Dr. Hugo Riemann's 'Katechismus der Kompositionslehre,' and the numerous admirable articles by Dr. Hubert Parry in Grove's 'Dictionary of Music,' as having been of great service to him.

As on so many previous occasions, the author has again to acknowledge the kind assistance he has received from his friend Dr. C. W. Pearce in the correction of the proofs. He has also to thank his friend and colleague, Professor Mahaffy, of Trinity College, Dublin, for many valuable suggestions.

The present volume will be followed, should the author's life and health be spared, by two volumes on the Orchestra, which will complete the series commenced six years ago with *Harmony: Its Theory and Practice.*

LONDON, *January*, 1895.

TABLE OF CONTENTS.

[*N. B.—The numbers refer in every instance to the* sections, *not to the pages.*]

CHAPTER I.—Introduction ... . *page* 1

Summary of preceding volume, 1, 2—The evolution of music, 3—Abstract music rarely to be met with, 4—The form of music influenced by the medium through which it is presented, 5—*Applied Form* defined, 6—Difference between vocal and instrumental music, 7—Two classes of instruments: polyphonous and monophonous, 8—Different kinds of vocal music, 9—Plan of the present volume, 10, 11—The best masters in composition, 12.

CHAPTER II.—Pianoforte Writing ... ... *page* 5

Considerations to be borne in mind when writing for the piano, 13—The piano the most useful instrument for the composer, 14—Its inherent defects, 15—Uniformity of tone-quality, 16—Its natural shortcomings stimulate the imagination, 17—Interlacing of the two hands, 18—Example by Liszt, 19—Sustained melodies best in the medium of the instrument, 20—The pedal, 21—Explanation of its mechanism, 22, 23—Increases the volume of tone, 24—"Sympathetic resonance," 25, 26—The principal use of the pedal; example by Schumann, 27—Repetition of melody notes as accompaniment, 28—The pedal used to obtain wider positions of harmony, 29—The soft (*una corda*) pedal, 30—Position of the harmonies in writing for the piano, 31—Variation in number of parts, 32—Number of voices in polyphonic music for the piano, 33—Passages in only two or three parts, 34—Treatment of broken chords and arpeggios, 35—Relaxation of the strict laws of part-writing, 36–38—Dissonances in arpeggios should be resolved in the octave in which they are taken, 39—Treatment of isolated low notes in the bass, 40—The technique of the piano must be considered while writing for it, 41—Composing at the piano, 42.

CHAPTER III.—The Dance Forms ... ... *page* 23

Why dance forms are studied first, 43—Difference between dance music and dance forms, 44—The old Suite, 46—Its indispensable movements, 47—All the movements were in binary form, 48—The *Allemande*, 49–51—The *Courante*, 52–55—The *Sarabande*, 56–59—The 'Double,' 58—The *Gigue*, 60–63—The *Gavotte*, 64–67—The *Passepied*, 68—Explanation of the term 'Trio,' 69—The *Bourrée*, 70—The *Minuet*, 71—Minuets with more than one Trio, 72—The modern Minuet, 73—The *Scherzo*, a development of the Minuet, 74—Innovations introduced by Beethoven, 75—Scherzos with two trios, 76—The ternary form abandoned, 77—The *Waltz*, 78–81—The modern 'Valse de Salon'; Chopin's Waltzes, 82—'Sets' of Waltzes, 83—The *Mazurka*, 84, 85—The *Polonaise*, or *Polacca*, 86—Example by Bach, 87—Ditto by Schubert, 88—The *Marche aux Flambeaux*, 89—The *Bolero*, 90, 91—The *Tarantella*, 92—The *March*, 93—March forms, 94-96—Rate of speed, 97—Example by Beethoven, 98—Modern Suites, 99—Directions for work, 100.

CHAPTER IV.—THE SMALLER INSTRUMENTAL FORMS ... *page* 63

The smaller forms mostly simple binary or simple ternary, 101—Pieces written for children, 102—The forms of Beethoven's Bagatelles, Op. 33, 103—Ditto of the first book of Mendelssohn's 'Lieder ohne Worte,' 104—Ditto of Schumann's 'Phantasiestücke,' 105—Modern pianoforte music, 106—The *Etude*, 107—Cramer's 'Studio:' harmonic framework of the fourth study, 108—Example of an Etude by Steibelt, 109—Ditto by Henselt, 110—The larger form of Etude: the studies of Chopin, Henselt, Heller, and Clementi, 111—The *Prelude*, 112—Its simplest form, 113—Example by Handel, 114—A Prelude in the form of an Etude, 115, 116—Preludes in the larger binary form, 117—Bach's organ preludes; the preludes founded on chorals, 118—Larger organ preludes, 119—Analysis of Bach's Prelude in F minor, 120–123—The largest forms, 124—Use of the fugato in a prelude, 125—The preludes of Beethoven, Mendelssohn, and Chopin, 126—The *Fugue*, 127—Outline of its form, 128, 129—The fugue form a modification of simple ternary, 130–133—Directions for work, 135.

CHAPTER V.—THE VARIATION FORMS ... ... *page* 85

Incidental variation, 136—Variation defined, 137—The *Ground Bass;* example by Purcell, 138—The *Chaconne*, 139, 140—The *Passacaglia*, 141—Beethoven's '32 Variations' a modern Chaconne, 142—The *Air with Variations*, 143—Form of the theme, 144—Its character, 145—Longer themes, 146—Strict and free variations, 147—The older and the newer style, 148—Strict variations, 149—Analysis of Mozart's Variations on "Je suis Lindor," 150–153—Other variations by Mozart, 154—Beethoven's variations, 155—Analysis of the 'Six Variations,' Op. 34, 156–162—Beethoven's later variations, 163—The variations of Schubert, Weber, and Mendelssohn, 164—The modern style of variation, 165—Rhythm of the variations, 166—Canonic variation, 167—*Double Variations*, 168—Variation on two themes, 169, 170—Variations in vocal music, 171—The Introduction, 172—General summary of principles, 173-176—The diversity of variation forms, 177.

CHAPTER VI.—THE OLDER RONDO FORM ... ... *page* 107

The larger forms, 178—The *Rondo:* meaning of the name, 179—Two kinds of Rondo, 180—Example by Couperin, 181—Analysis of the same, 182 Number of episodes, 183—Their key, 184—Rondo by Bach analyzed, 185, 186—The rondos of Haydn, &c., 187—Their development from the ternary form, 188—Minuets in rondo form, 189—Choice of keys for the episodes, 190, 191—Rondo by Haydn analyzed, 192–195—Analysis of Dussek's 'La Consolation,' 196, 197—Ditto of Mozart's Rondo in A minor,

199, 200—Beethoven's Andante in F, 201—Analysis of Beethoven's Rondo in C, Op. 51, No. 1, 202, 203—Ditto of rondo in Sonata, Op. 53, 204—Other examples, 205—Rondos with three episodes, 206—The principal subject only one sentence; example by Mozart, 207—Analysis of rondo from Mozart's trio in E flat, 208, 209—Irregular rondos; example by Beethoven, 210—The double variation sometimes a rondo, 211—Some pieces incorrectly described as rondos, 212—Directions to the student, 213.

CHAPTER VII.—THE SONATA FORM: THE EXPOSITION ... *page* 127

Definition of the *Sonata Form*, 214—It is found in other works besides sonatas, 215—The essential difference between a Rondo and a movement in Sonata form, 216—The old Sonata form: example by Scarlatti analyzed, 217—The "bridge-passage," 218—How to find the limits of the second subject, 219—The second part of the movement, 220—Modifications of detail, 221—Later examples of the old form, 222—The modern form developed by C. P. E. Bach, 223—Difference between the old and the modern Sonata forms, 224—The *Exposition* of a sonata movement; the first subject: example by Beethoven, 225—Ditto by Haydn, 226—Ditto by Schumann, 227—Ditto by Mozart, ending with a half cadence, 228—Ditto by Beethoven, 229—Its rhythmic construction explained, 230—Long first subjects, 231—Subjects with a preface, 232—The bridge-passage; how to know where it begins, 233—Example by Mozart, 234–236—Material of the bridge-passage: its course of modulation, 237—Very short bridge-passages, 238—The *second subject*, 239—Key of the second subject; the old rule, 240—Beethoven's innovations, 241—Second subject in the mediant, major and minor, 242—Ditto in the submediant, 243—Key of the second subject in a minor movement, 244—The practice of Beethoven, 245—Second subject in the dominant *major*, 246—Second subject in flat keys, 247—The "sections" of the second subject, 248—A second subject indivisible into sections, 249—Analysis of movement by Haydn, 250–252—Ditto of exposition of 'Eroica' symphony, 253—Many sections in the same key, 254—The second subject of a minor movement in two keys, 255—The first section in a different key from the following, 256—Change of *mode*, 257—Change of tonic, 258—Example by Beethoven (Op. 10 No. 3) analyzed, 259—Incidental modulation, 260—Unity of style, how obtained, 261—The second subject beginning in a remote key; examples, 262—This procedure peculiar to major movements, 263—An unusual close, 264—Determination of the limits of the second subject, 265—The *codetta*, 266—Repetition of the exposition, not obligatory, 267—Summary of the chapter, 268–274.

CHAPTER VIII.—THE SONATA FORM (*continued*): THE DEVELOPMENT, AND RECAPITULATION ... ... *page* 158

Freedom of the form in the second and third parts of a sonata movement, 275—The *Free Fantasia*, 276—How it differs from the second part of a genuine ternary form, 277—The free fantasia the test of a composer's genius; supremacy of Beethoven, 278—Analysis of free fantasia of his sonata, Op. 7, 279–281—Ditto of Haydn's symphony in G, 282–285—Thematic development, 286—The free fantasia in Beethoven's Pastoral Symphony, 287–290—Fragments of themes worked separately; example from Beethoven's Waldstein sonata, 291—Contrapuntal development, 292—Introduction of episode, 293—Examples, 294–297—A slow introduction brought in again during free fantasia, 298—Example by Clementi, 299—An episodical andante, 300—General principles for the construction of the free fantasia, 301—Choice of keys—302, 303—Course of modulation, 304, 305—Methods of thematic development, 306—Episode, 307—The return to the first subject, 308—Examples, 309-312—The *Recapitulation*, 313—The regular form, 314—The first subject; often with new counterpoint, 315—The Bridge-Passage, 316—Omission of the bridge-passage, 317—Key of the second subject, 318, 319—The second subject in more than one key, 320, 321—Treatment of the second subject in a minor movement, 322-326—Irregular recapitulations, 327—The first subject in the subdominant, 328—The second subject preceding the first, 329—Abridgment or omission of first subject, 330—Extension of first subject, 331—A first subject beginning in a different key from that in which it ends, 332—Abridgment of the second subject, 333—The second subject considerably altered, 334, 335—Exceptional key for second subject, 336—The entire recapitulation of a minor movement in the tonic major key, 337—Very irregular recapitulation, 338—The *Coda*, 339—Example by Beethoven, 340—New themes introduced in the coda, 341, 342—Alteration of tempo, 343—The infinite variety of the sonata form, 344.

CHAPTER IX.—MODIFIED SONATA FORMS ... ... *page* 195

Modified sonata forms defined, 345—*The Abridged Sonata Form*, 346—How it differs from the old sonata form, 347—Adagio from Beethoven's sonata, Op. 10 No. 1, analyzed, 348-353—Analysis of slow movement from Beethoven's sonata in D minor, 354—Ditto from Mozart's sonata in F, 355, 356—Mendelssohn's Presto Agitato in B minor, 357, 358—The exposition in this form never repeated, 359—The *Overture*, 360—Its old form, 361—The overture in sonata form, 362—The overtures of Mozart and Beethoven, 363-365—A slow introduction common, 366—Overtures by Weber, Spohr, and Mendelssohn, 367—Exceptional repeat of the exposition, 368—Modern opera overtures, 369—The *Concerto:* meanings of the word, 370—Form adopted by Mozart and Beethoven for the first movement; the double exposition, 371—The difference between the two expositions, 372—The second exposition often longer than the first, 373—Mozart's practice in this respect, 374, 375—Beethoven's method, 376—The second exposition more ornamented, 377—The first exposition ending on the dominant, 378—Entry of the solo instrument, 379—The second and third parts of the movement, 380—The Cadenza, 381—The modern concerto form introduced by Mendelssohn, 382—The *Sonatina*, 383—Example by Kuhlau analyzed, 384—Vague use of the name, 385, 386.

CHAPTER X.—THE MODERN RONDO (RONDO-SONATA) FORM *page* 212

The later Rondo form a modification of the Sonata, 387—The rhythmic form of the first subject, 388—Its song-like character, 389—The exposition, 390—Difference between second subject and episode, 391—Key of second subject, 392—Repetition of first subject at close of exposition, 393—Episode, 394—Recapitulation, 395—General summary of the form, 396—Analysis of rondo in Beethoven's sonata, Op. 14, No. 1, 397-399—Ditto in Beethoven's sonata, Op. 22, 400-402—Rondos without episode, 403—Analysis of Schubert's Rondo, Op. 107, 404-408—An irregular rondo analyzed, 409-410—This form always employed either as a separate movement or as a finale, 411.

CHAPTER XI.—MIXED AND INDEFINITE FORMS ... ... *page* 227

What are meant by mixed and indefinite forms, 412—MIXED FORMS, 413—Analysis of finale of Weber's sonata in D minor, 414, 415—Ditto of andante from same sonata, 416—Example from Mozart's sonata in D, 417, 418—Ditto from Beethoven's sonata, Op. 2, No. 1, 419—Other examples by Beethoven, 420–422—Schubert's Impromptu in F minor analyzed, 423, 424—Finale of Schubert's quintett, Op. 114, 425, 426—INDEFINITE FORMS, 427—The *Introduction*, 428, 429—The *Toccata*, 430, 431—The *Capriccio*, 432, 433—The *Intermezzo*, 434, 435—The *Fantasia*, 436—Fantasias in one movement, 437—The subjects in a fantasia recurring, 438—Fantasias with detached movements, 439—The *Sonata quasi Fantasia*, 440—Operatic fantasias and transcriptions, 441.

CHAPTER XII.—CYCLIC FORMS ... ... *page* 242

Definition of *Cyclic Form*, 442—The process of evolution, 443—The typical cyclic form, and its variations, 444—Unity of character, 445—The most important modern cyclic form developed from the Suite, 446—The three-movement form, 447—Usual order of movements, 448—All the movements in the same key, 449—Choice of key for the middle movement, 450–452—The slow movement in a key in the second degree of relationship, 453—Ditto in an unrelated key, 454—The slow movements of works in a minor key, 455–456—The *form* of the second movement, 457—The second movement in quick tempo, 458—Form of the finale, 459—Irregular arrangement of movements, 460, 461—The two-movement form, 462—Contrast in the movements, 463—The four-movement form, 464—General plan of the movements, 465—The order of the middle movements optional, 466—Four-movement works without a slow movement, 467—Deviations from the normal form, 468, 469—Different methods of obtaining unity, 470–472—Cyclic works in more than four movements, 473—The modern Suite, 474—Quartetts in five movements, 475—The *Serenade*, 476—The *Cassation* and *Divertimento*, 477—The *Concerto*: its regular form, 478—Concertos in four movements, 479—Irregular forms: Bruch's violin concertos, 480—Saint-Saëns' piano concertos, 481, 482—Liszt's concertos, 483—The *Symphonic Poem*, 484, 485.

CHAPTER XIII.—ORGAN MUSIC ... ... *page* 258

Some knowledge of the instrument desirable, 486—The manuals, 487—The registers, 488—Eight-feet stops, 489—Foundation stops, 490, 491—Mutation stops, 492—Compound stops, 493—Flue-stops and reed-stops, 494—Differences of quality, 495—The pedal organ, 496—Passages for the pedals, 497—Organ music generally written on three staves, 498—Combination of different manuals, 499—Sustaining power of the organ: *legato* and *staccato*, 500—The expressionless character of the instrument, 501—Pedal points, 502—Varieties of organ tone, 503—Directions for registering, 504—Alterations of tone quality, 505—Use of the pedals, 506—The melody on the pedals, 507—Polyphonic writing, 508—The forms of organ music, 509—Bach's organ sonatas, 510—Mendelssohn's organ sonatas, 511—The sonata form in organ sonatas, 512—Variety of the movements, 513—Widor's organ symphonies, 514—Smaller forms of organ music, 515—Duets for the organ, 516—The tone style of composition for the organ, 517.

CHAPTER XIV.—VOCAL MUSIC ... ... *page* 272

Writing for voices, 518—Association of music with words, 519—The accents of words and music must correspond, 520—Care in selection of words, 521—Position of cadences, 522—Example of faulty accents, by Handel, 523—Compass of the voices, 524, 525—The "registers," 526—Ineffective example, by Schumann, 527—Use of the upper notes of the voice, 528, 529—Unvocal writing, 530—Examples, 531, 532—Cross accents, 533—Vocal music without words: Solfeggi, 534—'Bouche fermée,' 535—Vocal forms: *Recitative*, 536—*Recitativo a tempo*, 537—Examples referred to, 538—Choral Recitative, 539—The *Strophic Song*, 540—The "durch-componirtes Lied," 541—Songs in ternary form, 542—Ditto in the older rondo form, 543. 544—Ditto in sonata form, 545—Songs with more than one movement: The *Scena*, 546–548—The accompaniments of songs, 549—Pieces for more than one solo voice: the vocal canon, 550—The *Glee*: the male alto voice, 551, 552—The *Part Song*, 553—The *Madrigal*, 554—The *Motett*, 555—The *Anthem*, 556—Ditto with orchestral accompaniment, 557—The *Church Cantata*, 558—The *Church Service*, 559—Fugal writing for voices, 560—Examples of good subjects, 561—The *Mass*, 562—The largest vocal works: Cantata, Oratorio, Opera, 563, 564—The indefiniteness of the larger vocal forms, 565.

APPLIED FORMS.

CHAPTER I.

INTRODUCTION.

1. In the preceding volume of this series, bearing the title of *Musical Form*, we treated the question of the gradual development of musical compositions from their simplest elements. It was seen in that volume how everything springs ultimately from the embryo, or germ, which we name the *motive.* We saw how by the combination of two motives we obtain a section, how two sections form a phrase, and how a second phrase added to a first makes a sentence, or period (*Musical Form*, Chapters II., III.). It was also shown that the four-bar phrase and the eight-bar sentence constituted the normal form, and that all sentences and phrases of any other length were not new and distinct forms, but merely variations of the normal form, of which we have just spoken.

2. Proceeding a little further, we showed that, by carrying on this process of building up, we obtained by the combination of two sentences the simplest of all complete forms—that known as the Binary Form. It was seen how the binary form could be expanded and modified in various ways without losing its essential characteristics. By adding an episode to an already complete binary form, and then repeating the first part of the movement, either entirely or partially, we obtained the Ternary Form—the only other typical form ; and in concluding the volume it was said that all the larger forms, which still remain to be noticed, were developed from one or the other of these two typical forms, the Binary and Ternary.

3. We have briefly summarized in these few words the contents of our last volume, in order to impress strongly upon the student a point which we have several times had occasion to mention—that all music is an *organic growth*, and that the binary and ternary forms are developed from the simplest motives by as natural a process of evolution as that by which an oak grows out of an acorn. When, later in the present volume, we deal with the

largest and most perfect of the forms, such as the Sonata form, we shall find the same process still carried on, though composers themselves may be often but imperfectly conscious of it. It is this development from simple motives, often by a process which might be compared to spontaneous generation, which gives unity of structure to the fugues of Bach and the symphonies of Beethoven.

4. Hitherto we have treated merely of form in the *abstract*. It is true that our illustrations have been taken from works of all kinds, vocal and instrumental; but in our analyses we have not concerned ourselves with the differences of structure resulting from the nature of the instruments, whether organ, pianoforte, orchestra, or vocal organs, which were the media employed by the composer for the presentation of his ideas. But, as a matter of fact, purely abstract music is very seldom to be met with. We see it in the examples of chord-progression, &c., to be found in theoretical treatises; but we can only point to one work in standard musical literature that may be truly considered to be abstract music. This is Bach's "Art of Fugue." Though in the best-known edition (that of Czerny) it appears as pianoforte music, it was not (excepting the two fugues for two claviers) written as such by the composer. This is seen very clearly from the fact that in the autograph all the fugues are written in open score—a procedure which Bach never adopted with his pianoforte or organ fugues—and that it contains passages which cannot possibly be played as they are written, by two hands.

5. When a composer sits down to write a piece of music, its form will be to a greater or less extent influenced by the nature of the instruments for which he is writing. For example, many passages which are perfectly easy for the piano are either difficult or impossible for the violin, and *vice versâ;* while in composing vocal music it is necessary to take into account the compass and capabilities of the voice or voices written for. As an illustration of what has just been said, let the student compare the solo part of Beethoven's violin concerto with the arrangement of the same work by its composer as a pianoforte concerto, and notice what important alterations are made in order to adapt the music to the technique of the keyed instrument. We do not mean to say that the *abstract form* of the work is changed; the sentences and phrases have the same number of bars as before, but very considerable modification is made in the details of the composition.

6. As distinguished from the abstract form treated of in our last volume, form considered in its relation to the medium through which it is presented to the hearer is called Applied Form and it is this with which we have now to deal. The same term is also used to describe the larger forms of instrumental and vocal music, which are developed out of the two typical forms,

the Binary and the Ternary, with which the student is already acquainted.

7. Music is broadly divided into two kinds—instrumental and vocal; and there is a very great difference in the treatment of the two. This will be seen at once, if we remind the student that, while all the notes of vocal music can be played on an instrument such as the piano, by far the greatest part of instrumental music cannot possibly be sung. This distinction, it should be added, is comparatively modern; instrumental music is of much more recent origin than vocal; and the first edition of some of the old madrigals describes the music as "apt for voices or viols."

8. Musical instruments may further be divided into two classes—those which are capable of producing complete harmony by themselves, and those which can only produce one note at a time. To the former class belong all keyed instruments, such as the piano, with its various precursors (harpsichord, clavichord, &c.), the organ, and the harmonium. In the latter class are included all wind instruments. The stringed instruments can, it is true, produce more than one note at a time; but it is impossible to obtain from them continuous full harmony, as from a piano or organ; we therefore include them in the second class. The first of these two classes we will call *polyphonous* instruments; the second, *monophonous* instruments. The harp, though really a polyphonous instrument, is seldom employed, except in the orchestra. The whole question of orchestral composition will be dealt with in later volumes of this series; the only instrumental music of which we shall treat in the present work will be that written for such polyphonous instruments as the piano and organ.

9. Vocal music also may be divided into that which is written for one voice, and that written for more than one. In the former case it is evident that, in order to obtain any complete harmonic effects, the music must have an accompaniment of one or more instruments. By far the most common accompaniment for a vocal solo is that of the piano; though examples are also to be met with of songs accompanied by the organ, harp, or guitar. Music written for more than one voice may be either accompanied or unaccompanied.

10. As a large part of the present volume will be devoted to the examination of music written for the pianoforte, it will be advisable in the first place to give the student some practical hints as to writing effectively for that instrument. We shall then speak in detail of the various forms of pianoforte music, beginning with the smallest. Some of these have been already met with in the last volume; others will be new to us. From the smaller forms, which will be found to be mostly either simple binary or simple ternary, we shall proceed to the larger forms, Rondo, Sonata, &c. We shall find that these are either extensions or modifications of the ternary form. Our study of instrumental

forms will be completed by some notice of the organ and organ music.

11. In treating of vocal music, it will be needful to give some explanation of the mechanism of the voice itself, and to follow this by an examination of the relation of words to music—a point on which the most serious mistakes are often made by students. The principal forms of unaccompanied and accompanied vocal music will then be spoken of, treating in the latter case only of music accompanied by the piano or organ.

12. It will be seen that the field of research covered by the present volume is very large; it embraces, in fact, the entire range of music, both vocal and instrumental; for the forms of orchestral compositions and of chamber music (that is, music written for two or more solo instruments) are in all essentials identical with the forms of pianoforte music. When, later, we come to speak of the orchestra, we shall not have to concern ourselves at all with the form of the music, but only with the means by which it is presented. Those who carefully study this and the preceding volume of the series will, it is hoped, know enough of the subject of musical form to need no further instruction than such as they can obtain for themselves by the examination of the works of the great masters. If these works are seriously approached with the requisite preliminary knowledge, more can be learned from them than from all the theoretical works that were ever written. Without in the least undervaluing the great services rendered to the cause of musical education by such distinguished theorists as Marx, Hauptmann, Lobe, or Dr. Riemann, we say unhesitatingly that the best masters in composition are Bach, Mozart, Beethoven, and the other immortal composers, who have brought our art to its present state of advancement. From the student's point of view, no text-books in the world can ever be so beneficial as a thorough study of the masterpiece of musical literature.

CHAPTER II.

PIANOFORTE WRITING.

13. It may be fairly assumed that every student who attempts composition will have at least some acquaintance with the pianoforte. We have no intention, therefore, in the present chapter of writing anything in the nature of a pianoforte school, or of saying anything about the *technique* of the instrument, in the sense in which that word is generally understood, as applying to fingering, touch, &c. There are, however, some general principles concerning the method of writing for the piano, and certain important considerations which the student should bear in mind; and it is of these that we are now about to speak.

14. If a musician has a practical acquaintance with one instrument only, there can be no question that the piano is the most useful one for him to know. It has the largest compass of any keyed instrument;* it is capable of executing any kind of passages that lie within the reach of two, or (in the case of a duet) of four hands; and music written for any other instrument, or combination of instruments, can be reproduced upon it, at least approximately, by being suitably transcribed. For these reasons it is most desirable that every student should have some knowledge of the piano.

15. On the other hand, there are certain shortcomings, inherent to the nature of the instrument, which the composer has carefully to take into account in writing for it. Foremost among these is the inability to sustain a sound of uniform strength. As soon as a note has been struck on the piano, the amplitude of vibration, and therefore the tone, of the sounding string begins to diminish. It is true that our modern grand pianos possess far more sustaining power than the instruments of the last century; but even with ours, the diminution of the tone very soon becomes perceptible. A *crescendo* on a holding note is of course absolutely impossible. It should be added that the sustaining power becomes continually less as we ascend to the higher part of the compass of the instrument.

16. Another point to be noticed with regard to the piano is, that its tone is almost uniform in quality throughout its entire compass. When we come to treat of orchestral instruments, it

* Of course it is possible on a large organ to obtain both higher and lower notes by means of 32-ft. and 2-ft. stops; but such cannot be used alone; and, in the ordinary sense of the words, the statement in the text is correct.

will be seen that their quality varies considerably in their different registers—grave, medium, and acute; in singers also there is a difference between the chest-voice and the head-voice. But on the piano, except with the extremely low bass notes, there is hardly any difference in quality, though, as said in the last section, the sustaining power varies in different parts of the instrument.

17. Dr. Marx, in his admirable "Kompositionslehre," has called attention to the fact that the very shortcomings of the piano to which we have just alluded are, from one point of view, an advantage to the musician. He says that there is no instrument which so readily calls upon the imagination and fancy, both of performer and hearer, to supply its natural defects. If, for instance, we play a slow and sustained melody, or succession of harmonies, we know that, as a matter of fact, there will be a *diminuendo* upon every note. But the mind carries on the preceding chord to the next one, as if it were sustained at a uniform strength. As an example, let anyone play the following passage from Schumann's "Humoreske":—

SCHUMANN: Humoreske, Op. 20.

The effect produced by this passage is to all intents the same as if it were played on the organ. Though there is a perceptible decrease of tone on each chord, the mind is hardly conscious of this, and the imagination supplies what is wanting, and carries on the sound of each chord undiminished to the next one.

18. The passage just quoted illustrates another point of pianoforte writing which may here be touched upon. It will be seen that the hands are here, so to speak, interlaced—the thumb of the left hand striking a higher note than the thumb of the right. Had facility of performance been the only point regarded, Schumann would have written the passage thus :—

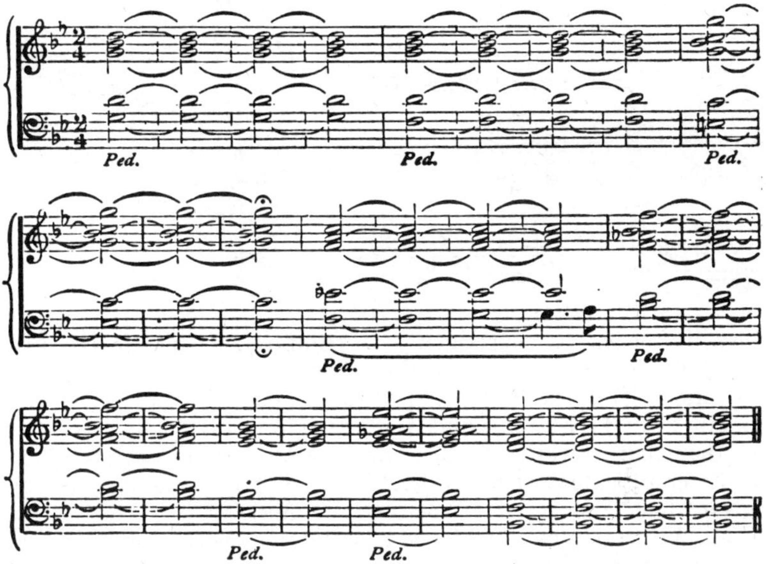

This would not only have been much easier, but it would have allowed the real bass of the harmony, which Schumann has written in small notes, to be sustained by the hand, instead of by the pedal. But if the student will play both the passages, he will find that the effect of the two is quite different. The composer's object here was to give a certain prominence to the melody in the middle voice :—

(We have reduced the length of the notes by one-half, and written in $\frac{4}{4}$ time, to show the melody more clearly.) This secondary melody produces here an effect somewhat analogous to that which it would have if given on the high notes of the violoncellos in the orchestra; and to obtain this, Schumann employs a somewhat constrained position of the left hand, which almost forces the player to bring out strongly the notes played by the thumb.

19. This effect of the interlacing of the two hands has been often employed by modern writers for the piano, and by none with more skill than by Liszt, the greatest pioneer in the domain of pianoforte technique that the world has yet seen. An extract from his transcription for pianoforte solo of Beethoven's symphony in C minor will illustrate this point.

LISZT: Transcription of Beethoven's Symphony in C minor.

Here, in order to reproduce the composer's idea, it is most important to mark strongly the *sforzando* on the single notes (D♯ and G♯) on the third beat of each alternate bar; and if the student will try it, he will find it impossible to do this in any other way than that in which it is here arranged. No rules can be given for the employment of such effects as these; the composer's feeling for what he requires will be the only guide.

20. We spoke in § 17 of the hearer's imagination helping him to supply the defects of the instrument in regard to sustaining power. In the upper part of its scale this deficiency is especially perceptible; it is generally, therefore, advisable not to write a *cantabile* melody at a high pitch. This can be sometimes done, as in the following passage by Beethoven :—

BEETHOVEN: Bagatelle, Op. 119, No. 11.

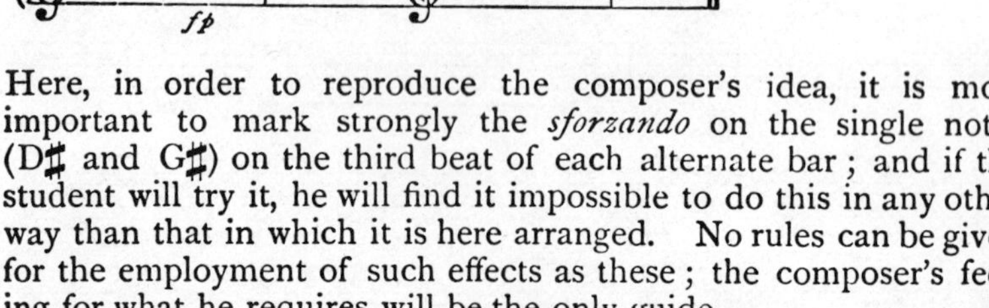

Here, as in the passage by Schumann quoted in § 17, we are not really conscious of the decrease of tone on the long holding notes, because the mind carries each one on till the following note of the melody is sounded. In the majority of cases, however, it is best to give such passages to the medium part of the instrument. Let the student examine Mendelssohn's "Lieder ohne Worte," and he will find that, with hardly an exception, the melodies are placed in that part of the instrument which has the most singing power.

21. The sustaining power of the piano is considerably increased by the correct use of the *pedal.* It would be hardly needful to refer to the proper function of the pedal, were it not for the common experience of pianoforte teachers, that when students see the pedal marked in a *piano* passage, they often take it to indicate the use of the soft (*una corda*) pedal (§ 30). This misapprehension probably arises from the fact that the right pedal (properly the "damper pedal") is so often spoken of as the "loud pedal." It is perfectly true that by putting down this pedal the tone (as we shall show directly) is increased; but this is not its principal function. A clear understanding of its correct employment is most important to anyone who wishes to write well for the piano.

22. Anyone who has even an elementary knowledge of the mechanism of the piano is aware that against each of the notes, produced by two or three strings in unison, is placed a piece of felt called a "damper." So long as the damper is pressing against the strings, they are unable to vibrate. When a key is pressed down, a hammer strikes the strings opposite to that key; the same movement lifts the damper off those strings, and allows them to vibrate while the key remains down. As soon as the finger leaves the key, the damper is released and falls back upon the string, stopping its vibration. If there were no dampers, each note would continue to sound after the finger had left the key, until the vibrations died away of themselves.

23. When the pedal is pressed down by the foot—and here let it be distinctly understood, that when the word "pedal" is used without qualification the damper-pedal is *always* meant—the dampers are lifted from the whole of the strings simultaneously. The result of this is, that now, when the finger quits a key, the damper, being held off by the pedal, does not fall back on the string; consequently the note that has been struck continues to sound as if the finger were still holding it down. Of this the student can convince himself by putting down the pedal and striking a chord *staccato.* The chord will be sustained until he releases the dampers by raising his foot from the pedal.

24. Now let him try another simple experiment. Let him, without putting down the pedal, strike a single note, for instance, the C below the treble staff, with moderate force. Then let him put the pedal down, and strike the same note again, with as nearly as possible the same strength as before. He will notice a perceptible increase in the volume of tone. This is because other strings of the piano, which are free to vibrate now that the dampers

are not pressing against them, are set in vibration by the phenomenon known as "sympathetic resonance."

25. For a full explanation of this phenomenon we must refer our readers to Chapter III. of Helmholtz's "Sensations of Tone," and content ourselves here with quoting his general definition :—

"This phenomenon is always found in those bodies which when once set in motion by any impulse, continue to perform a long series of vibrations before they come to rest. When these bodies are struck gently, but periodically, although each blow may be separately quite insufficient to produce a sensible motion in the vibratory body, yet provided the periodic time of the gentle blows is precisely the same as the periodic time of the body's own vibrations, very large and powerful oscillations may result. But if the periodic time of the regular blows is different from the periodic time of the oscillations, the resulting motion will be weak or quite insensible." (*Sensations of Tone*, p. 56.)

26. This law applies to the case we are now discussing ; the sound of the middle C struck by the finger sets in vibration the same note on all the other strings capable of producing it. We know that strings when vibrating sound, not only their fundamental tone, but some of their earlier produced upper partials (*Harmony*, §693). In the present instance, middle C is one of the earlier upper partials of all the following notes—

and it will be sounded with greater or less strength on each of these strings, if by raising the dampers we allow them to vibrate freely. Though each separate upper partial will be comparatively weak, yet together they will considerably reinforce the strength of the note struck. If a whole chord be sounded when the pedal is put down, the same process of course goes on with each note. This is the true reason of the pedal being called the "loud" pedal.

27. This, however, is a comparatively subordinate object of the use of the pedal. Its chief use, as said above, is to sustain the sound ; and by its proper employment the player is often able to obtain effects which without its aid would require three, or even four hands. The following passage illustrates this point :—

SCHUMANN : Etudes Symphoniques, Op. 13.

sf
cres.
f
sf
sf
sf
sf
f

It will be seen that in the first four bars of the above there are two sustained melodies, one above and the other below the harmony given in the semiquaver triplets; while, in the latter half of the extract, the melody of the bass is heard in three, and even in four octaves. It is obviously impossible to sustain these melodies except by the use of the pedal.

28. A more usual, and not less characteristic, employment of the pedal is seen in our next example :—

KULLAK: 'Les Fleurs Animées,' No. 5.

(The melody marked: the accompaniment *pp*)

Here a simple melody is sustained in the middle of the instrument, while both hands execute arpeggios above and below. Notice that the left hand in every bar strikes the note which has been already heard as a melody note, but with less force. This repetition of a note, given first as a melody and then as an accompaniment, is sometimes used with entire chords, as in the following passage :—

(*b*) S. HELLER : Etudes, Op. 45.

Here the real outline of the passage, as well as the actual melodic and harmonic effect obtained is this :—

(*c*)

Observe here another instance of the interlacing of the two hands spoken of in § 18.

29. One more use of the pedal still remains to be mentioned. It is often employed to obtain fuller harmony and wider positions of chords than would be possible without its aid. An excellent example of this effect is the commencement of the adagio of Mendelssohn's sonata in D, Op. 58, for piano and violoncello :—

MENDELSSOHN: Sonata, Op. 58.

30. A word should be said here as to the proper use of the soft (*una corda*) pedal. When this pedal is pressed down by the foot, the hammers are shifted a little to one side, so as only to strike one string for each key. Hence results a great difference not only in the volume but in the quality of tone; and the misuse of this pedal (unfortunately but too frequent) by incompetent players, in order to obtain a factitious and illegitimate *piano*, is as grave an offence against art as the no less common abuse of the damper pedal. But, for the production of a veiled and ethereal tone, the soft pedal is most useful. In the adagio by Mendelssohn quoted in our last paragraph, the opening bars are repeated near the end of the movement an octave higher, and *una corda*, with a charming effect. Other examples of the legitimate use of the soft pedal are to be seen in the slow movements of Beethoven's concerto in G, and of his sonata in B flat, Op. 106, as well as in many of Liszt's pianoforte pieces. We strongly advise students in writing for the piano to be very sparing in indicating the employment of the soft pedal.

31. A very important consideration in writing for the piano is the position of the harmonies. As a general rule, it is not good to have the hands too widely separated from one another, because the effect is thin, as in the following extract from the first movement of Beethoven's great sonata in B flat, Op. 106:—

BEETHOVEN: Sonata, Op. 106.

This passage is not quoted with any intention of fault-finding; it is quite evident that the composer's idea could not be otherwise expressed; but the great distance between the two hands, especially in the third and fourth bars, certainly produces a feeling of emptiness, if the passage is regarded simply in its sensuous effect on the ear. But in this case the imagination to some extent fills up the gap, and one is scarcely conscious of the real thinness of the passage. Here we see an illustration of what was said in § 17. In general, however, it will be best to keep the hands nearer together.

32. Except in polyphonic writing, such as fugues, it is not necessary to keep throughout to the same number of parts in writing for the piano. In this matter considerable freedom is allowed to the composer. A passage from one of Haydn's sonatas will illustrate this point:—

HAYDN: Sonata in E flat, No. 1.

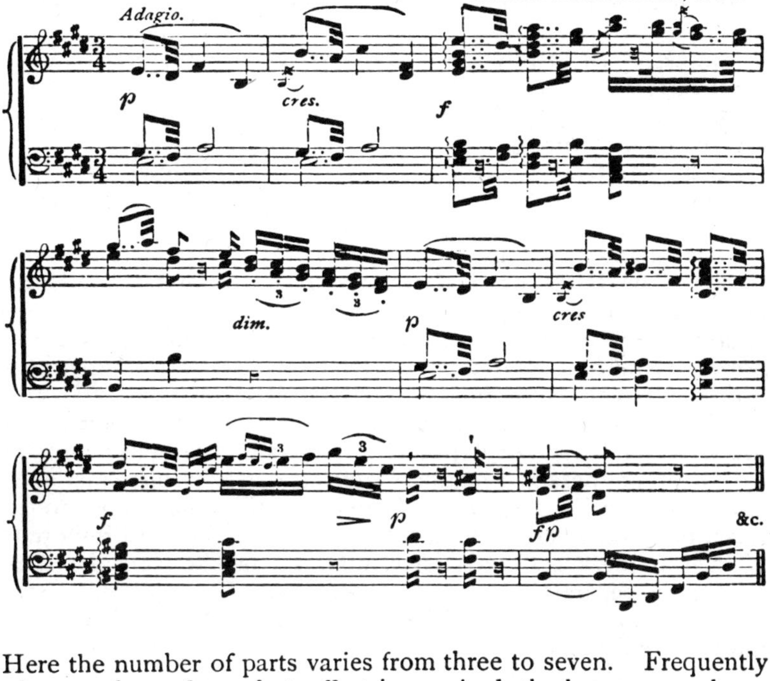

Here the number of parts varies from three to seven. Frequently when a *sforzando* or *forte* effect is required, the harmony, as here, becomes fuller. In such cases, it is not considered that consecutive octaves are produced by the filling up, though it will be better and safer for the student to avoid such doublings of the leading note as are seen in the third bar of the above passage. It is also best, in general, not to double such dissonant notes of the harmony as have fixed resolutions, though it must be added that in the pianoforte works of the great masters considerable licence is often to be found in this respect.

33. In polyphonic writing, it should always be remembered that each additional voice not only adds to the technical difficulty of the music, but also renders it less easy for the hearer to follow the progression of the separate parts. Considerably more than half of Bach's fugues for the clavier are for three voices only, and even in these we frequently find passages of considerable length written in two-part harmony. For example, in the great fugue in A minor, for three voices,

we find that, not reckoning the first part of the exposition before the third voice enters, there are more than 60 bars, or about a third of the whole fugue, in which only two notes are sounded at once.

34. It is not merely in fugues, however, that the preference of composers for writing for the piano in only two or three parts is exhibited. Many movements in the sonatas of Haydn and Mozart are chiefly in harmony of two or three parts only, though, as will be seen directly, the effect of fuller harmony is obtained by the way in which these parts are disposed. A very familiar example of this style of writing is seen in the Rondo of Beethoven's "Sonate Pathétique," more than half of which is in two-part harmony. The tendency of the modern school of piano writing, from Schumann onwards, is toward the employment of fuller chords; but the practice of the great masters sufficiently shows how possible it is to obtain excellent effects from the instrument without keeping all the fingers continually at work.

35. In writing for the piano in only two or three parts, large use is generally made of broken chords and arpeggios; and the treatment of these is a matter requiring considerable experience, but about which it is, unfortunately, all but impossible to lay down more than very general rules. Of these, the most important is, that in broken chords each note should be considered as forming a separate part of the harmony. The opening of the Rondo of the "Sonate Pathétique," above referred to, will illustrate our meaning :—

Beethoven : Sonate Pathétique.

If we examine the harmonic structure of the left hand part of this passage, we find it to be as follows :—

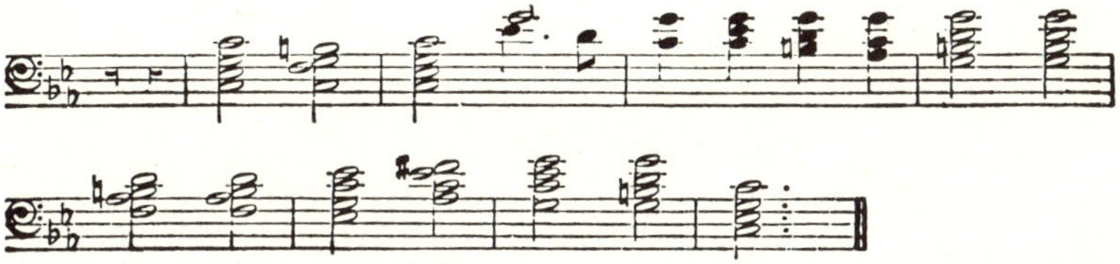

Here we have an example of what was said in § 32—that it is not always necessary to keep to the same number of parts in writing for the piano. But the point to which we wish particularly to direct the attention of the student is, the treatment of the dissonances. The chords of the dominant seventh in the first bar, of the dominant minor ninth in the fifth, and of the augmented sixth in the sixth, are all resolved as regularly as they would be in the strictest vocal writing.

36. It is, however, by no means uncommon, whether in arpeggios or in full chords, to find the rules of correct part-writing departed from, sometimes for technical, at other times for æsthetic reasons. We give one example of each :—

Beethoven : Sonata in E flat, Op. 7.

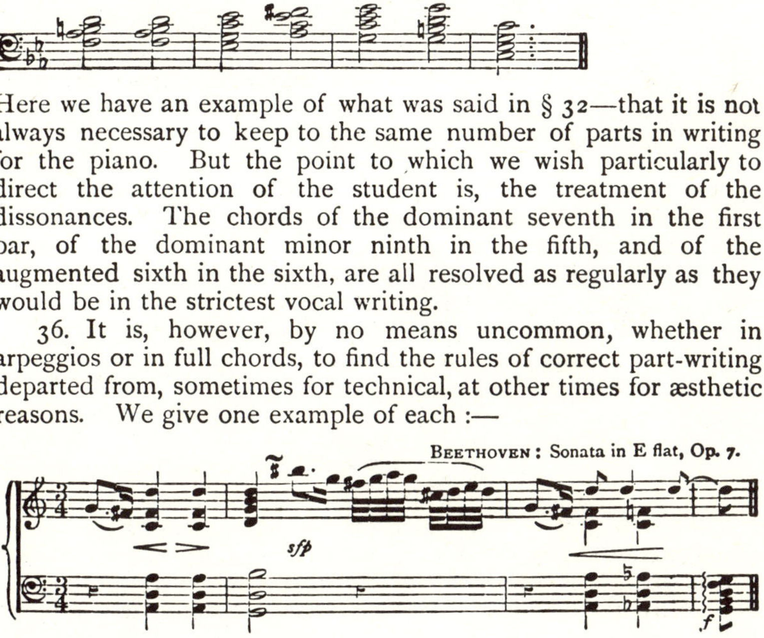

In the first bar of this passage is seen the second inversion of the chord of the seventh on D. The C is here resolved by the B in the left hand of the following bar. In the last chord but one is the fourth inversion of the dominant eleventh in the key of C. The C being the dissonant note against the D, should resolve by falling a semitone. But at the end of the last century, when this sonata was composed, it was unusual to write a stretch of a tenth on the piano, even for the left hand, as Beethoven has done in the second bar of our extract ; while a tenth in the right hand would have probably been almost without precedent. The general use of the tenth in pianoforte music was first introduced several years later by Weber. Beethoven, therefore, resolves his C in the lower octave, with a position of the chord which does not sound so well, owing to the major third low down in the bass. A modern composer would unquestionably have written the passage thus :—

37. In our next example

WEBER : Variations on " Vien quà, Dorina bella," Op 7.

there are in reality consecutive fifths between the second and third bars in the left hand. The harmony is evidently

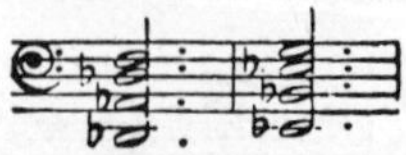

But the licence is here tolerated for the sake of euphony. It may be taken as a general rule that thirds in close position do not sound well in the lower part of the piano, nor, indeed, mostly on any instruments. Had Weber written the figure in the third bar

though the passage would have been grammatically more correct, the effect would have been so far inferior, that he was fully justified here in writing what he did, in spite of the fact that the strict letter of the law is broken thereby. Since the time of Weber and Chopin, who were the first freely to use widely dispersed positions of harmony on the piano, such passages as that just given as a correction of Weber's text have become almost obsolete, though they are often to be found in the works of older composers.

38. Another case in which consecutives are justified by broken harmony is seen in the following passage:—

Beethoven: Sonata in G, Op. 31, No. 1.

Here the semiquaver passage in the right hand is merely the harmony

with the notes played alternately, instead of together. The consecutive sevenths, therefore, in the right hand between the fourth and fifth quavers of the second bar, and the consecutive fifths between the sixth and seventh quavers, are only apparent, not real.

39. It will be seen, from the passages above given, that it is impossible to lay down hard-and-fast lines as to when and how far the strict rules of harmony may be relaxed in writing for the piano. Much must be left to the judgment and experience of the composer. Two general principles may be here added for the guidance of the student. First, it is hardly ever good to resolve dissonances, even in arpeggio passages, in a higher octave from that in which they are taken.* A pupil of the author recently wrote in a pianoforte piece the following—

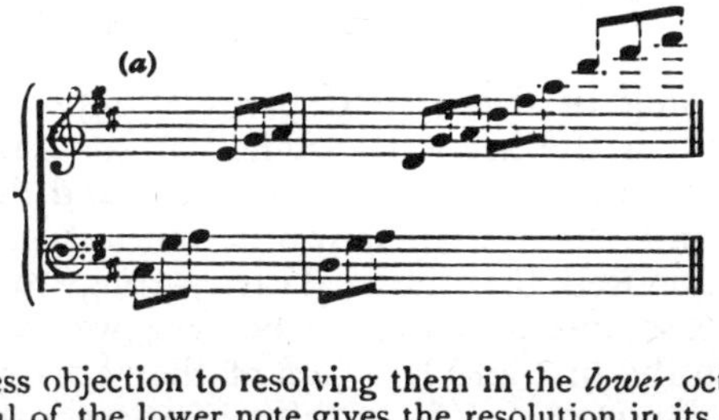

* There is less objection to resolving them in the *lower* octave, because the first upper-partial of the lower note gives the resolution in its correct position. Even this, however, is seldom good, and the rule given in the text had better be strictly adhered to by pupils.

Here the G in the second bar is a suspension, which is resolved two octaves too high. The correct manner of writing the passage would be :—

(*b*)

40. The other important principle to be mentioned here is that when, as in modern music so frequently happens with broken chords or arpeggios, the first note of a beat in the bass is in a lower octave than the rest of the harmony, we must consider it as if held on to the next accented note, and be careful in general to put that next note in the same octave. To illustrate this point, we quote the left-hand part only of a passage from an Etude by J. C. Kessler.

J. C. KESSLER : Etude in C sharp minor.

It is needless to give the right-hand part, as that does not affect the harmonic structure of the passage. It is quite evident that the real bass of the harmony is

If, at the beginning of the second bar, the upper E is taken as the first note (as in the second crotchet of the same bar), the seventh will be resolved an octave too high, and there will be a somewhat similar fault to that shown in our last paragraph. It must not be supposed that it is always wrong to change the position of the bass note into another octave; we see examples of such a change in the first and last bars of the above passage; but when this is done, it is best for it to be after a concord, and not after a discord.

41. One useful piece of advice has still to be given to the

student before concluding this chapter. We have already spoken of the necessity of considering the nature of the instrument in regard to its sustaining power and the quality of its tone. But it is also most important to bear in mind its technique, that is to say, to consider how the passages lie under the hands of the performer. A very common error with beginners is to write music which the Germans describe as "unklaviermässig," *i.e.*, unsuitable to the key-board. It is impossible to define in precise terms what is and what is not uncomfortable to play. In saying "uncomfortable," we do not mean merely difficult. Many passages are to be found (for example, in the works of Chopin and Liszt) which require a great deal of practice before they can be correctly played, yet which, when once mastered, are perfectly comfortable and most effective. This is because the composers we have named had an intimate knowledge of the technique of the instrument, and never lost sight of it when writing. But we also meet not infrequently with passages which are as ineffective as they are difficult, because the peculiarities of the instrument have been insufficiently considered. Such are the too frequent use of very full harmony in both hands, especially if accompanied by rapid changes in position. Many passages, even of single notes, which would be perfectly easy, for instance, on the violin are almost or quite impracticable on the piano, *e.g.*—

Stringed instrument players when composing for the piano are often disposed to think of their own instrument rather than of that for which they are writing; though it is not likely that any one would write so absurd a passage as that just given. The best safeguard against injudicious and ineffective writing is a practical knowledge of the piano; and this is not the least among the many reasons why an acquaintance with the instrument is so valuable to the composer.

42. While, however, it is very necessary that the student should think of the instrument for which he is writing, the practice of *composing at the piano* is to be strongly deprecated, even for beginners. We are perfectly well aware that some eminent composers, notably Meyerbeer, were in the habit of doing this; but that fact proves nothing in its favour. To every one who aspires to compose at all, notes of music ought to convey absolutely as distinct ideas as the letters of a word. Unless the symbols of musical notation call up in the student's mental ear just as clear impressions of a sound as the words of a book which he is reading to himself, and, conversely, unless he is able to write down unhesitatingly and correctly on music-paper any

succession or combination of sounds which may present themselves to his imagination, it is utterly useless for him even to attempt the simplest form of composition. Music picked out painfully and laboriously, a note or a chord at a time, on the piano, does not deserve the name of music at all. On the other hand, if the student has a free flow of ideas, the frequent stopping to try them over on the piano will only be likely to check inspiration. We by no means wish to discourage the habit of improvisation at the piano, provided that there is some plan and connection of ideas (see *Musical Form*, §§ 3, 4), and that the improvising does not degenerate into mere "maundering;" very often the imagination may be stimulated for composition by a "preliminary canter;" and, after writing, it will of course be well to play over a piece and see whether it is susceptible of improvement; but the act of composition itself should be a purely mental process without any aid from the external ear. Orchestral players often complain that modern composers write pianoforte passages for their instruments; may not this be in some cases the result of the music having been written at the piano? If the student finds himself unable to write without an instrument, he must first acquire the power—quite possible to everybody with natural musical aptitude—of what the late Dr. Hullah used to call "hearing with the eye, and seeing with the ear." Till he has done this, it is useless for him to try to compose; as soon as he can do it, he will no longer require the piano.

CHAPTER III.

THE DANCE FORMS.

43. THE first of the applied forms of which we shall treat are those known as the Dance Forms. We select them to commence with, not only because they are in general among the simplest and clearest of all forms, but also because, in consequence of the variety of their rhythmic figurations, commonly spoken of as their "rhythms" (*Musical Form*, § 180), the study and practice of them is very valuable in developing the musical feeling of the student.

44. It is necessary in the first place to call attention to the difference between Dance Music, in the strict sense of the term, and music merely written in dance form. In the former case, the music has to be so constructed as to correspond exactly to the regular steps of the dance. Hence we find that, with hardly an exception, dance music is written in regular four- and eight-bar rhythm throughout; we scarcely ever meet with a sentence or phrase of irregular length. But in music written in dance form, but not intended for dancing, irregular rhythms are by no means uncommon. Let the student compare the two examples from minuets by Mozart, given in §§ 314 and 264 of *Musical Form*. That quoted in § 314 was written for the Royal Balls, at Vienna. Here the steps of the dancers had to be considered, and the cadences occur at every fourth bar throughout the piece. But the minuet, of which we give the first two sentences in § 264, is taken from a string quartett. The composer no longer writes under the same restrictions; consequently, he is quite free to reduce his sentences to seven-bar rhythm by the elision of an unaccented bar. At the beginning of the trio of the same minuet (quoted in *Musical Form*, § 232) two four-bar phrases are extended to five-bar, by the insertion of an unaccented bar. The passage in § 314 is an example of dance *music*, while those in §§ 264, 232 are specimens of music in dance *form*.

45. The different varieties of dance forms are so numerous that it would be quite impossible, even were it desirable, to describe them all within the limits of one chapter. An entire volume would be required to do justice to the subject. As a matter of fact, the study of the greater number of these forms belongs rather to musical history than to practical composition;

we shall confine our attention to those which are of special importance, either as being parts of the old Suite, out of which our chief modern instrumental forms were developed, or because of their being frequently met with in the music of the present day.

46. The ancient Suite consisted of a series of movements in dance form, all of which were in the same key. In the larger Suites (such, for example, as Bach's so-called "English Suites") the first dance was usually preceded by a prelude; in smaller Suites (*e.g.*, in Bach's "French Suites") this movement was mostly wanting.

47. Every complete Suite of regular form contained four movements which were indispensable. These were the Allemande, Courante, Sarabande, and Gigue. Besides these, the composer was at liberty to introduce between the Sarabande and the Gigue any other dance forms that he chose. In the Suites of Bach, which are the most perfect existing models of the form, the additional dances most frequently introduced are the Gavotte, the Bourrée, the Passepied, and the Minuet.* We now proceed to describe each of the movements we have named.

48. In one respect all these dances resemble one another. They are all in the simple binary form treated of in Chapter IX. of *Musical Form*, and consist of two parts, each of which is repeated. The first part usually ends with a modulation; if the movement is in a major key, this modulation is to the key of the dominant; in a minor key the modulation is either to the key of the relative major or to the dominant minor, both being equally common. Sometimes, however, the first part does not modulate, but ends with a half cadence on the dominant, or (more rarely) with a full cadence in the tonic key. In the majority of these movements the sentences are of regular construction, that is, they consist of some multiple of 4—either 8, 12, or 16 bars; but occasionally we find extension of sentences, by the formulæ $6=4$, &c., with which the student is already familiar. An example of this will be seen in the Bourrée from Bach's sixth French Suite, given in § 327 of *Musical Form*.

49. The ALLEMANDE, the first of the four indispensable movements of the old Suite, has in general a less regular rhythmic construction than other dance forms—that is to say the cadences come at less regular intervals. This probably arises from the fact

* Many other dances are to be met with in the Suites of the old composers; we can here only mention some of their names, referring readers who wish for further information to F. W. Böhme's "Geschichte des Tanzes." Among the chief of these were the Chaconne, Loure, Pavane, Polonaise (not the modern Polonaise, to be described later in this chapter), Siciliana, Tambourin, Rigaudon, &c. A description of all these would occupy too much space, and would be of comparatively little use to the student. Of the Chaconne we shall have something to say when we come to speak of the variation form (Chapter V.).

that at the time of the development of the Suite the Allemande *as a dance* was entirely obsolete. It was a moderately quick movement in $\frac{4}{4}$ time—therefore a *compound* time (*Musical Form*, § 36) with two accents in each bar, and it always begins with one or more short notes before an accented beat, generally with a semiquaver or a quaver, less frequently with a group of three semiquavers (see Bach's Partita, II.), and exceptionally with a whole crotchet of up-beat (Bach, Partita III.). Its special characteristics are the continual movement (mostly in semiquavers, though sometimes triplet semiquavers or demisemiquavers are also to be met with) in the voices, and the general richness of the harmonies.

50. As an example of this form, we give the Allemande from Bach's fifth French Suite :—

J. S. Bach : Suites Françaises, No. 5.

(6=7)
(8)
(8a)
(4)
(8=4)
(8)
(4=2)
(4=2)
(4)
(6=7)
(8)

We said just now that the common time (C) of the Allemande was a compound time, with two accents in the bar. That this is the case, is proved by the position of the cadences, all of which, excepting the last of each part, of which we shall speak directly, come at the third beat of Bach's bars. Whenever in common time the last chords of the cadences are found at the third beat of the bar (unless with feminine endings) this proves the time to be compound. In order to show the rhythmic construction of the piece, we divide each bar of the original into two by means of dotted bars. The ends of the sentences and phrases are clearly defined by the cadences, and it will be seen that, as is so often the case, the bar-lines of the original do not indicate the position of the strong accents. The first two sentences are perfectly regular in their construction; but in the third Bach contracts his sentence by (6 = 7), so as to bring the final chord of the cadence at the beginning of a bar, and then restores the sentence to its normal length by the prolongation of the final chord. We have intentionally chosen an example containing a rhythmic irregularity; but in many cases Bach brings in his final chord at the regular distance, and therefore at the third beat of his bar.

51. The second part of this Allemande contains only two sentences, each of which is extended to twelve bars, the former by the addition of an after-phrase, the latter by the familiar formula (4 = 2) which is twice repeated. Those readers who have studied the preceding volume of this series will readily understand the system on which we have marked the accented bars. The close of the second part is an exact transposition into the key of the tonic of the corresponding passage of the first part; it should also be noticed that, though differently divided, the total lengths of the two parts is exactly the same. This is frequently, but by no means invariably, the case; if there is a difference, the second part, and not the first, should be the longer (*Musical Form*, § 345).

52. The COURANTE, which in a Suite follows the Allemande, is a movement in quick triple time, of which there are two distinct varieties, one in $\frac{3}{2}$, and the other in $\frac{3}{4}$ time. With Bach, both forms are equally common; Handel (whose Suites, it may be remarked in passing, are much less regular in form than Bach's, and seldom include all the four essential movements) always writes his Courantes in $\frac{3}{4}$ time. Like the Allemande, the Courante in both its forms begins with an up-beat—generally only a single note (quaver or semiquaver), occasionally with more than one. We will first speak of the Courante in $\frac{3}{2}$ time.

53. A special feature of this dance is the prevalence of dotted notes, and the fact that cross accents are always met with in the cadences at the end of each part, which are therefore in $\frac{6}{4}$ time. The first half of the Courante in Bach's fourth English Suite will show this clearly:—

J. S. BACH: Suites Anglaises, No. 4.

Here, though the movement is evidently in $\frac{3}{2}$ time, the cadence is unmistakably in $\frac{6}{4}$.

54. The cross accents we have just spoken of are sometimes in a Courante to be seen in other places than the cadence, as in the following example by Couperin:—*

COUPERIN: Pièces de Clavecin, Book 1.

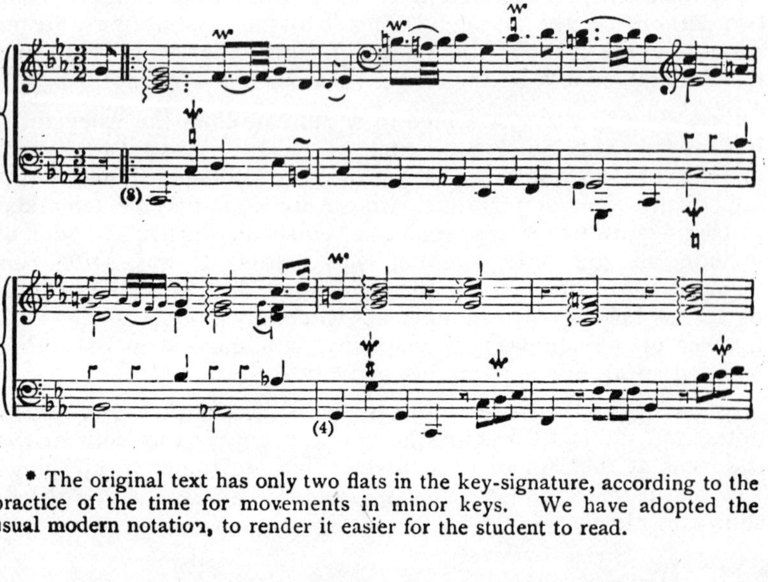

* The original text has only two flats in the key-signature, according to the practice of the time for movements in minor keys. We have adopted the usual modern notation, to render it easier for the student to read.

In this piece several of the bars are most distinctly in $\frac{6}{4}$ time, while others as clearly conform to the time-signature. This mixture of times was a frequent feature of the dance. In a Suite in E flat by Bach, we exceptionally find a Courante with the signature of $\frac{6}{4}$, containing cross-accents of the same kind.

55. The other kind of Courante, in $\frac{3}{4}$ time, is mostly simpler in construction, and generally consists largely of running passages, as in the following :—

J. S. BACH : Suites Françaises, No. 5.

It has been sufficient in all these examples to give only the first half of the pieces. The second half is in each case similarly constructed, and closes, of course, in the key of the tonic. Sometimes the second half is of the same length as the first, but not infrequently it is longer by one sentence, or one phrase. Also, as with the Allemande, it is by no means unusual to meet with extended sentences of irregular length.

56. The third movement of a Suite is the SARABANDE. This is a slow dance in triple time, written indifferently with $\frac{3}{4}$ or $\frac{3}{2}$ as the time-signature. It begins on the first beat of a bar, and its most characteristic features are the frequent occurrence of the rhythmic figure ♩ ♩. ♪| ♩ 𝅗𝅥 | or ♩ ♩. ♪| ♩. ♪ ♩ | and the prevalence of feminine endings to the cadences. Its rhythmic construction is usually far more regular than that of the Allemande or Courante; the first part usually consists of one sentence of eight bars (occasionally extended to twelve by the addition of a second after-phrase), while the second part mostly contains two eight-bar sentences. In only one of Bach's works (the 4th Partita) do we find any departure from this regular four and eight-bar formation; though in a few other of the Partitas we meet with so-called Sarabandes in which the characteristic figures of that movement are altogether wanting.

57. As our first example we give the first eight bars of the Sarabande in the sixth English Suite by Bach:—

J. S. BACH: Suites Anglaises, No. 6.

Here the characteristic figure is clearly seen in the first and fifth bars; the sentence ends with a half cadence in the tonic key.

The second part consists of two eight-bar sentences, the first of which ends with a full cadence in the key of F, while the second, of course, concludes in the key of the tonic.

58. It is not uncommon with Bach to find the Sarabande followed by a variation, known as a "Double." The subject of the Variation forms will be treated of in a later chapter of this volume; it is enough now to say that in the Double the melodies were ornamented while the harmony remained the same. As a specimen of this procedure we give the first four bars of the Double of the Sarabande of which we have quoted the commencement :—

J. S. BACH: Suites Anglaises, No. 6.

In two of Bach's English Suites (Nos. 2 and 3) we find similar variations entitled "Les agréments de la même Sarabande," *i.e.*, the embellishments of the same Sarabande. We occasionally, though much more rarely, find "Doubles" also to the Allemande and Courante.

59. As a particularly perfect and characteristic specimen of the Sarabande, we give a little known piece from Handel's 'Terpsichore.' It is written for stringed instruments, and we have compressed the score on two staves :—

Largo assai. HANDEL: 'Terpsichore.'

As in our last example, the first part ends with a half cadence in the tonic; but it is at least as common to find it end with a modulation to some nearly related key. In the second part of this Sarabande will be seen instances of the feminine endings spoken of above as a common feature of this dance.

60. The last of the four indispensable movements of the regularly constructed Suite was the GIGUE (also written "Gique," or, in its Italian form, "Giga"). This was a quick dance in triple time, most commonly $\frac{3}{8}$ or $\frac{6}{8}$, sometimes also $\frac{12}{8}$ or $\frac{12}{16}$. When intended for dancing, the rhythmic structure was mostly quite regular, as in the following simple example from Handel's ballet 'Terpsichore':—

HANDEL: 'Terpsichore.'

The first part of this Gigue consists of an eight-bar sentence regularly divided into two phrases of equal length. The second part contains only one sentence of eight bars extended to sixteen; the last eight bars can clearly not be considered as a new sentence, as they contain only repetitions and confirmations of the cadence. We have marked the eighth bar after the double bar as (8 = 4), because the inverted cadence here proves that the sentence is not completed; a new after-phrase is added, and the repetition of this after-phrase (8 = 4 again) gives sixteen bars as the whole length of the sentence. The point which we wish to emphasize is, that the cadences come regularly at every fourth bar throughout.

61. In the Suites of Bach, in whose works all the dance-forms are seen in their highest development, the Gigue often assumes larger dimensions, and much greater complexity. He frequently treats it in the free fugal style, in which, as we already know (*Musical Form*, § 269), there are great irregularities of rhythmic structure. To illustrate these, we give the Gigue from the third English Suite:—

J. S. BACH: Suites Anglaises, No. 3.

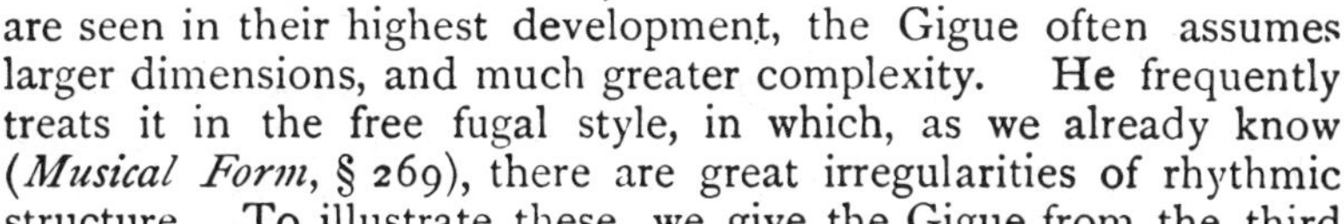

(8)
(4—5)
(8—1)
(4)
(8)
(4)
(4a)
(8)

(4)
(8)
(4)
(8)
(2)
(2a)
(4—5)
(8)
(4)

(4a)
(8=1)
(4=1)
(4)
(4a)
(8)
(4)
(6)
(8=5)
(8)

As $\frac{12}{8}$ is compound time, containing two accents in each bar, it is needful for our analysis to change it to $\frac{6}{8}$ by the addition of dotted bars throughout. It will be seen that, as is so frequently the case in compound time (*Musical Form*, § 37), the strong accents come, in the majority of cases, on the third beats of Bach's bars; the distinction between the strong and weak accents was often disregarded by the great composers. The first sentence of eight bars is quite regular; but at the entry of the third voice we see the conversion of an accented into an unaccented bar (compare the fugue by Bach in § 270 of *Musical Form*); a similar conversion (8 = 1) is seen at the end of the sentence, as is clearly shown by the position of the following cadences—our only guide in analyzing sentences and phrases. Notice the addition of a section to the fore-phrase at (4*a*), and the feminine ending of the fore-phrase at the fourth bar before the double bar.

62. The second part of this Gigue begins with the fugal treatment of the inverted subject. Here the rhythmic irregularities become more frequent than in the first part; the student who understands the principles laid down in Chapter VIII. of *Musical Form* will find comparatively little difficulty in following our analysis. It should be observed that in spite of the irregularity of the separate sentences, there is a certain uniformity in the outline of the piece as a whole, the first part containing altogether twenty bars of $\frac{12}{8}$ time, and the second twenty-four; both numbers, it will be seen, being multiples of 4. It will, however, be found quite impossible to divide it into regular eight-bar sentences, as many of the cadences will be in the wrong places.

63. In two instances Bach writes his Gigues in simple quadruple time—in the sixth Partita (₵), and the first French Suite (C), and in the fourth Partita we see a Gigue in $\frac{9}{16}$ time. These, however, are quite exceptional cases. The Gigue in the first Partita, though the time-signature is C, is only an apparent exception; the continual flow of triplets throughout makes it really in $\frac{12}{8}$ time. The student who wishes to write a Gigue had better use either $\frac{6}{8}$ or $\frac{12}{8}$ time, and will also do well (at least at first) to avoid complicated rhythms.

64. It was said in § 47 that between the Sarabande and the Gigue other dance forms were often introduced. A brief description of the most important of these will complete this portion of our subject. One of the most frequently met with is the GAVOTTE. This was a quick dance in duple time (two minims to the bar), beginning with a half-bar, which usually contained two crotchets, for one or both of which quavers might be substituted. In its early form, the first part of a Gavotte contained one sentence, and the second the same, both of normal length. An example of such a Gavotte is the following, from Couperin's "Pièces de Clavecin":—

Gayement. COUPERIN: Pièces de Clavecin, Book I.

65. In the works of Bach and Handel, the Gavotte frequently assumes larger dimensions. The example from Bach's 'Französische Ouverture,' given in § 323 of *Musical Form*, contains two eight-bar sentences in the second part; while in the sixth English Suite of the same composer, the first part of the Gavotte contains eight bars (one sentence), and the second twenty-four, these being not divided into three eight-bar sentences, but into two, each of which is extended to twelve bars. Still greater extension is to be seen in the Gavotte which forms the final movement to Handel's overture to 'Semele.' Here the first part contains twelve bars, and the second thirty-six; in other words, there are three sentences in the second part and one in the first, and each sentence is extended to twelve bars.

66. We give for our next example a Gavotte by Handel, in which we find a contracted. instead of an extended sentence—a rather unusual case:—

HANDEL: 'Ottone.'

The first two sentences of this piece are quite regular; but the third contains only six bars, and an examination shows us that the first section of the fore-phrase has been elided. The final sentence is again of the normal length.

67. Unlike the Allemande, Courante, Sarabande, and Gigue, the Gavotte was often followed by a second, similar to it in form and rhythm, but usually more or less contrasted in character. This second Gavotte was often indicated as "Alternativo," and after it was played, the first was to be repeated. If the first Gavotte were in a major key, the second would be in the same key; but if the first were in a minor key, the second would be either in the tonic major or in the relative major. It should be remembered that, while each Gavotte considered separately is in the simple Binary form, the two taken together form a movement in Ternary form (see *Musical Form*, §§ 314, 351). Sometimes (as in the third and sixth of Bach's English Suites) the second Gavotte was written on a "drone bass," *i.e.*, on a tonic pedal; in that case it was called a "Musette."

68. The PASSEPIED was a movement in $\frac{3}{8}$ time, beginning on the third quaver of the bar, and of a lively character. Handel seldom if ever uses it, but several beautiful specimens of the dance are to be found in the works of Bach. We give, as one of the most perfect in its form, the Passepied from the 'Französische Ouverture':—

J. S. BACH: 'Französische Ouverture.'

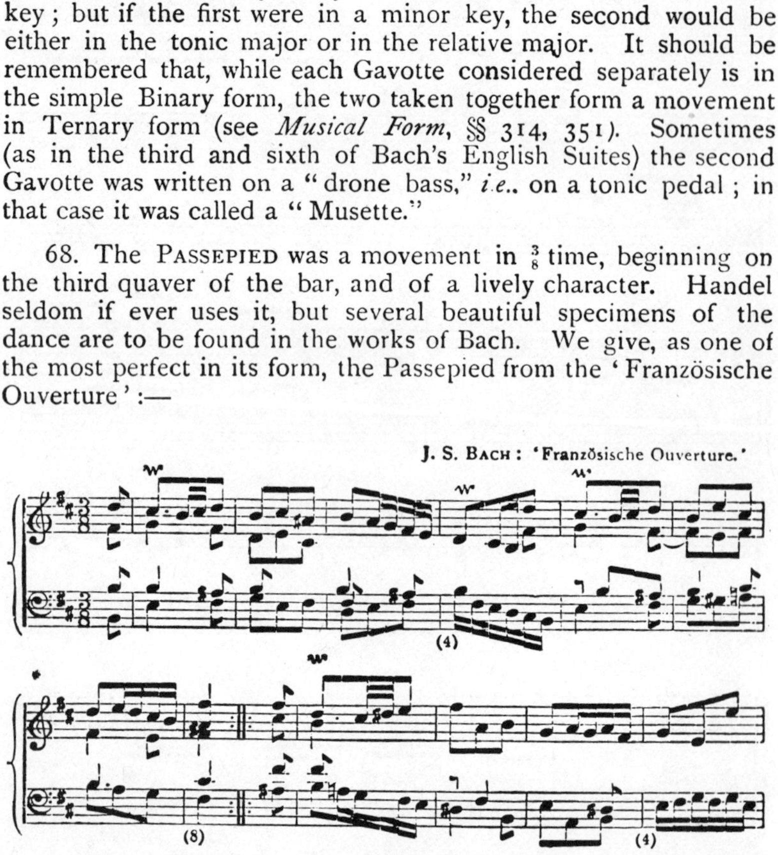

It will be seen that the first part of this piece contains one eight-bar sentence, and the second three. Extensions of sentences are comparatively rare in the Passepied; in general, the normal rhythm is adhered to.

69. Like the Gavotte, the Passepied is often followed by a second, after which the first is repeated. We quote the second Passepied which follows our last example, not only because of its intrinsic beauty, but because it illustrates a point of considerable importance:—

J. S. Bach: 'Französische Ouverture.'

Passepied I., Da Capo.

It will be seen that this second Passepied is written in three-part harmony throughout. This was often done by the older composers when one dance was followed by another of the same form, the method being adopted for the sake of obtaining contrast. The second movement, being in three-part harmony, was often described as the *Trio;* and this name continued to be used long after it had ceased to be the custom to write the second dance in three parts only. This is the explanation of the terms "Minuet and Trio," "Scherzo and Trio," &c., so often to be met with in modern compositions.

70. The BOURRÉE was a lively dance in duple ($\frac{2}{2}$) time, very similar in character to the Gavotte, from which, however, it is easily to be distinguished by the fact that it always begins on the fourth crotchet of the bar—the phrases and sentences therefore ending on the third crotchet—while the Gavotte always begins on the third crotchet. A second Bourrée, which may also be a Musette (§ 67), sometimes follows the first one. A good specimen of the Bourrée will be seen in § 327 of *Musical Form.* The RIGAUDON is almost, if not quite, identical with the Bourrée.

71. The last of the old dances to be described here is the most important of all, because it is the only one which has survived as an integral part of modern instrumental compositions. This is the MINUET. In its older form it was a rather stately dance in $\frac{3}{4}$ or $\frac{3}{8}$ time, beginning with an accented note, *i.e.*, on the first beat of the bar. Bach's minuets are always written in $\frac{3}{4}$ time; so are those of Couperin, with one exception. On the other hand, Handel shows a preference for $\frac{3}{8}$ time, though examples written in $\frac{3}{4}$ are not infrequent (see, for instance, the minuet from the overture to 'Berenice,' given in § 326 of *Musical Form*). The minuet was often followed by a second, which, if written in three-part harmony, was frequently described as a "Trio," the first being then repeated. The second minuet

might be either in the same key as the first, or in a related key. As an example of this form, we give the Minuet and Trio from Bach's third French Suite :—

J. S. BACH : Suites Françaises, No. 3.

It is seldom that in the minuet much rhythmic irregularity is to be seen; the most common is that which is shown here—the extension of a sentence by the addition of a second after phrase. Exceptionally, however, we find, in an overture in F for clavier by Bach, a minuet written in three-bar rhythm throughout.

72. When a minuet is followed by a trio, the form of the piece, considered as a whole, becomes ternary, as we have already explained. But occasionally more than one trio is introduced. A striking instance of this will be seen in the first of Bach's so-called "Brandenburg Concertos." The minuet of this concerto has three trios, the first and third being strictly in three parts, while the second is a Polonaise written in four-part harmony. After each trio the minuet is repeated. The third trio is written in $\frac{2}{4}$ time—an anticipation of the procedure of Beethoven and

Schumann. When a minuet has more than one trio, the form ceases to be ternary, and becomes a Rondo, as will be seen later in this volume (Chapter VI.).

73. The minuet in the works of more modern composers (from Haydn onwards) differs materially in character from the older minuet which we have been describing. In the first place, the *tempo* (which is always $\frac{3}{4}$) is considerably faster, and the stateliness of the old dance gives place to a feeling of merriment and sometimes, one might say, of jollity. This change was due to Haydn, to whom also is most probably owing the innovation of commencing on the third beat of the bar instead of the first, an alteration which gives greater lightness to the music. Handel never begins a minuet otherwise than on the first beat, and Bach only once.* But Haydn in his earliest quartetts sometimes begins on the third beat, as if experimentally, while in the later quartetts and symphonies we find a predominance of the newer form. With Mozart both are about equally common; but in Beethoven's works not more than one in four of the movements written in this form commences on the first beat. Besides this, as the minuet was now treated, not as a dance, but as an abstract dance-form, far greater irregularities in the rhythmic construction are admitted. As examples of the whole, or part, of minuets written in this modern, free style, we refer our readers to the passages quoted in *Musical Form*, §§ 232, 233, 240, 264, 283, and 285.

74. A still more modern development of the minuet is the SCHERZO, which we owe to the genius of Beethoven. It is true that this name had been applied to a minuet by Haydn, who, in his set of six quartetts, Op. 33, calls the minuets either "Scherzo" or "Scherzando." But the term is here used only to denote the character of the music as being "playful;" for these movements do not differ, except in name, from the corresponding movements which, in other works, Haydn calls "Minuets." But, with Beethoven, the character of the movement is changed. His scherzos are more fantastic, more *freakish* (if the expression may be allowed), than his minuets. It is difficult to define in words wherein the difference consists; but the student will feel it for himself if he will compare the scherzos of the first two piano trios of Beethoven's Op. 1 with the minuet in the third trio of the same set. Frequently, also, the form is considerably enlarged, most striking examples of this being the scherzo of the trio in B flat, Op. 97, and of the ninth symphony, which latter nearly approaches the complete "Sonata Form," to be spoken of in a later chapter.

75 Though in the further development of the scherzo it

* In the second Minuet (Trio) of his Claviersuite in E flat

almost, if not entirely, ceases to belong to the dance-forms of which we are treating in this chapter, it will be convenient to complete our notice of the subject in this place. Another innovation introduced by Beethoven was the writing of the movement in other than the $\frac{3}{4}$ time of the minuet, from which it was developed. In the string trio in C minor, Op. 9, No. 3, the Scherzo is in $\frac{6}{8}$ time; while in the piano sonatas in E flat, Op. 31, No. 3, and A flat, Op. 110, the Scherzo is written in $\frac{2}{4}$ time, and in the quartetts in B flat, Op. 130, and C sharp minor, Op. 131, the two Prestos ₵ are really scherzos in common time. In the Scherzos of the Pastoral and Choral Symphonies, both of which are in $\frac{3}{4}$ time, Beethoven writes the trios in common time.

76. We said above (§ 72) that with the older minuets more than one trio was occasionally introduced. The same thing is to be found in the more modern forms. Mozart, though he never writes more than one trio to the minuets of his quartetts or symphonies, has several times introduced two in his Serenades, Divertimenti, and other instrumental works. A familiar example will be found in the clarinet quintett. Beethoven only twice gives two trios to a minuet, and both times in his earlier works—the string quintett, Op. 4, and the trio, Op. 25, for flute, violin, and viola. On the other hand, he sometimes, after the minuet (or scherzo) has followed the trio, repeats the latter, and concludes with a second repetition of the minuet, as in his fourth and seventh symphonies, the trio in E flat, Op. 70, No. 2, and the quartett in E minor, Op. 59, No. 2. The first to introduce two trios in the scherzo of a symphony was Schumann; examples will be seen in his symphonies in B flat and C, and also in his pianoforte quintett in E flat. If more than one trio is introduced, it is advisable, for the sake of variety, that at least one of them should be in a different time from that of the scherzo.

77. In many examples of the modern scherzo the ternary form of the old minuet and trio is frankly abandoned. Here, again, the example was set by Beethoven in his pianoforte sonata in E flat, Op. 31, No. 3, and his great quartett in F, Op. 59, No. 1, both of which movements are in sonata form. Mendelssohn, who was especially happy in his scherzos, has followed in the same direction; excellent specimens of scherzos in this form will be seen in his "Scotch" symphony, his octett, and his piano trio in D minor. Chopin, in his scherzos for piano, adheres to the ternary form, but gives it larger dimensions. The composer of a scherzo is free to use his own judgment as to the form which he may select.

78. Coming now to speak of some of the more important of the modern dance-forms, the first to be noticed is the WALTZ (*Fr.* Valse, *Ger.* Walzer). This dance, of German origin, was also known, for that reason, as "Deutsche," the name being occasionally

met with as "Teutsche." The Waltz is invariably in quick triple time, mostly $\frac{3}{4}$, occasionally $\frac{3}{8}$, and may begin either on the first or third beat of the bar. Nearly fifty waltzes were written by Mozart, under the name of "Deutsche Tänze," all of which consist of two sentences, each of eight bars in length, each half being repeated; and each is followed by a trio (§ 69) of precisely similar construction, to which in one set of dances Mozart has given the name "Alternativo." These "Deutsche Tänze" are mostly written in sets, containing from six to twelve numbers in each, and a "Coda" is added at the end of some of the sets. The following example (written for orchestra, but transcribed here on two staves) will show the form clearly :—

MOZART.

79. Beethoven's waltzes, also entitled "Deutsche Tänze," are of the same construction as Mozart's. The same is the case with the majority of Schubert's. This composer was especially prolific in this form, having written more than 200 waltzes for piano solo, the majority of which have no trios, but consist merely of two eight-bar sentences. We quote one of these, as probably the first example of a syncopated effect which Gounod has popularized in his waltz in 'Faust,' and which has often since been imitated —

SCHUBERT: 12 Deutsche Tänze, No. 2.

80. In the earlier specimens of the waltz, such as those we have given, very little modulation is to be found, and that only to the most nearly related keys. Schubert was the first to enlarge the form in this respect. In many of his waltzes (*e.g.*, in some of

the "Valses sentimentales," Op. 50, "Valses nobles," Op. 77, and "Letzte Walzer," Op. 127) he modulates into keys in the second degree of relationship, and also considerably extends the form. The Waltz in F (No. 10, Op. 127) is one of the most striking examples of the free form adopted by Schubert:—

SCHUBERT: 20 Walzer, No. 10.

8va
fz
fz
fz
(4)
8va
8va
Trio.
Fine.
pp
(8)
(4)
pp
(8)
(4)
(4)
(8) Da Capo.

This waltz begins with two bars of the dominant, *ff* and in unison, serving as an introduction, and forming no part of the first sentence. Then follows the first part of the waltz, consisting of one eight-bar sentence modulating to the dominant. The second part contains three sentences, of which the first and third are preceded by a *link* (*Musical Form*, § 368). The first of these sentences is in A flat major, the second in E major, and the third in F. The following trio, in B flat, also contains three sentences, of which the second begins in G flat, modulating back to the dominant of the original key. It will be seen that no modulation, except that in the first sentence of the waltz, is to a nearly related key.

81. Irregular rhythmic formations, such as the link here seen, are rarely to be found in waltzes, though the addition of a four-bar phrase to a sentence is not uncommon. Quite exceptionally, however, in a little known waltz by Schubert in G flat, the first sentence consists of two phrases of six bars each. But in general, even in the larger waltzes, the rhythmic construction is perfectly regular, except sometimes in the introduction and coda.

82. The extension of form of which we have just given an example by Schubert prepared the way for the modern "Valse de Salon," of which Chopin's waltzes are perhaps the most perfect examples. These works are so well known and so easily accessible that it is needless to quote any of them here. Their forms are mostly very clear; the larger waltzes (Op. 18, Op. 34, Nos. 1 to 3; Op. 64, Nos. 2 and 3; Op. 69, No. 2; Op. 70, No. 3; and the waltz without Opus-number in E minor) are in ternary form, which in two cases (Op. 18 and Op. 34, No. 1) is considerably extended. The other waltzes are all in binary form, excepting Op. 42, in A flat, which is a kind of cross-breed between the binary and ternary forms, and belongs to the "mixed forms" referred to in *Musical Form*, § 396. More modern compositions of this class mostly follow the model of Chopin's waltzes.

83. Waltzes for dancing purposes (as distinguished from those composed simply as pianoforte pieces) are often written in *sets;* that is, four or five short waltzes, each generally consisting of two sixteen-bar sentences, sometimes of three (in which case the third is usually a repetition of the first), are arranged to follow one another, and are mostly preceded by an introduction, which need not be in waltz time or rhythm, and followed by a coda, containing a reference to some of the subjects already heard. This plan of construction is as old as Mozart; we find it in the first set of his "Deutsche Tänze" (No. 509 in Köchel's Catalogue), which contains six waltzes with trios, each one being connected with the following by a passage a few bars in length, and concluding with a coda seventy-five bars in length, partially founded upon the subject of the trio of the sixth waltz.

84. Another dance which requires a short notice, in consequence of the importance given to it by Chopin, is the MAZURKA. This is a dance of Polish origin, in rather quick $\frac{3}{4}$ time, the special feature of which is the accentuation of the weak beats of the bar, especially in the accented bars (the second and fourth) of a phrase, sometimes in other bars also. This will be seen in the following examples, which are the beginnings of two of Chopin's mazurkas:—

CHOPIN: Mazurka, Op 7, No. 3.

We have omitted the first eight bars, which are merely introductory, and do not show the characteristic rhythmical figure of the dance. It will be noticed that in all the accented bars strong emphasis is given to the third crotchet, and that the first beat of the bar is generally subdivided.

85. Our next example shows also the accentuation of the second beat:—

CHOPIN: Mazurka, Op. 6, No. 3.

Here again we have omitted the first eight bars for the same reason as in our last quotation. We should add that the rhythmic figure is not always so clearly defined by Chopin as in the examples just given. These will suffice to show the character of the mazurka, which seldom contains rhythmic irregularities such as are seen in the above passage. The smaller specimens are in simple binary, and the larger in simple ternary form. We refer students who wish to investigate them more thoroughly to the complete collection of Chopin's mazurkas, of which several good editions are published.

86. A dance of considerable interest from its employment by the great composers is the POLONAISE, or POLACCA. This dance is of Polish origin, like the mazurka, which it also resembles in being in triple time, though much slower than the dance just named. A very characteristic feature of the Polonaise is seen in the feminine endings of all the principal cadences. This is less pronounced in the older specimens of this form than in the more modern; in the best examples, such as those of Beethoven, Weber, and Chopin, the tonic chord in the chief cadences is deferred to the third beat of the bar, as in the following cadence from Weber's "Grande Polonaise," Op. 21 :—

Like the other dances of which we have been treating, the Polonaise is in simple binary form, which may be extended to ternary form by the addition of a trio. Sometimes, as for example in Chopin's favourite Polonaise in A flat, Op. 53, the form is of considerable development. In the same composer's Polonaise in F♯ minor, Op. 44, a mazurka is introduced as the trio; this, however, is an exceptional case.

87. As Chopin's Polonaises are generally accessible, we prefer to give two less known examples, the first one showing the older form :—

J. S. BACH: Suite in B minor.

The Suite from which this movement is taken is written for strings and flute. We have transcribed the score on two staves, but several crossings of the inner parts are not shown in our arrangement. The flute doubles the melody in the upper octave. The first part contains exceptionally only four bars, the repetition of which completes the eight-bar period. The feminine endings of the cadences are here not very decided, and consist merely of changes in the position of the tonic chord. In the original score this Polonaise is followed by a "Double" (§ 58) of a peculiar kind; instead of being a mere ornamentation of the melody, as usual, the melody is itself made the bass of the Double, and a florid counterpoint for the flute is added above it.

88. Our next example is the first of a set of four Polonaises written for pianoforte duet by Schubert, and illustrates some of the more modern features of the dance:—

SCHUBERT: Polonaise, Op. 75, No. 1.

It will be seen that every sentence ends with the characteristic cadence referred to in § 85. Another point often to be noticed in the Polonaise is the rhythmic figure of accompaniment  which we see here in the second part, and which was probably borrowed from the Spanish Bolero. Other examples of a similar accompaniment will be found in Beethoven's Polonaise for piano solo, Op. 89, and in Chopin's Polonaise in C♯ minor, Op. 26, No. 1.

89. An interesting variety of the Polonaise is the MARCHE AUX FLAMBEAUX (*Ger.* "Fackeltanz"), a stately processional music used in some royal courts at weddings. In rhythmical structure and in its cadential formulæ it is identical with the form already spoken of; but the finest models of this variety (those written by Meyerbeer) are more extended in their development, containing several trios, or episodes, and therefore belonging (like the minuets referred to in § 72) to the Rondo form.

90. The BOLERO is a Spanish dance in $\frac{3}{4}$ time, having some resemblance to the Polonaise, but differing from it in the absence of the feminine endings to the cadences, and somewhat more lively

in character. It is characterized by the peculiar rhythmic figure of the accompaniment ( or ) which we saw also in Schubert's Polonaise, § 88), and in general this figure is heard for one or more bars before the melody of the Bolero itself begins. It will be well to remind the student that such introductory bars form no part of the first sentence (*Musical Form*, § 265).

91. As a specimen of this dance we give the first sentence of the Bolero in Weber's 'Preciosa':—

Weber: 'Preciosa.'

Another good example will be found in the ballet in the first act of Auber's 'Masaniello.' Chopin's Bolero in A minor, Op. 19, though containing the characteristic figure of the dance, is irregular in its rhythmic construction, as it begins with two five-bar phrases.

The explanation, of course, is that the piece, though written in dance form, was not intended for dancing.

92. The TARANTELLA is a Neapolitan dance in rapid $\frac{6}{8}$ tempo. It usually commences with an up-beat, though examples are not infrequent (*e.g.*, Chopin's Tarantelle, Op. 43, and Heller's in A flat, Op. 85, No. 2) of the theme beginning on the accent. The dance is so generally known that it will suffice to give the commencement of one as an example :—

AUBER : 'Masaniello.'

The SALTARELLO, of which a very fine specimen will be found in the finale of Mendelssohn's Italian Symphony, is closely related to the Tarantella.

93. Though not itself a dance, the MARCH is so nearly akin to the dances in its form that the present chapter is the proper place for treating of it. Like the various dances, the march was originally designed to accompany regular steps—those of soldiers when marching. For this reason it was always written in duple or quadruple time, with strongly marked rhythmical figures, and in general with the normal construction of four and eight bars. The older marches, such as those to be seen in Handel's operas, were

in small binary form, divided into two parts, each of which was repeated. The same form is to be seen in the marches by Mozart, though with somewhat more extended developments, and in the march in Beethoven's 'Fidelio.' Not infrequently the march was followed by a trio, sometimes by more than one; the form then became ternary or rondo, as the case might be.

94. Just as we have seen that from the dances were developed the dance-forms, so from the marches grew the march-forms; that is, pieces written in the time and with the rhythmical figures of the march, but which were not intended for marching purposes. Of these the numerous marches by Schubert for piano duet are examples. They are all in ternary form (with a trio), but differ largely in their dimensions, some of them being developed at considerable length. To the same category belongs the War-March of Priests in Mendelssohn's 'Athalie,' which, though part of the incidental music to Racine's tragedy, is directed in the score to be played "before the 4th act." The magnificent march in Spohr's symphony 'Die Weihe der Töne,' and the Funeral Marches of Beethoven, Chopin, and others, are also specimens of march *form*, as distinguished from the march proper.

95. In theatrical and operatic music the form of the march is largely influenced by dramatic considerations. Thus, the unusual length of the grand march (with chorus) in the second act of 'Tannhäuser'—211 bars of rather slow quadruple time—arises from its having to accompany an elaborate procession upon the stage. On the other hand, most operatic marches (*e.g.*, those in the first act of Mozart's 'Clemenza di Tito,' and in the third act of Weber's 'Euryanthe') are comparatively short.

96. A march can begin either on the fourth or first beat of a bar, the former being, perhaps, the more common. In the somewhat rare case in which a march is written in $\frac{2}{4}$ time, it commonly begins on the last quaver. Schubert's two marches, Op. 121, are exceptionally written in $\frac{6}{8}$ time; in the first the theme begins on the first quaver of the bar, and in the second on the last.

97. With regard to their rate of speed marches differ widely. Religious marches, such as those in Gluck's 'Alceste' and Mozart's 'Zauberflöte,' are of course in slow time, as also are the funeral marches of Handel, Beethoven, and Chopin. On the other hand some of the "Quick Steps" (*Ger.* Sturmmärsche) approach nearly to a *presto*, and we find almost any intermediate rate of speed in the marches by the best composers. But the form itself differs but little in the various specimens, and in the majority of cases it will be found to be the simple binary or ternary form.

98. So many collections of marches are published that it is needless to give many specimens here. For the sake of completeness, we conclude with a short and very characteristic march by Beethoven:—

BEETHOVEN: 'Egmont.'

This march is a specimen of a very simple binary form. The first four bars are introductory; the first sentence begins at the fifth bar, which we therefore mark as (5 = 1). The march contains three sentences, one in the first part and two in the second, the third sentence being the repetition of the first. There is no trio.

99. We mentioned in § 46 that the ancient Suite consisted of a series of dance movements, sometimes preceded by a prelude, all of which were in the same key, though the mode sometimes alternated between the major and the minor. Composers of the present day sometimes write pieces to which they give the name of Suites, but which have little in common with the old form beyond the name, and which may be therefore called MODERN SUITES. In these the movements are not always in the same key. For example, Joachim Raff's Suite for piano, Op. 91, contains a Fantasia and Fugue in D minor, a Gigue with variations in the same key, a 'Cavatina' in B flat, and a March in D major. Of these movements, neither the Cavatina nor the March is a dance, and the name "Suite" is applied here, and in similar cases, so loosely, that it is hardly too much to say that it may be given to any work consisting of a series of movements, some of them being dances, which are not in sonata form.

100. The student can now exercise his invention and ingenuity in the composition of dances after the model of those shown and described in this chapter. He should be careful to keep the form as clear and distinct as possible—for instance, not to write a waltz so that it might be mistaken for a mazurka, or *vice versâ;* each dance has its own special characteristics, which must be considered in writing. We also strongly recommend that, with very rare exceptions, the normal four- and eight-bar rhythm should be strictly adhered to. One of the chief advantages to be derived from the

writing of dance music is the cultivation of the rhythmic feeling, especially in students with whom this is naturally at all vague or uncertain. When the smaller dance forms are mastered, and the larger ones are to be attempted, occasional extensions, &c., of sentences may be introduced ; but it should not be forgotten that rhythmic irregularity is less suitable to dance music than to almost any other form of composition

CHAPTER IV.

THE SMALLER INSTRUMENTAL FORMS.

101. WE have now to speak of the smaller instrumental forms, other than the dance forms described in the last chapter. These are mostly, though not exclusively, met with in music written for the piano, and, with a few exceptions, are composed on a plan with which the student is already acquainted—that is to say, they are generally either in simple binary or in simple ternary form. They occur under such various names that it is impossible to give an exhaustive catalogue of them; we must content ourselves with a short account of such as are most frequent; if the construction of these be understood, little difficulty will be found in analyzing others, whatever they may be called; for the difference is rather in name than in form.

102. With the exception of the Etude, the Prelude, and the Fugue, of which we shall speak later in this chapter, but few of the forms now to be noticed will require detailed description. As was said in *Musical Form* (§ 379), nearly all small pieces—of course we are now excluding rondos and movements in sonata form—are written either in the simple binary or the simple ternary form. Among the shortest and most concise of these are the various pieces written for the use of children. The great composers have thought it not beneath their dignity to compose such works. We need only instance Schumann's "Kinderscenen," Op. 15, and "Album für die Jugend," Op. 68; Mendelssohn's "6 Kinderstücke," Op. 72, and, of more recent date, Heller's charming "Album pour la Jeunesse," Op. 138. With very few exceptions, these are written in the simple binary form, while the exceptions are almost exclusively in ternary form.

103. In pieces of somewhat large development, under whatever names they may be known, the same two forms are almost always to be found, sometimes in a modified shape. As an illustration of this, we take Beethoven's "7 Bagatellen," Op. 33, and describe the form of each. We select this work, because the music is easily accessible, and the forms are sufficiently varied to be fairly representative of the class of pieces of which we are now speaking. No. 1 (Andante grazioso, in E flat, $\frac{6}{8}$) is in simple ternary form; the first part extends to the second double bar; the episode beginning in E flat minor is only twelve bars in

length. A "link" of six bars leads to the repetition of the first part, slightly more ornamented, and followed by a short coda. No. 2 (Scherzo, Allegro, C major, $\frac{3}{4}$) is an ordinary scherzo with trio, and therefore (*Musical Form*, § 314) in simple ternary form. No. 3 (Allegretto, F major, $\frac{6}{8}$) is a simple binary form, repeated with a little embellishment. No. 4 (Andante, A major, $\frac{2}{4}$) is, like No. 1, in ternary form; but the first part on its repetition is varied by additional entries of the subject in the bass. No. 5 (Allegro ma non troppo, C major, $\frac{3}{4}$) is again a very clear ternary form, with a coda of fifteen bars. No. 6 (Allegretto quasi Andante, D major, $\frac{2}{4}$) is another ternary form, with a very short middle section of only one sentence, which is extended to ten bars by a cadential repetition. No. 7 (Presto, A flat major, $\frac{3}{4}$) is less regular in structure than the other numbers. It resembles a scherzo of two sentences, followed by a trio in the same key, after which the scherzo is repeated in a varied form, then the trio unchanged, and again the scherzo with further variation. The principal theme appearing not less than three times, the movement seems to belong to the rondos, of which we shall speak later in this volume. On the other hand, the two sentences (bars 21 to 36), which we have spoken of as "trio," are so little contrasted with the principal theme that they can scarcely be considered episodical. The fact is that the form is here somewhat indeterminate, and it would probably be no less correct to consider the whole piece as far as bar 36 as a larger binary form repeated with ornamentation, as in No. 3. It is not uncommon to meet with movements such as this, of which one cannot define the class with certainty.

104. It is evidently impossible to treat of all the varieties of form to be found in the enormous number of small pianoforte pieces existing. We will take two other well-known collections, and explain their construction, and the student ought then to have little difficulty in analyzing others for himself. We first take the first book of Mendelssohn's "Lieder ohne Worte." No. 1 (Andante con moto, E major, C) is a simple binary form, the first sentence being repeated. No. 2 (Andante expressivo, A minor, $\frac{3}{8}$) is also a binary form, with a rather long coda. No. 3 (Molto Allegro e vivace, A major, $\frac{6}{8}$) is in a condensed sonata form, which, as will be seen when we treat of this form later in this volume, is a modification of the ternary form. No. 4 (Moderato, A major, C) is again a simple binary form, preceded by a short introduction, which is repeated as a coda. No. 5 (Poco agitato, F sharp minor, $\frac{6}{4}$) is another condensed sonata form, but less regular than No. 3; while No. 6 (Andante sostenuto, G minor, $\frac{6}{8}$) is a simple binary form.

105. The other collection of pieces that we shall examine is Schumann's "Phantasiestücke," Op. 12. The first piece ("Des Abends") is in binary form, each part being repeated, and the

second repeat written out in full. No. 2 ("Aufschwung") is given complete in *Musical Form*, § 386, and is there shown to be in ternary form. No. 3 ("Warum") is a small binary form; the piece contains only two extended sentences, the first of sixteen bars, and the second of twenty-six. No. 4 ("Grillen") has the form of a Minuet and Trio, and is therefore ternary; on the repetition the middle portion of the first part, which at first appeared in F minor, is transposed into B flat minor. No. 5 ("In der Nacht"), the longest of the set, is a large ternary form, with an extended middle section beginning at the "Etwas langsamer," in F major. Nos. 6, 7, and 8 are also in simple ternary form, which is so clear as to require no explanation.

106. Of the twenty-one separate pieces contained in the three collections we have just been examining, we find that eighteen, or six out of seven, are either in simple binary or simple ternary form. As our selection was made quite at random (for we chose the first sets of pieces that happened to occur to us), it is probable that the result obtained gives us a fair average, and thus bears out what was said in § 101. If, instead of taking our specimens from the works of the great composers, we examine the pianoforte music of the present day, we obtain similar results. The form may be more or less disguised by repetition or variation; but when we analyze it we shall generally find either the simple binary or the simple ternary form as the basis underlying the piece. We now pass on to notice a few forms which possess special features of their own, and shall first direct our attention to the ETUDE, or STUDY.

107. As indicated by its name, the Etude was in the first instance a piece written merely to afford practice to the student in overcoming some technical difficulty. In the simplest kind of exercises nothing else is aimed at; and we accordingly find that they have no complete form in the sense in which we have been using that word. Take, for example, the two following, from Czerny's universally known "101 Exercises":—

(a) CZERNY: 101 Exercises, No. 1.

CZERNY: 101 Exercises No. 38.

The first of these Exercises is intended to give equality of power to the fingers; the second is a study in arpeggios. It will be seen that neither forms a complete musical sentence; both consist simply of alternations of tonic and dominant harmony.

108. The examples just given show the most elementary kind of Etude. Excepting in such little pieces written for beginners, we generally find the form more clearly marked, though irregularities of rhythmic construction are by no means infrequent, especially in studies written with a purely technical object. Such, however, in the case of modern studies are the exception. One of the first composers who endeavoured to give artistic interest to technical work was J. B. Cramer, in his celebrated "Studio per il Pianoforte." The plan adopted in most of these studies is to take a particular figure and employ it more or less continuously throughout the whole piece, as an ornamentation of some clearly defined harmonic outline. An example will best illustrate our meaning. Cramer's Studies are so universally accessible that it is needless to quote any of them in full here. We will take No. 4 in the first book, beginning:—

The pattern of triplet semiquavers announced in this bar is continued to the end of the piece, as also is the figure of staccato quavers in the left hand. We here give the harmonic framework of the whole study:—

CRAMER: Studio, No. 4. (Outline.)

The student should compare this with the original text. As the time-signature ($\frac{24}{16}$) of the right-hand part is the compound time of $\frac{8}{8}$, it is clear that we have here two accents in the bar, and that the time is therefore compound also in the wider sense of the term given in *Musical Form*, § 36, because it is quadruple, and not duple. This is also proved by the fact that most of the cadences come on the half bar, which is never the case in a genuine duple time, except with feminine endings. In order to show the true structure of the sentences, we therefore divide each bar by means of dotted bars. It will be seen that the piece is in simple binary form, some of the sentences being extended. We have not marked any rests or indications of staccato in the left hand part, because we wish to impress on the student what we have often had occasion to mention—the mental effect of rests. It must never be forgotten that during a rest the mind always retains the impression of the preceding harmony.

109. Let us now adopt the opposite process, and, instead of analyzing an Etude, put one together, beginning with the harmonic outline. We will suppose that the piece is to be a study on broken chords, with practice for the weaker fingers of the right hand. We begin by writing down, or if not, by at least having in our minds, the harmonic progressions. Let us make the first sentence, thus:—

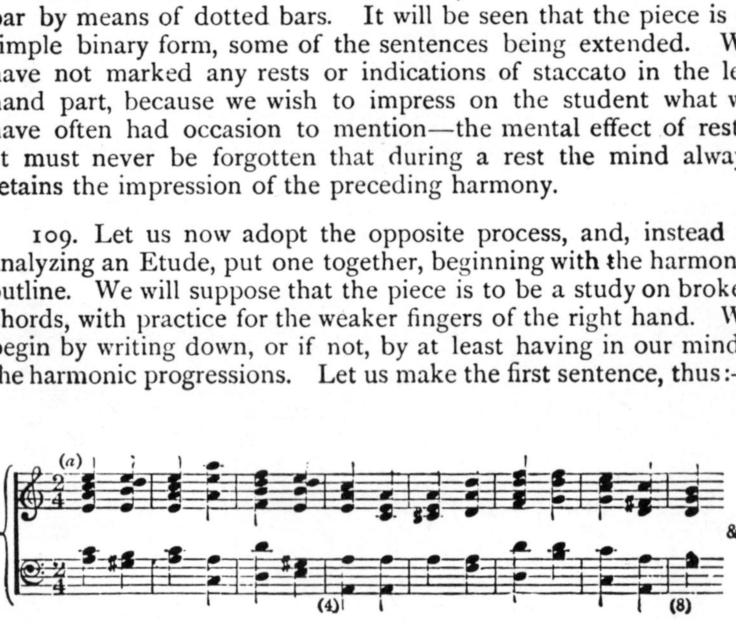

This passage is the framework of the commencement of a study by Steibelt. The inaccurate harmonic progression in the right hand between the third and fourth bars is an illustration of what was said in Chapter II. of this volume (§§ 36–39) of the freedom which composers allow themselves in writing for the piano. Steibelt fills up the above outline in the following manner:—

STEIBELT: Etudes, Op. 78, No. 68.

110. One other example, of more recent date, will suffice for this part of our subject. It is the opening sentence of a study by Henselt; it will be needless to give the harmonic outline, which is perfectly clear:—

HENSELT: Etude, Op. 2, No. 3.

111. It must by no means be imagined that an Etude is always worked out on one pattern, as in the examples we have hitherto given. Often a larger form is adopted, with much greater variety of figure. In such cases there will be little if any difference between an Etude and the smaller forms that we have previously described, excepting that, as the Etude is written with a didactic purpose, a larger amount of technical difficulty may probably be found. The Etudes of Chopin and Henselt, for example, are with hardly an exception beautiful little pieces, in simple binary or simple ternary form, in which are introduced the special technical effects characteristic of their composer's styles. Stephen Heller's Etudes (among the most charming of any existing) were avowedly written less as studies for executive difficulty than to teach correct phrasing, and a good style of playing. In Clementi's celebrated "Gradus ad Parnassum" we find many numbers which are quite as much æsthetic as technical in their scope. Some are regularly developed sonata movements in form; others are complete canons or fugues. On the title-page of the "Gradus" Clementi describes the pieces as "*Exercises* in the strict and elegant styles." An examination of a very large number of Etudes of all styles, and of different dates, justifies the generalization that the Etude may be written in any form that the composer may select, while, as a matter of fact, the great majority are either in the simple binary or simple ternary form.

112. A very important form, from its frequency, is the PRELUDE; at the same time it must be said that there is perhaps hardly any name for a composition which is applied in so many different ways. To such an extent is this the case, that it is almost impossible to lay down any fixed rules for the student as to what a Prelude should or should not contain. All that can be done here is to give a description of some of the chief kinds of Preludes to be found in the works of the great masters,

with such remarks as may be necessary to explain their construction.

113. The etymological meaning of the word "Prelude" is a piece played before something else—in other words, an introduction. Sometimes this consists of only a few chords, as in the short Prelude (entitled "Fantasia") to Bach's great Fugue for Clavier in A minor :—

J. S. BACH : Fugue in A minor.

It may be well to add, for the information of students, that the "Arpeggio" indicates that the chords are to be played in the following, or some similar manner :—

We have here a simple harmonic progression of the nature of an improvisation, which evidently is not of the usual four- and eight-bar construction.

114. A more extended example of the same kind of Prelude will be seen in the first Suite of Handel's "Suites de Pièces pour le Clavecin" (First Collection), in which similar arpeggios to those just shown are interspersed with passing notes and other ornamentations. The piece is too long to give in full ; we quote the first half only :—

HANDEL : Suite de Pièces, No. 1.

Here again it is perfectly obvious that there can be no question of normal rhythmic structure. In pieces of this kind, as in many examples of the Fantasia, there is no regular form. Another Prelude by Handel, very similar in character to the above, is that in B flat which opens the first Suite in the Second Collection.

115. Another kind of Prelude frequently to be met with in the works of Bach closely resembles the Étude in the persistence with which one rhythmic figure is worked throughout. In such cases the form is mostly the simple binary, the plain harmonic progressions being more or less elaborately ornamented. As an example of this form we give the framework of the first Prelude of the "Wohltemperirtes Clavier":—

Bach: Wohltemperirtes Clavier, Prelude 1. (Outline.)

By comparing this outline with the original it will be seen that the Prelude is written in pure five-part harmony almost throughout. It contains three sentences, the first, which ends with a full cadence in the dominant key, being extended to eleven bars; the second is of normal length, and the third is extended to sixteen bars. The simple binary form here is quite clear.

116. It is comparatively seldom that each harmony extends over a whole bar, as in the example just given. Usually the changes are more frequent. To illustrate this, we give the beginning of the sixth Prelude in the same work :—

BACH : Wohltemperirtes Clavier, Prelude 6. (Outline.)

Here it is evident that the crotchet is the unit of measurement, not the minim, as in the first Prelude. The time is therefore quadruple, and in order to understand the rhythmic structure we divide each bar into two by dotted bars. (Compare the examples in §§ 50, 61, and 108.) Here we find a piece beginning in the middle of a sentence (*Musical Form*, § 266); for after the cadence with which the Prelude opens we have to the end of our extract a perfectly regular eight-bar sentence, of which it is clear that the first bar forms no part. This Prelude again is in simple binary form, with various extensions of its sentences in its latter half.

117. In other Preludes of the "Wohltemperirtes Clavier," especially in the second book, we see the larger binary form in which each part is repeated. We gave one of these in § 330 of *Musical Form.* Even finer and more extended examples are the Preludes in G sharp minor (No. 18), and B flat (No. 21) of the second book. No. 5 (in D major) is a very remarkable anticipation of the modern sonata form, to be treated of later in this volume.

118. In Bach's Preludes for the organ we find further varieties of form. Of the distinctive characteristics of organ music we shall speak later in this volume (Chapter XIII.); at present we are concerned merely with the essentials of the form, and not with the manner of its presentation. Many of the smaller Preludes are founded upon chorals, and in these we find great diversity of treatment. Sometimes the melody is merely accompanied by a florid counterpoint, as in the three Preludes on the choral "Wer nur den lieben Gott lässt walten" (Peters, V. 56, 57)*; at other times the choral itself is treated in canon, and accompanied by free parts. Of this the prelude on "Liebster Jesu, wir sind hier" (quoted in *Double Counterpoint*, § 399) is a good example, while others, more extended, are those on "Gottes Sohn ist kommen" (Peters, V. 20), and "Dies sind die heil'gen zehn Gebot" (Peters, VI. 50). Many of the preludes are in fugal form, while some are elaborate Fantasias, among the finest examples of the latter being "Ein' feste Burg" (Peters, VI. 58) and "Komm, heiliger Geist, Herre Gott" (Peters, VII. 4).

119. The organ preludes not founded upon chorals are nearly all in simple binary form, sometimes comparatively short, sometimes extended to considerable length. In only one case—the first of the "Eight small Preludes and Fugues" (Peters, VIII. 48)—do we find the form we referred to in § 117, which Bach so frequently employs in his Clavier Preludes, in which each part is repeated.

120. As a fair average specimen of the large binary form used by Bach in the organ preludes, we will analyze that in F minor (Peters, II. 29):—

J. S. BACH: Organ Prelude in F minor.

* For the identification of the preludes spoken of, we give references to the Peters edition of the organ works. The Roman numerals indicate the volumes, and the Arabic the pages.

(3)
(3a)
5
(4)
(4a)
(6)
(6a)
10
(8—1)
15
(4)
(6)
(8)

20
(4)
25
(8)
(2)
(4)
30
tr
(8)
35
(3)

(3a)
(4)
(4a)
40
(6)
(6a)
(8)
45
(4)
50

(8=1)
(2)
(3)
(3a)
55
(4)
(4a)
60
(8)
(4)
65

We have numbered every fifth bar for convenience of reference. Though, as will be seen directly, the two-part form of this prelude is perfectly clear, its rhythmic analysis offers considerable difficulty, as, indeed, is almost always the case with polyphonic music (*Musical Form*, § 269).

121. The first part of this binary form extends to bar 32, ending with a full close in C minor. Though it contains four sentences, they are not each of eight bars' length. In the first sentence we find at bar 4 the insertion of an unaccented bar (3*a*); for the cadence at bar 5 shows the end of the fore-phrase. Bar 6 repeats the cadence of bar 5, and is therefore (4*a*). Similarly bar 9 is a repetition of bar 8, and is (6*a*), and the first sentence ends at bar 11. The next sentence is contracted, ending in bar 17. The cadence of the fore-phrase is found at bar 14; counting back from this point, we find that bar 11 is (8 = 1); while between bars 16 and 17 an unaccented bar (7) is elided. The third sentence extends to bar 25, and is regular in construction, while in the fourth sentence an unaccented bar (3) is elided after bar 27.

122. Before proceeding to analyze the second part of this very fine prelude, let us look at the thematic structure of the first part. The first eight bars are built entirely on the motive

the first three notes of which furnish the material for much that follows (see bars 11 to 13, and 21 to 24); as the student who understands what was said about the development of the motive in Chapter VII. of *Musical Form* will readily see. Two other motives are also employed—

and the ascending scale passage in the bass of bar 17, with its counterpoint in contrary motion—

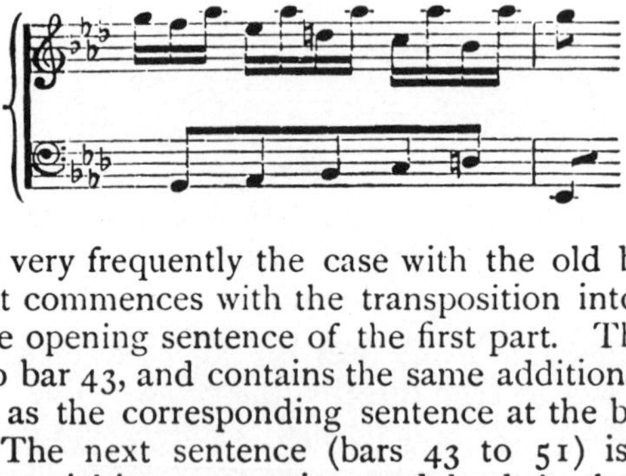

123. As is very frequently the case with the old binary form, the second part commences with the transposition into the dominant key of the opening sentence of the first part. This sentence extends here to bar 43, and contains the same additional bars (3*a*), (4*a*), and (6*a*), as the corresponding sentence at the beginning of the prelude. The next sentence (bars 43 to 51) is normal in length and sequential in construction, and leads back to F minor, the tonic key. Sequence is also a prominent feature of the following sentence (bars 51 to 60), which is prolonged by additional third and fourth bars. The last sentence, which extends from bar 60 to the end of the piece, is more complex in its construction than any of the preceding, and furnishes a good example of the kind of difficulties to be met with in the analysis of music of irregular rhythmic structure. The first part is simple enough; down to bar 68 the construction is normal; but the inverted cadence in this bar ($\begin{smallmatrix}7 & 6\\3 & 4\end{smallmatrix}$ with feminine ending) shows that the sentence is not completed at its eighth bar, which has therefore a double function. Looking ahead, we see there is no other cadence till the end of the piece; we therefore count backwards from the last bar. Bar 75 is evidently (7) and the preceding bar (6), while the florid cadence in bars 71 to 73 is only a free prolongation of

the harmony of bar 70, which is therefore (5), and we see that bar 68 is (8 = 4), the following bar being (4*a*) because it is simply a repetition of the preceding harmony.

124. In some of the other organ preludes we see still larger developments of the binary form. In the great Prelude in C minor (Peters, II. 56) the first part contains 49 bars, and the second 95. In the Preludes in E minor (Peters, II. 64), B minor (II. 78), and E flat (III., 2), we find such a number of themes that these pieces cannot be classed as simple binary, but would deserve the name of "Fantasia" which Bach has used in many cases, both with his organ and clavier works, for the movements preceding his fugues. The same name might even more appropriately be applied, in consequence of the irregularity of its construction, to the Prelude of the great Fugue in A minor (Peters, II. 54), which begins :—

125. It is not uncommon in the larger forms of prelude, as seen in Bach's works, to find extensive use made of *fugato* passages (*Fugue*, § 358). The organ Prelude in B minor referred to above is an instance of this, and several other good examples will be found in the preludes of the English Suites. Of the form of the fugues which so frequently follow the preludes we shall have something to say directly.

126. The same diversity of form and character which we have found in the Preludes of Handel and Bach is also to be observed in those of more modern composers. Beethoven's "Two Preludes through all the Major Keys" (Op. 39) have no regular form at all, but are like improvisations on short themes of two bars each, with almost incessant modulation. His Prelude in F minor is more regular, and an imitation of the contrapuntal style of Bach's Preludes. Mendelssohn's Preludes (Six Preludes and Fugues for Piano, Op. 35 ; Three Preludes and Fugues for Organ, Op. 37 ; Three Preludes, Op. 104, and Prelude in F minor (without Opus-number) are very diverse in form, the simple binary being the most frequent. Chopin's 24 Preludes (Op. 28) are again widely different from each other, both in form and character. The majority of them resemble short Etudes, but some (*e.g.*, No. 6, 7, and 20) are in small binary form, while one (No. 15, in D flat) is a regular ternary movement. It may, in fact, be said that a composer in writing a prelude is free to adopt almost any form that may seem good in his own eyes, so long as he abstains from writing in the larger instrumental forms (Rondo, Fugue, or Sonata forms), for which the name "Prelude" would be inappropriate.

127. Though not strictly speaking one of the smaller instrumental forms, the FUGUE is so frequently found in connection with

the Preludes of which we have just spoken, that the present is the most suitable place for saying something about its form. The details of fugal construction have been fully dealt with in an earlier volume of this series; but, for the sake of those readers who may not possess that volume, it will be well to say a few words here upon the subject.

128. It is scarcely needful to remind the student that a fugue is a composition founded upon one subject (except in the case of double or triple fugues), which appears successively in all the parts in turn. The appearance of the subject in the second voice (termed the "Answer") will be at the distance of a fourth or fifth above or below the subject, and in general the subject and answer will enter alternately till each voice is engaged. This part of the fugue, which is entirely confined to the two chief keys of the piece,* tonic and dominant, or (more rarely) tonic and subdominant, constitutes the exposition of the fugue, which is sometimes followed by a second exposition, called the counter-exposition, in which the entries are in different order (*Fugue*, § 207).

129. The exposition, or counter-exposition, is succeeded by an episode—that is, a passage in which for a time neither the subject nor the answer is heard. Modulations are mostly made by means of the episodes, which introduce entries of the subject in other keys than those of the exposition. These are called "middle entries." Their number varies in different fugues; sometimes two or more of such entries will be introduced in succession, forming groups of middle entries; in other cases each entry will be divided from the next following by an episode (see Bach's Organ Fugue in G minor given on page 38 of *Fugal Analysis*). After these various middle entries the music returns to the key of the tonic, in which at least one entry of the subject is heard.

130. In this very brief outline of a fugue we have said nothing about such matters as real and tonal answers, counter-subject, entries by inversion, augmentation, or diminution, or stretto, because these matters do not in the least affect the construction of the fugue from the point of view from which we are now regarding it. We are merely considering its general form as a whole; and the student will have little difficulty in seeing that we have here a ternary, or three-part form—not the simple ternary spoken of in Chapter X. of *Musical Form*, but an "applied" ternary form.

131. To understand this clearly, let us bear in mind what is the essential peculiarity of the ternary form as we know it. The first part is a simple binary form; the second part consists of an episode *in some different key* from the first part; while in the third part the first subject, either complete or in part, returns in the tonic key. Now we have no exact analogy to this in a fugue, for the

* We sometimes find *incidental* modulations to other keys in the course of the subject (*Fugue*, §§ 40, 41), but these do not affect the general rule here given, as each entry will end in one of the two principal keys.

word "episode" is used in a different sense, and the episodes of a fugue, instead of being strongly contrasted with its principal ideas, are generally developed from them (*Fugue*, Chapter VII.). But if we look at the ternary form from the point of view of its course of modulation, we shall see the analogy at once. The first part of the ternary form is in the tonic, and nearly related keys; the second part is the modulating portion to other keys than those of the first part; and the third part brings back the keys of the first part.

132. Now let us apply this to a fugue. The first part consists of the exposition (and counter-exposition, if there be one), in the two keys of the subject and answer. The second part, termed the "middle section" of the fugue, begins with the first episode that modulates, or with the first entry of the subject in some other key than those of subject and answer, if (as occasionally happens) there is no modulation till after the first episode. The third part ("final section") of the fugue commences with the return of the subject in the original key, provided that this be not followed by another entry in some other key than that of tonic or dominant. In that case the entry in the tonic will form part of the middle section. An example of this will be seen in Bach's Fugue in E minor given in § 298 of *Fugue*.

133. If the student will examine the collection of fugues in *Fugal Analysis*, he will find the three sections marked in each case. We refer him to that volume for fuller information than we have space to give him here. We have, however, said enough to show that every regularly constructed fugue is written in a modification of ternary form. Such irregular fugues as are not in this form have been described and explained in *Fugue*, Chapters XI. and XII.

134. Nearly all small instrumental pieces belong to one or other of the forms we have been describing in this chapter, unless they are Variations, Rondos, or Sonata movements, each of which we shall now proceed to discuss. The irregular formations sometimes to be found will be dealt with in a later chapter, under the heading of "Mixed Forms."

135. The student may now begin to compose pieces in the various small forms described in this chapter. He will be allowed a great amount of liberty in the details, but there are two important points that he should bear in mind. First, he should have a definite outline of the piece in his mind before he begins writing, and not put down whatever happens to come into his head. This especially refers to the course of modulation, which should always be carefully thought out, and well balanced. The other point to be particularly regarded is *clearness of tonality*. If the music is so vague as to leave any doubt as to what key it is in, or if it is so restless that there is a new modulation every bar or two, the effect will most certainly be weak and unsatisfactory.

It ought to be added that we are not including the fugue among the forms which the student can attempt merely after reading this chapter. To write a fugue it will be needful to study the volume on Fugue in the present series, or some other work treating of the same subject.

CHAPTER V.

THE VARIATION FORMS.

136. IN speaking of the Simple Ternary Form in Chapter X. of *Musical Form*, it was said (§ 359) that in the third part of a piece written in this form the chief subject was often varied or embellished, and we gave in the same section an Adagio from one of Haydn's quartetts which illustrated this point. Variation of this kind, which is of almost constant occurrence in the ternary form, may be termed *incidental* variation. We have now to speak of the variation as an independent form of itself—a form, it should be added, of considerable importance, and of almost infinite variety.

137. By the word "Variation" in its musical sense is meant the presentation of the same thought, or series of thoughts, under different aspects. Thus the many developments of a motive which we showed in *Musical Form* (§§ 172–176) are from one point of view *variations* of the motive. The word is, however, employed in a somewhat different way when we speak of the Variation form. In this a simple theme, which is in almost all cases a small binary form, is announced, and then repeated with modifications of melody, harmony, time, key, or any combination of these, as many times as the composer may choose. The variations may either constitute an independent piece by themselves, or they may form one movement of a larger work, such as a sonata, quartett, or symphony.

138. The simplest, and probably the oldest, form of variation is that known in England as a GROUND BASS, and abroad by its Italian name, *Basso ostinato* (*i.e.* "obstinate bass"). This is a composition in which a theme, generally of four or eight bars, though occasionally of other lengths, was continually repeated, every time with different upper parts. The harmonic framework usually underwent little change, but fresh melodies were superposed. Many good examples of this form will be seen in the old instrumental works of early English composers, such as Blow and Henry Purcell. The Ground Bass was also frequently used in vocal compositions. As an interesting example we give the air "When I am laid in earth," from Purcell's 'Dido and Æneas':—

PURCELL: 'Dido and Æneas.'

Here the variations are not separated from one another, but continuous, as is almost always the case with a Ground Bass. It is worthy of notice that the chromatic scale descending from tonic to dominant, with which this theme begins, was also used in a slightly different form as a "Ground" by Handel in the opening chorus of 'Susanna,' founded on this theme,

and by Bach in his Church-Cantata "Weinen, Klagen," the first chorus of which he subsequently developed into the sublime "Crucifixus" of his great Mass in B minor. In the latter work the bass assumes the following form :—

Other good examples of a Ground Bass will be found in Handel's choruses "To song and dance" ('Samson'), "Almighty Ruler" ('Joshua'), and "O Baal, monarch of the skies" ('Deborah').

139. Closely allied to the Ground Bass are the CHACONNE and PASSACAGLIA (*Fr.* "Passecaille"). Both of these were originally dances, and the former is to be found in the Ballet music of some of Gluck's operas. But in the instrumental works of Bach and Handel we meet with them as variation forms. In Handel's "Suites de Pièces" we find a "Passacaille" (*sic*) in the seventh Suite of the first book, with fifteen variations, and in the second book there are two Chaconnes, both in G major, the themes being nearly identical, the former of which has twenty-one, and the latter no fewer than sixty-two variations. To illustrate this form we quote the theme and the first few bars of some of the more characteristic variations of the second Chaconne :—

CHACONNE. HANDEL: Suites de Pièces, Book 2.

&c.
Var. 41.
Var. 45.
&c.
&c.
Var. 51.
Var. 55.
&c.
Var. 59.
&c.
Var. 62.
&c.

Most of these variations contain no change of harmony, the alterations being mostly in melodic outline (as in Variations 7, 23, 32, &c.), or in rhythmic figure (as in Variations 4, 9, and 41). We give the last variation in full; it will be seen that it is a little canon in the octave, the harmonic outline of which closely resembles, except in the third bar, the original theme. The whole of the piece may be examined with advantage by those who wish to see how much can be done with a very common, not to say threadbare, sequence of chords.

140. Bach's treatment of the Chaconne and Passacaglia is freer than Handel's. His well-known Chaconne for violin without accompaniment consists of a theme of eight bars, of which the second half is a slightly varied repetition of the first, with thirty variations, in some of which the harmonic treatment is very free. In several of the variations the mode is changed from minor to major, and the piece ends with the repetition of the theme in its original simple form, the final cadence being altered, to make a more satisfactory close.

141. In Bach's great Passacaglia in C minor for the organ we find even greater freedom. The work is founded upon the following Ground Bass, which, it will be seen, is of the normal eight-bar construction:—

This theme is first announced by the organ pedals without any harmony, as in the example by Purcell, given in § 138. Above this bass Bach then proceeds to write variations. In the first four the bass remains unchanged, and different harmonies are added above it. In the fifth, ninth, and tenth variations, the bass is itself varied by the introduction of rests and ornamental notes. In the eleventh and twelfth variations the theme appears as a melody in the upper part instead of the bass, and in the thirteenth variation we find it in the middle of the harmony, with one part above and one below. In the fourteenth and fifteenth variations the long notes of the theme are no longer present, but its harmonies are suggested by broken chords and arpeggios. From the sixteenth to the twentieth variation the subject reappears in its original form in the bass, with new counterpoints in the upper parts. An elaborate double fugue of 124 bars, founded upon the beginning of the theme,

concludes the work.

142. Before leaving this part of our subject, it will be well to notice here a more modern example of the Chaconne. We refer to Beethoven's Thirty-two Variations for Piano in C minor. This piece is so generally familiar that it will only be necessary to say a few words about it. The subject, with its descending chromatic scale in the bass,

of which we have given the harmonies, has much resemblance to that quoted in § 138. Our space will not allow us to give an analysis of these variations; we strongly advise the student to make one for himself, and to notice the different ways in which Beethoven changes the harmonic framework, while never so far disguising the original as to render the theme unrecognizable. Of Beethoven's other variations we shall speak later in this chapter.

143. A much more common form than that of the Ground Bass or Chaconne (at least, with modern composers) is that known as the "Air with Variations," or simply "Variations." This may be either an independent piece of itself, or it may form part of a larger work, such as a sonata, quartett, or symphony. The same general principles apply to the writing of variations in both these cases.

144. The first thing to be considered in variations is the choice of the theme. It is not every subject that is equally well suited for variation. If it be too short, the piece as a whole is likely to be scrappy and fragmentary; if it be too long, the music will probably become discursive and rambling. As a matter of fact, a theme that is to be varied will be almost always in simple binary form, and in the majority of cases will be found to consist of two sentences of eight bars each. The thirty-two variations by Beethoven, spoken of in § 142, offers one of the few modern examples of a theme consisting of only one sentence.

145. It is further desirable that the theme to be varied should

(a) T.S., the abbreviation of *Tasto solo*, indicates that there is no harmony above the bass.

be simple, and at the same time sufficiently striking in character to be easily recognized in the different metamorphoses it has to undergo. To this end *variety of cadence* will be found very helpful. It is true that we sometimes find very beautiful variations in which this point is disregarded—a familiar example being the variations of Mozart's sonata in A; but this piece is successful in spite of, not because of, the monotony of the cadences, all of which are either half closes or full closes in the tonic key.

146. It was said just now that the majority of themes for variations were of sixteen bars in length. Examples of such themes will be seen in §§ 316, 317 of *Musical Form*. But it is by no means uncommon to find more extended binary forms taken as the subjects for variations. The variations by Mozart, referred to in the last paragraph, are an example of this; so are the variations in Beethoven's sonata in A flat, Op. 26, and his Variations in F, Op. 34, and on Diabelli's Waltz, Op. 120. For the simpler variations, which should be studied first, the small sixteen-bar theme will be best adapted.

147. Dr. Marx in his "Composition" divides variations into two classes—Formal- and Character-variations. Under the former name he includes those in which the original form of the theme is more or less closely preserved, though there may be changes of rhythm, of mode (from major to minor, or *vice versâ*), of harmony, or of the form of accompaniment, while by character-variations he means those in which there are important changes in the original form of the theme, such, for instance, as its conversion into a March, a Waltz, or a Fugue. It is, however, often very difficult to decide in which of these two classes many variations should be included; it will be simpler, therefore, to speak of variations as Strict or Free; by the former are meant those in which the outline of the theme is more or less closely adhered to; by the latter those in which it is widely departed from. Nearly all the variations by Mozart, and the majority of those by Beethoven, belong to the former class, while Schumann's "Symphonic Variations," Op. 13, afford an excellent example of the latter.

148. It would be both interesting and profitable to trace the gradual development of the variation form from the simple "Doubles" of the old Suites (§ 58) to the very free variations of modern composers. This, however, our space will not allow, and we must refer students to the admirable article on "Variations" by Dr. Hubert Parry, in the fourth volume of Grove's *Dictionary of Music*. The general tendency towards ever-increasing freedom of form will be seen in the successive examples that we are about to mention.

149. In the earlier examples of what we have termed the "strict" variation, the harmonic outline is mostly preserved intact, while the variations gradually become more elaborate or florid.

Look, for example, at Handel's Variations in E, known as "The Harmonious Blacksmith." The piece is so familiar that quotation is superfluous; it will be remembered that the theme mostly moves in quavers; in the first variation we have broken harmony in semiquavers for the right hand; in the second, similar passages for the left hand; in the third variation we find triplet semiquavers for the right, and in the fourth, for the left hand; while the fifth and last variation contains ascending and descending scale passages in demisemiquavers. The changes of harmony are very slight and unimportant.

150. Though in the strict variations of later composers (Haydn, Mozart, or Beethoven) we find the harmonic outlines less closely adhered to, the same general principles are observed. As an illustration of this, we give the commencement of some of Mozart's variations on the French air 'Je suis Lindor.' We select this piece because it is one of which the composer evidently thought well, as he frequently selected it to play at his concerts, and mentions it in one of his letters as a piece "which has something for everybody." The first part of the theme is the following—

Allegretto. MOZART: Variations on 'Je suis Lindor.'

The second part of this theme also consists of one sentence, the after-phrase of which is extended to five bars by repetition of its first bar, and then repeated with a varied cadence. On this air Mozart has written twelve variations, which we proceed to describe.

151. The first variation shows the melody embellished by auxiliary and passing notes, and accompanied by simple chords in the bass, with a change of harmony at the third and fourth bars:—

Var. I.

In the second variation, the theme appears in almost its original form in the right hand, accompanied by moving semiquaver passages of scales and arpeggios for the left :—

The third variation shows more florid embellishments of the subject, as will be seen from the first bars,

while in the fourth we see triplet semiquavers in the right hand, with "cross-hand" passages for the left, such as are often to be found in the music of Mozart's time :—

The fifth and sixth variations present the theme in a simple form, but with broken octaves, in the fifth for the right, and in the sixth for the left hand. Quotation is unnecessary.

152. Variation 7 (Maestoso) shows the theme in a new aspect. The bold chords with which it opens are followed by scale passages for both hands alternately, the harmonic outline remaining practically unchanged :—

Var. 7. *Maestoso.*

The eighth variation is in the tonic minor key. It was usual in this form to change the *mode* from major to minor, or *vice versâ*, for at least one variation. An early example of this will be seen in Handel's Chaconne in G major (not the one quoted in § 139) with 21 variations, in which the variations Nos. 9 to 16 are in the key of G minor. More frequently however, the change was only made, as here, for one variation :—

Var. 8. *Minore.*

153. The ninth and tenth variations are the counterparts of one another. In the former the dominant is sustained in the treble, and in the latter the tonic in the bass through nearly the whole variation :—

Var. 9. *Maggiore.*

Var. 10.

The eleventh variation shows a special characteristic of Mozart's treatment of this form. In fourteen out of fifteen sets of variations from his pen (not counting those which are single movements of larger works, such as sonatas and quartetts) we find one variation *Adagio*—nearly always the penultimate variation of the set. The effect is to change the character of the theme, though its melodic and harmonic outlines are generally closely reproduced. These slow variations are always elaborately ornamented, and are in many cases the most beautiful of the whole. We give the commencement of the present one :—

Var. 11. *Molto adagio.*

The final variation is free (§ 147). Here the time is changed to $\frac{3}{4}$, and the form to that of a minuet :—

Var. 12. *Tempo di Menuetto.*

This final variation is extended by means of a short coda.

154. The analysis of these variations by Mozart will, it is hoped, enable the student sufficiently to understand the older variation form. If he will procure Clementi's sonata in B flat, Op. 12, No. 1, he will find, as the finale of that sonata, a set of variations on the same theme, which it will be very interesting for him to compare with the variations by Mozart that we have just been examining. We recommend him also to analyze for himself Mozart's variations on "Unser dummer Pöbel meint" and "Ein Weib ist das herrlichste Ding," as well as those in the sonatas in A major and D major.

155. In the hands of Beethoven the variation form was considerably enlarged. One of the most striking characteristics of this greatest of all composers excepting Bach was his power of extending and modifying, without ever destroying, the forms employed by his predecessors. The larger number of his variations for piano solo are early works; in these he mostly follows the lines laid down by Mozart, though he only exceptionally (as in the variations to "Vieni amore" and "Tändeln und Scherzen") avails himself of the *Adagio* variation, which Mozart uses so effectively. But in his more important variations we find much greater freedom. As an interesting example, we give an analysis of the "Six Variations on an Original Theme," Op. 34.

156. The theme on which these variations are founded is, as usual, in the simple binary form. It commences with a sentence of the normal eight-bar construction, ending with a full close in the tonic key. This is followed by a phrase of four bars modulating to the dominant, and extended to six bars by a double repetition of its cadence, after which the first sentence is repeated without modification. We quote the first four bars:—

BEETHOVEN: 6 Variations, Op. 34.

157. A peculiarity of this piece is that Beethoven introduced into it an innovation which neither he nor, so far as we are aware,

any later composer has ever repeated. No two consecutive variations are in the same key or in the same time. The first variation is in D major; the harmonic outline of the theme undergoes but slight alteration, but it is very elaborately embroidered with florid ornamentation in the upper part. The *tempo* is approximately the same as that of the theme:—

Var. 1.

158. In the second variation we find an entire change in the spirit of the music. The dotted rhythmic figure in the first bar, and the semiquaver arpeggio and scale passage in the third are strongly contrasted with the dreamy, almost religious, character of the subject. This contrast is intensified in the second part of the variation; the theme is, in fact, completely metamorphosed, though the harmonic outline is in the main unchanged:—

Var. 2. *Allegro ma non troppo.*

159. Again another strong contrast! To the vivacity of the second variation succeeds the tranquil flow and repose of the third, in G major, with the quietly moving *legato* quavers in both hands. Yet the resemblance to the original theme is never for a moment obscured; the harmonic outline of every bar remains unchanged, though chromatic notes (both passing and harmony notes) are frequently introduced:–

160. In the fourth variation the theme is again transformed—now to a stately minuet:—

161. Now let us pause for a moment to notice the order of keys which Beethoven has hitherto observed. It will be seen that each variation is alternately a minor and a major third lower than the preceding, and stands therefore in the second degree of relationship (*Musical Form*, § 83) to that which has gone before it. As the keys are all major, it is clear that lowering the tonic a minor third always leads to a key with more sharps, and a major third always to one with more flats. In the fifth variation Beethoven again lowers his tonic a minor third; but he *changes the mode.*

This variation is therefore in the relative minor of the preceding, and takes the character of a funeral march :—

162. A "link" of six bars of the chord of C major, to which at the fourth bar the dominant seventh is added, leads back to the original key of F for the final variation :—

This variation is followed by a long coda, the latter part of which is really, though not so entitled, a seventh variation in which the theme (Adagio molto, $\frac{2}{4}$) is heard alternately in the right and left hands, and even more elaborately ornamented than in the first variation. We strongly recommend this piece to the attention of the student as an excellent example of the free style of variation. We also advise the study of Beethoven's 'Fifteen Variations and Fugue' (Op. 35) and of the variations in the sonatas Ops. 26 and 57, and of those in the great Trio in B flat. We cannot too often repeat that more is to be learned from a careful analysis of existing masterpieces than from any number of text-books.

163. In Beethoven's later works he developed the variation form still further. We find great freedom in the variations of the pianoforte sonatas, Ops. 109 and 111, and of the string quartetts in E flat, Op. 127, and C sharp minor, Op. 131. Most remarkable of all are the Thirty-three Variations on a Waltz by Diabelli, Op. 120, which Dr. Hubert Parry * excellently describes as "transformations rather than variations." In many of these, the theme is so far changed that its recognition is not easy; sometimes hardly anything remains beyond the final cadence of each sentence. We have not here space to analyze this great work, but we must refer our readers to the excellent article by Dr. Parry, already referred to. Those who can read German will also find an interesting analysis of the variations in the third volume of Marx's "Composition."

164. The variations by Schubert, Weber, and Mendelssohn,† though extremely interesting as illustrating the technique of those composers in pianoforte writing, present little new as regards the variation form. For the most part they would be classed among the strict rather than the free variations, though it must be acknowledged that it is very difficult, if not impossible, to draw a hard and-fast line of demarcation between the two styles. In the variations which form the middle movement of Weber's sonata in D minor, Op. 49, is to be seen an innovation worth noticing. The theme, which is preceded by an introduction four bars in length, consists of two eight-bar sentences, and is followed by four variations. Between the second and third variation is introduced an episode of 31 bars, and between the third and fourth a second episode of 16 bars. Here, therefore, we see a modified variation form, approximating to the older Rondo form which will be spoken of in the next chapter.‡

165. The more modern composers, such as Schumann, Brahms, and Raff, almost invariably write their variations in the free rather than in the strict style. The finest examples by Schumann are the "Etudes Symphoniques en Forme de Variations," Op. 13, the Variations for two Pianos, Op. 46, and those which form the slow movement of the string quartett in F, Op. 41, No. 2. Of these the variations for two pianos are the most regular, and the most

* See his article "Variations" in Vol. IV. of Grove's "Dictionary of Music."

† We recommend the student to examine the following variations by these masters:—

SCHUBERT: Andante con moto from Sonata in A minor, Op. 42; Impromptu in B flat, Op. 142, No. 3; Variations on "Death and the Maiden" in the String Quartett in D minor.

WEBER: Variations on "Vien quà, Dorina bella," Op. 7; Variations on the Romance from 'Joseph,' Op. 28; Variations on "Schöne Minka," Op. 37.

MENDELSSOHN: Variations Sérieuses, Op. 54; Variations in E flat, Op. 82; Variations in B flat, Op. 83; Variations in D, Op. 17, for piano and violoncello.

‡ This movement is analyzed in a later chapter of this volume (§ 416).

perfect as regards their form, while the "Etudes Symphoniques" are the richest in their artistic contents. In this great work, which is too well known to need analysis, freedom is carried almost to an extreme. As in the Thirty-three Variations by Beethoven, spoken of in § 163, often nothing but the bare harmonic outline of the original theme remains. The same is the case in many of the variations by Brahms,* and with Raff's brilliant "Giga con Variazioni" in his Suite, Op. 91.

166. In the large majority of cases (though numerous exceptions are to be met with) the length of the sentences, even in variations in the free style, will be the same as in the original theme. This is the case in 22 out of 33 variations in Beethoven's Op. 120, while in many other cases, when there is a difference it arises from the repetition of one of the phrases or sentences. As a general rule, the maintenance of the rhythm unchanged is one of the simplest as well as one of the best methods of preserving the unity of the composition. It should be added that this does not apply to the *final* variation, which, at least in modern compositions, is almost always extended by means of a coda.

167. A kind of free variation not yet spoken of is Canonic Variation. This is sometimes employed incidentally, as in the seventh of Beethoven's Fifteen Variations, Op. 35; but the finest examples are those by Bach in his 'Thirty Variations' for clavier, and his "Canonic Variations for Organ on the Choral, 'Vom Himmel hoch da komm' ich her.'" Extracts from both these works will be found in *Double Counterpoint and Canon*, §§ 353, 369–371, and 402–405. The 'Thirty Variations' may be described as an anticipation by a hundred years of the free variations of Beethoven, Schumann, and Brahms. Though they are inimitable, they will none the less repay study.

168. When, as is so frequently the case, the theme for variations consists of two eight-bar sentences, each of which is repeated, it is not uncommon to meet with what may be described as *Double* Variations. In these, instead of the repetitions of each half being identical, a second variation of the first half precedes the first variation of the second half. The third variation in the Andante of Beethoven's sonata in F minor, Op. 57, is a familiar example of this. Arpeggios and scale passages in demisemiquavers for the left hand accompany sustained notes in the right hand during the first eight bars; on the repetition of the sentence the sustained notes are given to the left hand, and the moving passages to the right. At other times much greater alterations are made, as in the following example from Beethoven's sonata, Op. 109:—

* Variations on a Theme by Schumann, Op. 9; Two Books of Variations, Op. 21; Variations and Fugue on a Theme by Handel, Op. 24; Variations for Orchestra on a Theme by Haydn, Op. 56.

BEETHOVEN : Sonata, Op. 109.

At (*a*) we give the first sentence of the theme ; at (*b*) are the first four bars of the second variation. The figure here shown is continued to the end of the sentence (the eighth bar), but instead of this sentence being repeated it is followed by an entirely new variation, as at (*c*). The second sentence of the theme is then treated in the same way, being first varied after the model at (*b*) and then as at (*c*). Here therefore we have double variations—in fact two variations in one.

169. A form of variation differing in some respects from any yet noticed is that to which Haydn appears to have been partial, as it is frequently met with in his quartetts and symphonies. This is a different kind of double variation to that just noticed, being written upon two themes, instead of one. In this form each theme has always the same tonic, but the mode is changed. One of the best examples is to be seen in Haydn's charming symphony in C

major (No. 3 of Rieter-Biedermann's edition). The slow movement is built upon two themes, each of which is a simple binary form. The first theme, of sixteen bars, is given complete in *Musical Form*, § 316. This is followed by a second theme in F minor, also containing two sentences, the first of normal length, and the second extended to fourteen bars. As with the first theme, each sentence is repeated. We next find a variation of the first theme, followed by a variation of the second theme. The second theme, however, does not end as before with a full cadence, but with an interrupted cadence, leading back, through a codetta of six bars, to the first theme, of which a second variation is then given, and a coda of 26 bars concludes the movement, the plan of which is as follows :—

(*a*) First theme (F major).
(*b*) Second theme (F minor).
(*c*) Variation of first theme.
(*d*) Variation of second theme.
(*e*) Second variation of first theme, followed by coda.

170. Haydn's Variations for the piano in F minor furnish another example of this same form, which will be familiar to many of our readers. Curiously enough, it was never employed by Mozart, and only once by Beethoven—in the second movement of his piano trio in E flat, Op. 70, No. 2. Since the time of Beethoven it seems to have been almost entirely disused.*

171. The variation form is occasionally to be found in vocal as well as in instrumental music. A once very popular example of this is to be seen in the air "Ah ! je veux briser ma chaine," in the second act of Auber's 'Diamans de la Couronne,' which is nothing but a brilliant set of *vocalises* for the soloist, and offers no special features for remark in its form. Far more interesting from an artistic point of view is the finale of Beethoven's Choral Symphony, which consists of an introduction and a series of free variations on the theme of the 'Ode to Joy.'

172. We have just spoken of the variations in Beethoven's symphony as preceded by an introduction. This, though by no means necessary, can always be used if the composer wishes. It is seldom to be met with unless the variations form an independent piece, and not merely one movement in a "cyclic form," that is, a work consisting of several movements. There are no rules as to the form which this introduction shall take ; in general it has the character of an improvisation or a fantasia. In the Choral Symphony the introduction to the variations consists of a recitative for the basses of the orchestra interrupted by reminiscences of the preceding movements of the symphony. A very good example of

* The author of this book has adopted it for the slow movement of his second Organ Concerto ; but he is not aware of any other instance of its employment by a contemporary composer.

an introduction to variations is found in Beethoven's Variations for piano, violin, and violoncello, Op. 121, which is chiefly a development of the theme of the first bar :—

Another specimen will be found in Chopin's Variations for piano and orchestra on "La ci darem," Op. 2.

173. We conclude this chapter with a general summary of the chief points which the student should bear in mind in beginning to write variations for himself. He should first of all be careful in the selection of the theme which he intends to vary. This should be of moderate length—preferably of two, or at most three eight-bar sentences,—it should be varied in its cadences, and of sufficiently distinctive character to be easily recognizable on its repetition in a varied form. This last stipulation applies chiefly to the strict variations.

174. Among the principal means of varying a theme are the following :—

I. Ornamentation of the melody without alteration of the original harmony. This is the simplest kind of variation, and that which is most frequently found in the older examples of this form. It includes the embellishment of the melody by auxiliary and passing notes, diatonic or chromatic, the dispersing of the harmony by means of arpeggios and broken chords, various combinations of these devices, &c.

II. Changing the harmony of the theme, either with or without modification of its melodic form. When this is done, it will be mostly advisable to introduce few or no changes in the melody, not only because thus it remains easier to recognize, but still more because the effect thus produced is often much more striking. As examples of this may be instanced the sixth variation in Beethoven's Fifteen Variations, Op. 35, and the sixth of Weber's Variations on "Vien quà, Dorina bella." If only this and the preceding method of varying be used, the variations will in general be strict.

175. III. By changing the *tempo* and the rhythmic figuration of the theme, as in the example by Beethoven analyzed in §§ 156-162, we obtain further variations, departing much more widely from the original form of the subject. We shall then have *free* variations. Not infrequently such variations take an entirely new form (March, Minuet, Polacca, Valse, &c.), or even, as in Beethoven's "Thirty-three Variations," are transformed to a Fughetta or Fugue. In such cases, the bond of connection with the theme is sometimes the general harmonic outline, at other times little more than the rhythmic structure of the music, and the

position of the cadences. In variations of this kind, more skill is required to preserve the artistic unity of the work than in the simpler and stricter variations previously described.

176. IV. It is mostly advisable, whether the variations be strict or free, that the length of their sentences shall be the same as in the theme. This is the usual practice of the great masters, and an observance of this rule will conduce greatly to the clearness of form of the composition. The exceptions to be met with are almost always in free, seldom if ever in strict variations. The final variation is in general extended by a coda; here the rule just given does not apply, though in most cases the variation itself which precedes the coda will be of the same length as the theme.

177. Of all existing forms there is none which shows such infinite diversity as (from its very nature) does the variation form. It has therefore been impossible to deal with it exhaustively. All that has been attempted has been to show the fundamental principles underlying the form, and to illustrate the application of these principles by reference to the works of the great composers.

CHAPTER VI.

THE OLDER RONDO FORM.

178. HAVING in our preceding chapters dealt with the most important of the smaller instrumental forms, we have now to treat of those larger forms which are the developments from the earlier and more primitive varieties, especially from the dance forms. It would be highly interesting, did our space permit, to trace the gradual growth of instrumental music from the simplest binary form to the modern sonata and symphony; but this would be beyond our scope, as the present volume is not a history of music, but a text-book of composition. The historical side of the question cannot be altogether overlooked; but we can only refer to it incidentally, as bearing on our examples; and students who wish to investigate the matter thoroughly must go elsewhere for their information.

179. The first of the larger forms of which we have to speak is the RONDO (*Fr.* "Rondeau"). This was originally a dance, the music to which was sung, while the performers danced in a circle, holding one another's hands. The music began with a chorus; one of the dancers then sang a solo, after which the chorus was repeated as a refrain. Other solos followed, the chorus being repeated after each. The chorus itself was called the 'Rondeau,' and the various solos 'Couplets.' The Rondeau, as a dance measure, was always in common time. Before long, movements in triple time were also composed in this form; and, although these could not be used for the dance, the name 'Rondo' was still applied to them. The dance itself is long since obsolete; but the name and the musical form remain to this day. In general terms, then, a Rondo may be described as a piece of music with a refrain—that is, in which the principal subject recurs at the end of each division of the piece. It is to be met with both in instrumental and vocal music.

180. There are two kinds of Rondo, differing so widely from one another that it will be needful to keep them quite distinct. The older Rondo form is the direct descendant of the dance described in the last section; the more modern Rondo is a modification, or variation, of the sonata form, of which we have as yet said nothing. It is the former of which we shall treat in this chapter, deferring our notice of the latter until the sonata form has been explained.

181. We said above that the name 'Rondeau' was applied

not only to the composition as a whole, but also to the principal subject, which served as the refrain. In the older examples of the form which we have examined, the name is always spelt in the French way, as we have spelt it here; the Italian form 'Rondo' is almost universal in modern compositions. In many examples by Couperin we find the name given on each resumption of the principal theme, while the connecting episodes still retain the name 'Couplets,' given to them when the music was vocal, as explained in § 179. As a very characteristic example of this form, we give the Rondeau from the Eighteenth Suite (or, as he calls it, 'Ordre') by Couperin :—

COUPERIN : Pièces de Clavecin, Ordre 18.

(8)
2e Couplet.
(4)
(8)
(4)
Rondeau.
(8)
(4)
(8)
3e Couplet.

We have given the rhythmic analysis, that the construction may be more easily followed.

182. The principal subject, here called 'Rondeau,' is a regular sentence, eight bars in length. This is generally the case in these older rondos; that in Bach's second Partita, in which the subject is sixteen bars long, is only an apparent, not a real exception; for the sixteen bars of $\frac{3}{8}$ time in that piece are really the equivalent of the eight bars of $\frac{6}{8}$ seen in the present example, as the principal accents come only on every second bar. (Compare the sixteen-bar sentence by Schubert, quoted in *Musical Form*, § 72.) The episodes ('Couplets') are less regular in

length The first contains only six bars, the first section of the fore-phrase being elided. This episode is in the dominant key. The second episode is longer; it consists of a complete sentence in the key of D minor, followed by another abridged sentence of six bars, similar in construction to the first episode. In this a return is made through the dominant key to the chief subject. The third episode, which is in the tonic key, and contains no modulation, consists of only one sentence, the after-phrase of which is repeated in a varied form. The unusually large number of embellishments in the right-hand part are characteristic of Couperin's style.

183. The rondo just analyzed contains three episodes. In these older rondos there was no fixed number of episodes; in the majority of cases we find two, three, or four; but a much larger number is occasionally to be seen. In Couperin's eighth Suite is a Rondo in B minor, containing no fewer than eight 'Couplets.' This piece, however, is a Passecaille (§ 139), and, though Couperin has given it also the title of 'Rondeau,' it is in reality a combination of the rondo and the variation forms.

184. It will be seen that in the rondo given above no two episodes are in the same key. This is an important point to be considered in composition; the episodes should always be contrasted with the principal subject in their character, and mostly in their key also. It is, however, not unusual to find a *final* episode in the key of the tonic. This would be very bad for a first episode; towards the close of a piece, after the course of modulation is ended, a digression without leaving the tonic key is admissible.

185. We will now analyze the "Rondeau" of Bach's Partita in C minor, to which we referred incidentally in § 182, and which illustrates some points in the construction of the older rondos not shown in the example by Couperin. Our space will not allow us to give the movement here; but this is the less necessary, as the work is readily accessible in the Peters edition. This piece is much more regular in its rhythmic construction than the rondo by Couperin. The principal subject, in C minor, consists of one sentence of sixteen bars, without any modulation; the fore-phrase ends in the eighth bar with a half cadence, and the after-phrase at the sixteenth, with a full cadence. There are three episodes, each being a complete sixteen-bar sentence; the first begins in E flat major, and modulates to F minor, the fore-phrase ending with a full cadence in that key, while the after-phrase, instead of ending with a full cadence (as was the case in all the episodes in Couperin's rondo), finishes with a half cadence in C minor; the return of the chief subject is thus more closely connected with what has preceded.

186. After the repetition of the chief subject comes the second episode. This is in the key of the relative major; the

fore-phrase ending with a half cadence (feminine ending), and the after-phrase with a full cadence in E flat. We then have the chief subject, now with the fore-phrase varied, though the after-phrase retains its original form. The third episode is in G minor, and is in strong contrast with those that have preceded. The chief subject then appears for the last time, but now with a new variation, not only of the fore-phrase, but of the after-phrase also. This variation of the chief subject of a rondo on its subsequent appearances is a very frequent and characteristic feature, not only of the form we are now discussing, but of the rondos of Mozart and Beethoven.

187. The older rondo form, as found in the works of more modern composers, from Haydn onwards, though resembling in many respects the rondos just analyzed, has special features of its own. These will be best understood if we consider the rondo as an extension of the ternary form by precisely the same process by which the ternary form was developed from the binary. Those who have studied Chapter X. of *Musical Form* will remember that the ternary form contains the three following parts:—

(1) Principal subject, which is in itself a complete binary form of at least two sentences.

(2) Episode, which may be, but is not of necessity, also a complete binary form.

(3) Repetition of chief subject, entire or in part, with or without variation or embellishment.

188. Now if to an already complete ternary form we add a second episode, and then once more repeat the whole or part of the chief subject, we have exactly the older rondo form, as we find it in the works of Haydn, Mozart, Dussek, or Beethoven, and their successors down to the present time. It is evident that a rondo of this kind will contain five parts, instead of the three met with in the ternary form. The student will never have any difficulty in distinguishing between the two forms, if he will only remember that *in a ternary form the principal subject never occurs more than twice, and in a rondo never less than three times.*

189. Though not properly to be classed among rondos, a moment's thought will show us that a minuet or scherzo which contains two trios will be really in rondo form. Take, for exampl the Minuet in Mozart's clarinet quintett, or the scherzo of Schumann's symphony in B flat. The two trios in these works correspond to the two episodes spoken of above. After each trio the minuet or scherzo is repeated, giving us in all the three appearances of the chief subject, which is the special characteristic of the rondo form.

190. When a minuet has two trios, it is not uncommon to find one of them in the same key as the minuet itself. This is the case in the clarinet quintett of Mozart, referred to in the last

paragraph. But in a genuine rondo the episodes are almost invariably in different keys from the chief subject; and the next question to be considered is, which are the most suitable keys for the episodes? The answer is very simple: the episodes may be in any key the tonic of which is consonant to the original tonic; but the keys most frequently employed are the following:—

For a rondo in a major key (1) the subdominant, (2) the relative minor, (3) the tonic minor, and, somewhat less frequently (4), the dominant.

For a rondo in a minor key (1) the relative major, (2) the tonic major, (3) the submediant major, (4) the dominant minor.

191. In addition to the keys just named, we occasionally find an episode in a key that is in the second degree of relationship. For example, in Beethoven's Rondo a Capriccio in G, Op. 129, one of the episodes is in E major. Such cases are comparatively rare; and the student will do well, in his first attempts at composing a rondo, to restrict himself to the keys we have given above. It ought to be hardly necessary to remind him that, as the same modulation should never be made twice in succession, the two episodes must never be in the same key.

192. As an example of the form we are now describing, we give the Rondo from Haydn's sonata in D major, No. 7 of Breitkopf & Härtel's edition. We select this movement, not only because it is perfectly clear and regular in its construction, but also because it is short:—

HAYDN: Sonata in D, No. 7.

(8)
(1)
(8)
(4=2)
(4)
(6a)
(6b)
(8)
(4)
(8)
(4)
(8=4)

(4)
(8)
(4)
(5=1)
(4)
(8)
(4)
(7)
(7a)
(8)
decres.
p
(8a)
(8b)
(8c)
(8d)
(8e)
(8f)
(4)

tr
f
(8)
(4)
tr
p
(8)
f
(4)
(8=4)
p
(8)
f
(4)
(8=4)
(8)
(8a)

The principal subject of this rondo is a small binary form of two sentences, the first, of the normal length, ending in the dominant, and the second extended to twelve bars by the addition of a second after-phrase. As is very frequently the case in older examples of this form, each sentence is repeated.

193. The first episode is in the tonic minor. Like the chief subject, it is a complete binary form, the first sentence ending in F major, and regular in length, and the second returning to D minor. This second sentence contains twelve bars; but there is not here (as in the second sentence of the principal subject) an additional after-phrase; instead of this, each phrase, as will be seen from our analysis, is extended by two bars. This episode is followed by an exact repetition of the whole of the principal subject.

194. It is evident that it would have been quite possible for the movement to end here. Had it done so, it would have been a very good example of a short and simple ternary form. The addition of a second episode makes the piece into a rondo. This new episode is in the subdominant key. It is worthy of notice that when one of the episodes of a rondo is in the subdominant, it is almost invariably the second, and not the first episode for which this key is chosen. The reason no doubt is that the subdominant being the key out of which the tonic is derived as a dominant, an early modulation into it has a tendency to reduce the real tonic to a subordinate or secondary position, and thus to confuse the feeling of the tonality. It is exceedingly rare, and certainly not advisable, to make a first principal modulation to the key of the subdominant.

195. The second episode of the rondo we are examining is, like the first, a complete binary form. It is followed by a connecting sentence, of irregular construction, serving as a "bridge-passage" to reintroduce the original key and the chief subject. In this subject the accompaniment is now varied in the repetition of the first, as well as throughout the second sentence. The movement has no coda, the end of the chief subject being only followed by two repetitions of the tonic chord.

196. Very similar in form to the example just given, though on a considerably more extended scale, and in slow time, is Dussek's favourite Andante known as "La Consolation." The piece is preceded by an introduction (§ 172), constructed of material quite independent of the subjects of the rondo itself. It is needless to quote a movement so generally familiar as this; a short analysis will be sufficient. The chief subject of the Andante is a short binary form, each part of which is repeated. The first part contains one sentence, and the second two, all being of the normal eight-bar construction. The first sentence ends, not, as usual with a major subject, in the dominant, but in the key of the relative minor, G minor. The first episode is in the tonic minor key. It is, like the chief subject, a complete binary form, the first

part (one eight-bar sentence) closing in the relative major (D flat), and the second part (two sentences of fourteen and eight bars respectively) ending with a full cadence in B flat minor. Both parts of this episode are repeated.

197. The principal subject then recurs; the first sentence is given in its original form and then repeated with a variation in triplet semiquavers; the two following sentences are only given once, but varied like the first by triplets. The second episode, in E flat, also consists of two sentences, both repeated; the first modulates to the dominant (B flat), and the second ends with a full close in E flat. This episode is therefore again a complete binary form. It is followed by a rather long bridge-passage of eighteen bars, leading back to the principal subject, of which we find now a second variation, in demisemiquavers, after which a coda of fifteen bars concludes the piece.

198. If we compare "La Consolation" with Haydn's rondo, we cannot but be struck with the great similarity of the general outline. In both pieces not only the principal subject, but both the episodes, are of complete binary form, with repetition of both parts. An even more important point of resemblance is seen in the order of modulation. In each case the first episode is in the tonic minor, and the second in the subdominant major. In both pieces also, a bridge-passage connects the second episode with the final return of the principal subject. The two movements may be taken as types of one of the common varieties of the older rondo form.

199. In the majority of rondos, however, the different sections of the work are not so clearly separated from one another by double bars as in the examples we have just analyzed. In Mozart's Rondo in A minor, for instance, a beautiful specimen of this form, which students will do well to examine, the chief subject is a binary form, thirty bars long, without repetition of either of its parts; an episode in F major, thirty-four bars in length, which immediately succeeds, is followed by a bridge-passage of sixteen bars leading back to the repetition of the chief subject, of which only the first sentence is now given, but with new ornamentation. The second episode is in A major; its first sentence of nine bars is repeated; but the second sentence (15 bars) leads into another long bridge-passage through which the return is made to the key of A minor, and the final appearance of the chief subject. The whole of this is now heard, with further embellishments, and a coda of twenty-four bars concludes the rondo.

200. To avoid misapprehension, it should be said that when we speak of the subject being in A minor, the first episode in F, and so on, it is not to be inferred that the music remains in those keys throughout the whole of the subject or episode, as the case may be, but only that those are the principal keys, from which incidental modulations are made.

201. Very similar in its general form to the rondo just spoken of is Beethoven's Andante in F, beginning:—

Here the first episode modulates to, and is mostly in the key of the dominant, while the second, consisting of two sentences, each repeated, is in the key of the subdominant. The principal subject is varied on each repetition, and the coda is of unusual extent and importance.

202. A few new features will be seen in the next example we will take—Beethoven's Rondo in C, Op. 51, No. 1. The principal subject, beginning

(*a*) BEETHOVEN: Rondo in C, Op. 51, No. 1.

consists of two sentences, the first eight bars long, and the second extended to nine. The first episode is in the dominant key and begins at bar 17, thus—

(*b*)

It ends at bar 38 with an inverted cadence in G over a tonic pedal, and is followed by a bridge-passage, leading back through the harmony of the dominant seventh of C to the return of the principal subject in bar 43. Of this only the first sentence is now repeated, with some florid ornamentation in the after-phrase.

203. The second episode, in C minor, begins at the 51st bar, and is in strong contrast to what has preceded it:—

(*c*)

Modulating first to E flat, and touching afterwards on F minor and G minor, it ends with a full cadence in C minor at bar 72, and is followed by another long bridge-passage, in which at bar 75 the chief subject is introduced in the key of A flat, with a new variation in triplets.* Only a fragment of the subject is heard in this key, the close of the first sentence being altered, so as to finish with a half-cadence in C minor at bar 83. Alternations of the dominant and tonic harmony of C minor lead back to the principal subject in C major at bar 91. The whole of the first sentence is now repeated with some slight variation, and also the first six bars of the second sentence. At bar 105 Beethoven commences his coda with a sudden modulation to D flat, returning at bar 116 to the original key of C major, in which key a new idea is introduced, but only briefly treated. The rondo ends with a reminiscence in the bass (bar 131) of the opening theme.

204. One of the grandest examples of this form, and also one of the most extended in its developments, is the Rondo of Beethoven's great sonata, Op. 53. The principal subject, which is of extreme simplicity,

BEETHOVEN: Sonata, Op. 53.

(a)

and is twice repeated with varied accompaniment, extends to bar 62. It is followed by a passage of eight bars, which should be regarded as a *codetta*, rather than as a bridge-passage; for by the latter term is meant a passage leading directly into what follows. The eight bars (62 to 70) in this rondo do not do this, but are merely cadential in the key of C, and therefore a continuation or prolongation of the close of the preceding subject. The first episode, which begins with a unison passage in broken octaves,

(b)

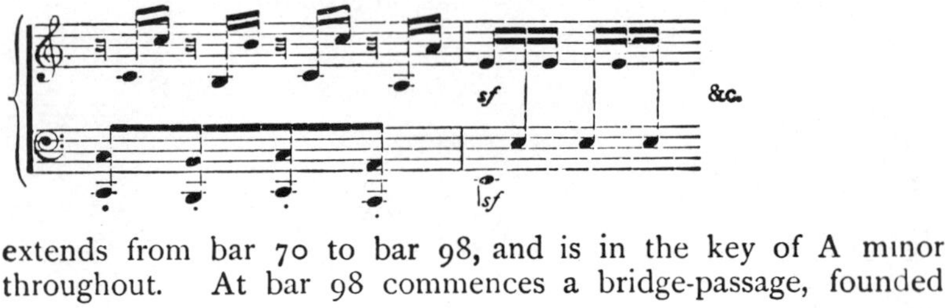

extends from bar 70 to bar 98, and is in the key of A minor throughout. At bar 98 commences a bridge-passage, founded

* It is very rare with modern composers to find the chief subject of the rondo in any but the tonic key. C. P. E. Bach, however, often introduces his chief subject in many different keys, sometimes even in those unrelated to the principal tonic. See, for instance, his Rondo in E major, in the third book of the 'Sonaten für Kenner und Liebhaber.'

upon the first four bars of the principal subject, and leading back to the return of that subject in bar 113. This is given in its complete form, and without a note of alteration, and on its conclusion in bar 175 it is followed immediately by the second episode, the principal key of which is C minor, and which (like the first episode) begins in unison :—

(*c*)

This subject on its immediate repetition is accompanied by semiquaver triplets, written in free double counterpoint in the octave. The second episode modulates through A flat and F minor, and after returning to C minor ends at bar 220. It is followed by an unusually long bridge-passage of 92 bars, which deserves to be carefully analyzed. On examining it the student will find that it is almost entirely developed from the first four bars of the chief subject. It modulates freely, and entirely through flat keys :—A flat (bar 221), F minor (bar 225), D flat (bar 229), E flat minor (bar 242), F minor (bar 246), B flat minor (bar 257), E flat minor (bar 263), D flat (bar 271), and C minor (bar 275). After alternations of tonic, dominant, and supertonic harmony in this key, the dominant chord is reached in bar 295, to which at bar 299 the dominant seventh is added, and this harmony is continued till the final return of the principal subject in bar 313. Only the last 32 bars of this subject now reappear, and at bar 344 the coda begins with a repetition of the short codetta seen in bars 62 to 70. This codetta is now considerably extended and leads into the *prestissimo* (bar 403), in which the chief subject is given by diminution. It should be noticed that though the notes of the subject are written of the same length as at first, the difference in the *tempo* reduces them to about half their original time value. This is clearly shown by the entry of the subject in minims at bar 485, where the notes have approximately their original length. Let the student notice that much of this *prestissimo* is again developed from the commencement of the chief subject; this will be clearly seen in the left-hand part of the passage beginning at bar 441. The entire movement is an exceptionally fine example of the capabilities of this older rondo form in the hands of such a master as Beethoven.

205. Other excellent examples of this form are to be found in the final movements of Weber's sonata in C, Op. 24 (the so-called "Moto Continuo") and Schubert's sonatas in D major, Op. 53, and G major, Op. 78. Of more modern composers, Schumann was very partial to the form, which he sometimes treats with considerable freedom. His popular 'Arabeske' (Op. 18) is a very familiar example, with its principal subject in C major, and its two episodes in E minor and A minor respectively. We also refer

students to Nos. 2 and 8 of the 'Kreisleriana' (Op. 16), Nos. 1, 2 and 3, of the 'Nachtstücke' (Op. 23), and No. 3 of the 'Three Romances' (Op. 28) as good specimens of this form. It should be mentioned in passing that in No. 2 of the 'Kreisleriana' the first episode is in $\frac{2}{4}$ time, while the rest of the movement is in $\frac{3}{4}$. Though not very often to be met with, a change of time for one of the episodes is quite allowable for the sake of contrast.

206. In describing this form we said in § 188 that as it contained two episodes, with three appearances of the chief subject, it naturally divided into five parts. This is the case in all the rondos that we have been analyzing; but though it is the form to be met with in the large majority of cases, we occasionally find rondos with three episodes. Two of Dussek's finest sonatas furnish excellent examples of this. In his sonata in E flat, Op. 75, the rondo has three episodes, the first modulating to the key of the dominant, the second to the relative minor, and the third to the subdominant. In the same composer's last sonata (known as "L'Invocation") the rondo, in F minor, has the first episode mostly in A flat, the second in B flat minor and D flat major, and the third in F major. Schumann's Novellette in D major (Op. 21, No. 5) is another instance of a movement in rondo form with three episodes.

207. In all the examples hitherto examined the principal subject of the rondo has been a complete binary form, consisting of at least two sentences. But we occasionally meet with rondos in which the principal subject is only one sentence in length. This is the case in the Rondo of Mozart's little sonata in C major, written for beginners ("Für Anfänger"). This movement, which will be readily recognized by its commencement—

is quite short, containing only 73 bars, and is noticeable for the perfect regularity of the four- and eight-bar periods throughout. Only at the final cadence is one additional bar of tonic harmony appended. In this rondo the chief subject, of eight bars, is repeated, and the first episode (in the dominant key) sounds far more like a continuation than a contrast, especially as the last four bars of the principal subject are used in a slightly modified form. The episode is also eight bars long, and a bridge-passage of four bars brings back the chief subject. Then follows a second episode in A minor, also largely founded upon the opening theme; after which the chief subject recurs, and is followed by a short *coda*. Had not Mozart expressly called this movement 'Rondo,' we should certainly not have so regarded it; for one of the most distinctive features of the rondo form—contrast of episode—is almost entirely wanting. As it is, we are compelled in analyzing it as a rondo to consider the chief subject as ending in bar 8 ; otherwise there is only one episode, and the piece is no longer a rondo. Had not the composer himself so described it, we should have said that the movement was in ternary form.

208. In general, if after one eight-bar sentence ending in the tonic (as in the movement we have just been discussing) the first modulation, supposing the piece to be in a major key, is to the key of the dominant, it is better to regard what follows as belonging to the chief subject rather than as episode, because in the majority of cases the music will be more of a continuation than a contrast. As an illustration of this we will take the rondo of Mozart's lovely trio in E flat for piano, clarinet, and viola. It opens with a sentence of eight bars, the melody of which is first given to the clarinet, and then repeated on the piano:—

MOZART : Trio in E flat.

(*a*)

At bar 17 there is a modulation to the dominant, and the clarinet continues with the following theme:—

(*b*)

This certainly suggests a continuation of, rather than a contrast to what has preceded, and a little later, at bar 36, we find further evidence to support this view in the introduction of the first two bars of the opening sentence treated in imitation between the clarinet and the viola:—

(*c*)

For the sake of clearness we have omitted the arpeggios in the piano part, which fill up the harmony. At bar 59 the first sentence is repeated by the piano alone, and we have now a complete binary form, of rather unusual extent—66 bars.

209. The first episode begins at bar 67 with a bold subject allotted to the viola :—

(*d*)

If the student will compare this with the example (*b*) in the preceding paragraph, he will see at once what we mean by the difference between continuation and contrast. This episode consists of two sentences, each of which is repeated ; and at bar 91 a bridge-passage, seventeen bars in length, leads back to the original key, and the first return of the principal subject (bar 108). Of this, as often happens when, as here, it is of considerable extent, only the first sentence is repeated, now as a viola solo, accompanied by quaver triplets for the piano. To this immediately succeeds the second episode in A flat, beginning at bar 116 thus :—

(*e*)

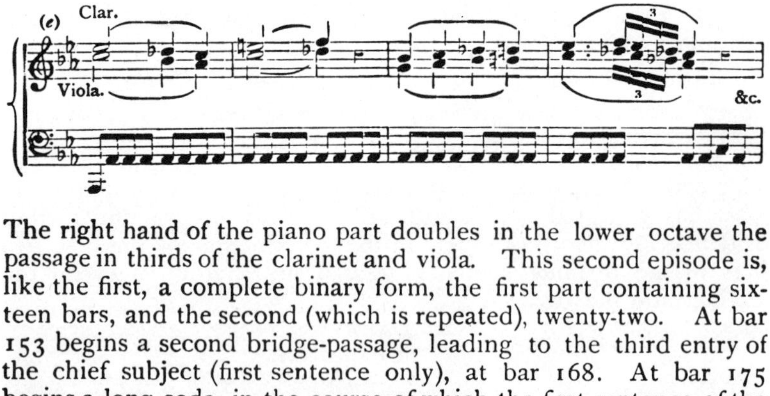

The right hand of the piano part doubles in the lower octave the passage in thirds of the clarinet and viola. This second episode is, like the first, a complete binary form, the first part containing sixteen bars, and the second (which is repeated), twenty-two. At bar 153 begins a second bridge-passage, leading to the third entry of the chief subject (first sentence only), at bar 168. At bar 175 begins a long coda, in the course of which the first sentence of the chief subject once more makes its appearance (bar 185). Toward the end of the coda (bar 212), a portion of the second bridge-passage is heard in the tonic key.

210. We sometimes find rondos so constructed that it is very difficult, if not impossible, to decide with certainty how they should be analyzed. Take, for instance, the rondo of Beethoven's sonata in D, Op. 10, No. 3. Two analyses are here quite possible. We may consider the chief subject as consisting (like that in Mozart's rondo spoken of in § 207) of only one sentence, ending on the first note of bar 9. In that case, there will be three episodes, beginning respectively at bars 9, 33, and 64. But this analysis is open to objection ; first, because the passage commencing at bar 9 has its

first six bars in the tonic key, and a first episode will always be in some other key than the tonic; and secondly, because the third episode (bar 64) is in the first part of it a mere repetition of the first episode, while its second part brings forward no new subject, and is merely free thematic treatment of the first three notes of the principal subject. If, on the other hand, we regard the chief subject as a large binary form, the second part of which begins at bar 9, and which ends at bar 33, we are met by the difficulty that we find no proper second episode. After the episode which begins in B flat at bar 35, the chief subject recurs at the end of bar 55; its second part modulates through G major (bar 68) to B minor (bar 72); but the passage between bars 72 and 83, where the chief subject makes its last appearance, cannot, as we pointed out just now, be considered as episode, because it contains no new material. The fact is that we have in this movement a rondo of irregular construction; and we have analyzed it in some detail to show the student that it is quite impossible to lay down any rules for these larger forms which shall be applicable in all cases. The more extended the form, the more room there is for variation in the details; and although the rules given in this chapter are observed by composers in the large majority of instances, numerous examples are, nevertheless, to be found in which they are more or less widely departed from.

211. In analyzing Dussek's "La Consolation" in §§ 196, 197, we called attention to the variation of the theme on each repetition. The double variation form on two themes, spoken of in the last chapter (§§ 169, 170), may be regarded as a variety of the rondo form. Here, as we saw, we have three appearances of the chief subject; but instead of two episodes, we have one episode repeated in a varied form. The minuet or scherzo with two trios (§ 76), or with one trio repeated, as frequently with Beethoven, is another variety of the rondo.

212. Sometimes pieces are called rondos which are not so in reality. Mozart's Rondo in D,

has no resemblance whatever either to the form described in this chapter or to the other rondo form to be spoken of later. It is a regularly constructed sonata-form movement, a form of which we shall treat in the next chapter. The same is the case with another movement by Mozart, entitled in some editions 'Rondo in B flat':—

This also is a complete sonata movement. The popular "Rondo alla Turca" of Mozart's sonata in A is also distinctly not a rondo, but is in ternary form. Mendelssohn's 'Rondo Capriccioso,' again, has much more of the 'Capriccio' than the 'Rondo' about it. It departs so widely from any acknowledged rondo form that it ought rather to have been entitled simply 'Capriccio.'

213. The student will, it is hoped, have now a sufficient idea of the construction of a rondo to be able to write one if he desires. We recommend him, above all things, to aim in the first instance at clearness of form. The different parts of the movement should be readily recognizable, without their being of necessity square cut, or of uniform length. In constructing his episodes, let him not forget that they should be well contrasted with the principal subject, while not destroying the unity of his work as a whole. Exactly how this is to be effected cannot be taught; it is here that his musical feeling must come to his aid. If he has a natural aptitude for composition, he will not be likely to go far astray; if not, he had much better leave it alone.

CHAPTER VII

THE SONATA FORM: THE EXPOSITION.

214. WE have now to treat of the most important, and, with perhaps the single exception of the fugue, the most artistic of the larger forms—that commonly known as the SONATA FORM. The word 'Sonata' is derived from the Italian verb *suonare*, "to play," and was originally applied to instrumental music—"that which was played," as distinguished from '*Cantata*'—vocal music, "that which was sung." But in its modern sense the word 'Sonata' is restricted to a composition for one or two instruments, containing at least two movements, of which one is generally, though not invariably, in the form to be described in this chapter. The different movements to be found in a sonata will be spoken of later in this volume, when we come to deal with Cyclic forms (Chapter XII.); for the present it will suffice to say that by the sonata form is meant that form which is to be found in the very large majority of the first movements, very frequently also in the finales, and sometimes in the middle movements as well.

215. It is not merely in sonatas that this form is met with. There are very few trios, quartetts, quintetts, or symphonies in which it is not employed for at least one of the movements; and it might just as appropriately be called 'Symphony Form,' indeed this name is occasionally given to it. It is also found, with modifications which will be described in a later chapter, in many overtures and concertos. From the frequency of its employment in first movements, it is sometimes called "first movement form." But the name "Sonata Form" is far the most usual; and if the student will remember that it is by no means the only form to be found in a sonata, but that it describes that which is generally met with in the first movement, there can be no confusion from its employment.

216. Before proceeding to speak in detail of the construction of a movement written in sonata form, it will be well to point out the essential difference between this form and the older rondo form treated of in the last chapter. We know that in a rondo there is always one principal subject—never more than one—and that between the appearances of this subject are interspersed

episodes of a more or less strongly contrasted character. The essential characteristic of the rondo form is *diversity.* In the sonata form, on the other hand, there are always two principal subjects, and although incidental episodical matter is frequently introduced, there are no independent episodes of the kind with which we are familiar in the rondo. The place of episode is supplied chiefly by the development of material to be found in the principal subjects themselves. In other words, the special characteristic of the sonata form is *unity.* For this reason some theorists describe it as a "movement of continuity"—an appropriate but rather clumsy name, while they call the ternary and older rondo forms "movements of episode." How the unity of which we have spoken is to be obtained will be seen when we come to describe the different parts of a movement in sonata form.

217. In the early part of the last century the name 'Sonata' was frequently given to a piece consisting of only a single movement, of binary form. The so-called 'Sonatas' of Domenico Scarlatti are of this kind; and, as the modern sonata movement springs directly out of this older form, we analyze a short example by Scarlatti, that the student may be able to follow more intelligently the larger forms to be afterwards examined.

D. SCARLATTI: Sonata in G.

(4)
(4a)
tr
(8=5)
(8)
(8a)
(8b)
tr
tr
(4)
(c)
(8)
(8a)
(2)
(2a)
(4)
(d)
(4a)
(8)
(2)
(2a)
(4)

This movement consists of two parts, the first containing 37 bars, and the second 41. The first part opens with a subject in the key of the tonic, consisting of a single eight-bar sentence extended to twelve bars by the repetition of the after-phrase. At (*a*) begins a passage modulating to the key of the dominant to introduce the second subject. Such a passage we call a "bridge-passage" (§ 195); it differs from the "link," that we have several times met with, in this respect—that a link is a passage connecting two sentences, but itself, from its want of cadences, forming no part of a sentence, while a bridge-passage will contain at least a complete phrase or sentence, and connects not merely two sentences, but two distinct subjects, or (in the case of a rondo,) a subject and an episode. In sonatas, whether of the older form now under notice, or of the more modern structure, as seen in the works of Beethoven, a bridge-passage of greater or less extent is almost invariably interposed between the first and second subjects.

218. The bridge-passage of the present sonata, though containing eight bars, does not form a complete sentence, because each pair of bars is repeated, as shown by our analysis (2, 2*a*, 4, 4*a*). At (*b*) the second subject is introduced; it is in the key of the dominant, and, like the first subject, it consists of only one sentence. By means of various repetitions it is extended to 17 bars.

219. Here the student may naturally enquire, How are we to know exactly where the second subject begins? The answer is generally very simple. In the first part of a sonata movement the second subject is always in some other key than the tonic—we shall presently discuss the question which are the proper keys to be used—but when this subject reappears later in the movement it will be in the tonic key. All that is needful in most cases—exceptions will be dealt with later—is to look at the latter part of the movement, and to see how much of what is at first in the dominant (or whatever other may be the key of the second subject,) is found transposed into the key of the tonic. In the present case everything from (*b*) down to the double bar which ends the first part of the movement is found later, at (*d*), trans-

posed, with very trifling modification, into the key of G, while the bars preceding (*b*) are not so transposed. We therefore know that the second subject begins at (*b*).

220. The first part of this sonata, then, is thus constructed: First subject, in G; bridge-passage, modulating to D; second subject in D, with a passing touch upon the minor mode. The second part of this movement is the exact converse of the first. It begins with the first subject, of twelve bars, in the key of the dominant; then follows at (*c*) a new bridge-passage, constructed on the same material as the first one, but now modulating from the dominant back to the key of the tonic, and extended by four bars; lastly, at (*d*) we have the second subject transposed into the tonic key. It was usual, with the older sonatas, to repeat both parts of the movement, just as in the old dances (Allemandes, &c.,) which were the germs out of which this form developed.

221. We have chosen for our illustration a particularly perfect* example of this old form; but it will be well to add that in many cases the construction is somewhat less clear than in the movement we have given. Especially do we frequently find modifications of the first subject when it appears in the second part of the movement. Sometimes it is only hinted at, and its thematic material is differently treated. As examples of this, let the student examine the preludes Nos. 9 and 12 of the second part of Bach's 'Wohltemperirtes Clavier,' both of which are in modified old sonata form. It is seldom, also, that the different parts of the movement are as distinctly marked off from one another as in the piece we have been analyzing.

222. The sonatas of Scarlatti date from the first half of the last century; for the composer (born 1683, died 1757) was a contemporary of Handel; but the form continued in use till considerably later, being only gradually supplanted by the more modern sonata form of which we shall speak presently. Examples of the older form may be seen in Clementi's sonatas in B flat, Op. 10 No. 3 (finale), and in G, Op. 38 No. 1 (first movement), in the two allegros of Haydn's sonata in G (No. 21 of Breitkopf and Härtel's edition), and in some of the earlier symphonies and sonatas of Mozart. Probably the latest instance of its employment is the finale of Schubert's sonata in A minor, Op. 164. At the present time it is entirely obsolete.

223. The invention, or, perhaps we should rather say, the development of the modern sonata form is usually attributed to Carl Philip Emanuel Bach. It is true that he was the first to introduce it systematically; but his illustrious father, who seems to have anticipated, by a kind of prophetic instinct, nearly all modern discoveries, has left us at least one or two movements which are

* "Perfect" that is, as regards its form; but the harmony, with its consecutive fifths and octaves, is very faulty.

perfect examples of this form. One is the prelude in D, No. 5 of the second book of the 'Wohltemperirtes Clavier;' another will be seen in the prelude in G beginning

J. S. BACH: Prelude and Fughetta in G.

If, after reading this and the following chapter, the student will examine the two movements here referred to, he will find that they both fulfil all the requirements of the modern sonata form. It is none the less true that the general introduction of this form was due to Emanuel Bach and Haydn.

224. The essential points of difference between the older and the modern sonata form are two. In the older form, as we have seen, at the end of the first part, the first subject reappears at once in the same key in which the second subject has just been heard. In the modern form, the first subject, when repeated, is in the tonic key, as at first; occasional exceptions will be noticed in the next chapter, when we come to speak of the recapitulation. But a far more important difference is, that in the later form the reappearance of the first subject does not follow the close of the first part immediately, but is preceded by developments, more or less extended, of the material announced in the first part. After this comes the recapitulation, in which both first and second subjects are generally reintroduced in the tonic key. The effect of this addition is to change the form of the movement. The older sonata form is, as we have seen, a large binary; the modern becomes a modified ternary, the three parts being (I.) the exposition, or the announcing of the first and second subjects; (II.) the development of these subjects, which takes the place occupied in the regular ternary form by the episode; (III.) the recapitulation of the first and second subjects. The student will see how appropriate the name "applied form" is to a movement of this kind; it is a free application of the more regular ternary form which he has already studied. We shall now treat in detail of these three parts of a sonata movement, beginning with the exposition. As we shall draw our illustrations from symphonies, quartetts, &c., as well as from sonatas, it will be well to remind the student of what we said in § 215—that the name 'sonata form' applies equally to all other compositions written on the same model.

225. The exposition of a sonata movement consists of three parts: the first subject, the bridge-passage, and the second subject. In the older examples of the form to be found in the works of Haydn and Mozart, and also in many specimens by Beethoven,

the first subject contains one, or at most two sentences, either or both of which may be extended beyond the regular eight-bar formation; it usually ends either with a full cadence or a half-cadence in the key of the tonic. We first give a few examples of first subjects that end with a full close in the tonic key.

BEETHOVEN: Sonata, Op. 10, No. 2.

This subject consists of a single sentence, extended to twelve bars by the addition of a second after-phrase. The inverted cadence in B flat at the eighth bar proves that the sentence is not completed there.

226. Our next example contains two sentences.

HAYDN: Quartett, Op. 64, No. 5.

The first sentence is quite regular in form; the second has an additional after-phrase. It is seldom that a subject twenty bars long is to be found which, like this one, contains not the least trace of a modulation.

227. Our third illustration is somewhat different.

SCHUMANN: 1st Symphony.

Here the two sentences are both of the normal length ; but the after-phrase of the first modulates to the dominant key ; while the fore-phrase of the second is in the key of the subdominant.

228. Less frequent than the ending with a full cadence, yet still not uncommon, is the ending of the first subject with a half cadence in the tonic key.

MOZART : Symphony in G minor.

This subject consists of one extended sentence; for the passage following the full cadence in G minor has evidently the character of a continuation of what has preceded, and must be regarded as a new after-phrase rather than as a new sentence

229. We seldom in a first subject meet with modulation beyond the nearly-related keys. Beethoven, however, sometimes introduced a sequential repetition of the opening phrase at a distance of a tone or a semitone. The commencement of the Waldstein Sonata is a good illustration of this.

BEETHOVEN: Sonata, Op. 53.

Here the first four bars are repeated a tone lower, in B flat. Similar passages are to be seen in the same composer's sonatas, Op. 31 No. 1, and Op. 57—the transposition in the latter case being a semitone higher. In the passage we are now examining, it will be seen that the half cadence is on the dominant of C *minor*. The major key reappears in the following bar.

230. A word must be said in passing on the manner in which we have marked the division of the phrases here. In *Musical Form* (§ 39,) it was said that the accented bars were those in which the cadences occurred. It will be seen that at the beginning of this extract the change from dominant to tonic harmony occurs at the third and seventh bars, and not, where we have indicated the (4) and (4*a*), at the fourth and eighth. It would be quite possible to assume that each phrase begins with the elision of an unaccented bar, and that the fourth bar is prolonged over two. But further investigation has convinced the author that, while the rule above referred to applies in the large majority of cases, there are exceptions in which it is preferable to look at the passage *as a whole*, and to consider the phrase as commencing with an accented bar and ending with an unaccented. To this we have an exact analogy in poetry; phrases commencing with an unaccented bar correspond to the iambic metre (⏑ –|⏑ –|⏑ –|⏑ –), while those in which the accented bar comes first are the equivalent of the trochaic (– ⏑|– ⏑|– ⏑|– ⏑). In such cases, however, the application of

the general law is seen as soon as we reckon by what we may call the "larger metre," *i.e.*, throw two bars into one. For instance, in the passage just quoted:—

The opening of Beethoven's eighth symphony, with its trochaic metre—

Beethoven : 8th Symphony.

is a similar case. The third and seventh are evidently the accented bars of this passage; but they are really the accented halves of the second and fourth bars of the "larger metre"—

231. Though in general a first subject is rather short, we sometimes find it of considerable length. The first subject of Beethoven's sonata in A, Op. 2 No. 2 is 32 bars long, and that in his Pastoral symphony contains 53. In such cases as these it will be generally found that the length results from the repetition of a few motives or phrases, and not from the presentation of many different themes.

232. Occasionally the first subject is preceded by a few introductory, or prefatory bars. The opening of Weber's sonata in

C, Op. 24 (quoted in § 268 of *Musical Form*,) is an illustration of this; here the subject does not begin till the last crotchet of the fourth bar. A still more striking example is the commencement of Beethoven's 9th symphony, in which the first subject does not enter till the sixteenth bar. This is, of course, an altogether different case from that in which the introduction forms a separate movement in different time, as, for instance, in Beethoven's first and second symphonies.

233. The first subject of a sonata movement is followed by the bridge-passage, by which modulation is made leading to the key of the second subject. It is important to know exactly where the first subject ends, and the bridge-passage begins. For example, in the Waldstein sonata, quoted in § 229, it looks at first as if the passage immediately following the pause belonged to the first subject. The same is the case in Mozart's symphony in G minor (§ 228). In general there is no difficulty in determining the limits of the first subject, if it is remembered that it nearly always ends with a full close or a half close in the tonic key, and that *as soon as the music begins to modulate toward the key of the second subject*, we have reached the bridge-passage. The last full cadence or half cadence in the tonic key before the commencement of such modulations shows the end of the first subject.

234. To make this clear, we quote the bridge-passage in Mozart's G minor symphony, beginning with the last note of the first subject—the last bar of our extract in § 228:—

MOZART: Symphony in G minor.

The key of the second subject in this movement is B flat, which, as we shall see presently, is the most usual key for the second subject of a sonata movement in G minor. The bridge-passage therefore modulates toward that key. Its first bars are a repetition of the opening of the first subject, but a variation of the harmony at the fourth bar induces a modulation to B flat, and thence to F major. The bridge-passage ends with a cadence in that key, which, it need hardly be said, is the dominant of the key in which the second subject is to appear.

235. The above passage illustrates two points: first, that when the first subject ends with a half cadence on the dominant, the bridge-passage frequently begins with a repetition of the opening bars. For other examples of the same procedure see the first movements of Beethoven's sonatas in C, Op. 53 and F minor, Op. 57, and the last movement of the sonata in C♯ minor, Op. 27 No. 2, in all of which the bridge-passage opens with the commencement of the first subject.

236. The other point shown by this extract is the ending of the bridge-passage on the dominant harmony of the key in which

the second subject is going to enter. Though occasional exceptions are to be met with, it would probably be safe to say that in nine cases out of ten the bridge-passage ends in this same way. With the older composers we sometimes find it end with a half close in the tonic key—that is, on the tonic chord of the new key. In Haydn's sonata in B flat (No. 14 of Breitkopf and Härtel's edition,) it finishes thus, and the second subject follows immediately in the key of F. A similar case will be seen in the first movement of Beethoven's sonata in C, Op. 2 No. 3.

237. No rules can be given as to either the length or the material of the bridge-passage. The only general principle to be laid down is, that the modulations should be *toward* the key of the second subject, and not *away* from it. For instance, if a movement began in C major, and the second subject were, as usual, in G, it would be very unwise to go through the keys of F or B flat (which lie on the opposite side of the tonic) in the bridge-passage. On the other hand, we often find the second subject approached through its tonic minor, as for instance in the first movement of Mozart's sonata in F beginning

Here the first subject ends in bar 22 with a full cadence in F, the bridge-passage begins in D minor, and at bar 29 modulates to C minor, continuing in this key till it comes to a half cadence in bar 40. The second subject enters in C major at the next bar.

238. The bridge-passage is occasionally very short, consisting of only a few bars. Thus in Beethoven's sonata in F, Op. 10 No. 2, of which we quoted the first subject in § 225, the bridge is only six bars in length, and it ends, not on the dominant of C (in which key the second subject enters), but the dominant of its relative minor, A minor. Even shorter is the bridge in the first movement of Schubert's unfinished symphony in B minor. The first subject ends at bar 38 with a full cadence in the tonic, and the entire bridge-passage is

followed immediately by the second subject in G major.

239. In most modern sonata movements the second subject, which follows the bridge, is of considerably greater extent than the first. We have seen that the first subject seldom contains more than two sentences, or if it contain more, that this will generally be the result of repetitions. But in the second subject it is by no means unusual to find three, four, or even more sentences, each containing some entirely new thought. Of this we shall give

examples later. Some writers therefore speak of "tributaries to the second subject," "concluding subject," &c., but this nomenclature often renders it difficult to define the limits of the second subject itself. We therefore prefer to use the term in a wider sense, and to include under the general name "second subject" everything contained between the end of the bridge-passage and the close of the exposition. The term "group of second subjects" would be more strictly accurate, but awkward; and there will be no confusion if the student remembers that the second subject almost always contains at least two distinct ideas, and frequently more.

240. The first question which we have to consider is, what are the proper keys in which to introduce the second subject? We have already seen (§ 224,) that the older sonata form, out of which the form which we are now discussing was developed, was a simple binary, on a rather large scale. In this form the first principal modulation was always to a nearly related key—almost invariably to the dominant in a major movement, and in a minor movement either to the relative major or to the dominant minor. In all works in sonata form down to the time of Beethoven (in the compositions of C. P. E. Bach, Haydn, Mozart, Clementi, Dussek, &c.,) this relationship of keys prevails; and although, as will be seen directly, Beethoven and his successors have at times employed other keys for the second subjects, yet in the large majority of cases, they too adhered to the practice of the great composers who had preceded them.

241. The great innovation made by Beethoven in the sonata form was the introduction of the second subject in a major movement in a key which was in the second, instead of in the first degree of relationship to the tonic. These keys, as the student will know (*Musical Form*, § 83), are those which are at the distance of a major or minor third above or below the tonic. But Beethoven does not take any one of these four keys at random for a sufficiently obvious reason. Two of them contain more flats (or fewer sharps) in their signature than the tonic. It should be remembered that every major key is derived from keys that contain more flats than itself; thus C is the dominant of F, and the mediant of A flat. On the other hand, keys containing more sharps are generated from the tonic; G is the dominant, and E the mediant of C, both being found as upper-partials of that note. If therefore a modulation is made into a flatter key, the tonic at once sinks into a subordinate position as a derived key. For this reason Beethoven never introduces his second subject in the key of the subdominant, and only in one single instance in the flat submediant,—in the first movement of the quartett in B flat, Op. 130, where the second subject is in G flat major. The movement is irregular in form, and can hardly be taken as a precedent; but it should be noticed that the key of G flat is too remote from the

tonic to cause such a feeling of disturbed tonality as would have been the case had the second subject been in E flat. In every other instance of a modulation to a key in the second degree of relationship, Beethoven goes to the *sharp* side of his tonic—either the major third above or the minor third below.

242. As examples of major movements in which the second subject is in the key of the mediant, the student should examine the first movements of the pianoforte sonatas in G major (Op. 31 No. 1) and C major, Op. 53, both of which subsequently modulate to the mediant *minor*, and end in that key. Less frequently the major mediant continues to the end of the exposition, as in the finales of the piano trio in E flat, Op. 70 No. 2, and the string quartett in F, Op. 135. Occasionally the second subject is throughout in the mediant minor—the relative minor of the dominant (finale of symphony in A; first movement of quartett in E flat, Op. 127). There is no example in Beethoven of a second subject in the key of the flat mediant—the *minor* third above the tonic.

243. The submediant is also to be found in several of Beethoven's works as the key for the second subject. In the first movements of the great trio in B flat, Op. 97, and the piano sonata in the same key (Op. 106), the second subjects are in G major; in the first movement of the quintett in C, Op. 29, the second subject begins in A major, but alternates between that key and A minor, the exposition ending in the latter. In the first movement of the symphony in F (No. 8,) the second subject begins in the submediant (D major), and then modulates to and closes in the dominant. The flat submediant, as already mentioned, is only once employed by Beethoven for a second subject.

244. With movements in a minor key, we find in the older sonata form (as in the Suite forms from which it was developed) that the relative major and the dominant minor are about equally common as keys for the second subject. Scarlatti shows a decided preference for the latter. Of eighteen sonatas in minor keys by him which we have examined, the second subject is in the dominant minor key in thirteen cases, and in only five is it in the relative major. With C. P. E. Bach the proportions are nearly equal, but modern composers far more frequently select the relative major, though, as will be seen directly, numerous examples of the dominant minor are also to be met with. Haydn and Mozart almost invariably introduce their second subject in the relative major key; we have only met with one instance in each composer of the employment of the dominant minor—in the first movements of Haydn's 'Farewell Symphony' in F sharp minor, and of Mozart's string quartett in D minor, No. 13.

245. Beethoven uses the dominant minor key much more frequently for his second subject, chiefly (though not exclusively) in his piano sonatas. Let the student examine the sonatas in F

minor, Op. 2 No. 1 (finale), in C sharp minor, Op. 27 No. 2 (finale), in D minor, Op. 31 No. 2 (first and third movements), and in E minor, Op. 90 (first movement), and he will see this key-relationship of the two subjects in each case. But, as with the major key, Beethoven also introduces his second subject sometimes in the key of the submediant (see the first movements of the Choral Symphony, the quartett in F minor, Op. 95, and the piano sonata in C minor, Op. 111). His example has been followed by Schubert in the first movements of his 'Tragic Symphony' (No. 4), and of the unfinished symphony in B minor, and by Brahms in his piano quintett in F minor.

246. Another innovation due to Beethoven is the employment of the dominant *major*, instead of the dominant minor for the second subject in a minor movement. This is only found once in his works—in the first movement of the 'Kreutzer' sonata in A minor, in which the second subject opens in E major, though it very soon modulates to E minor, in which key it ends. But the example set by Beethoven was followed by later composers, one of the most familiar instances being the first movement of Mendelssohn's trio in D minor, in which the second subject begins in A major, though the latter part of it is in A minor. Schubert in two sonatas in A minor, Op. 143 (first movement), and Op. 164 (finale), has the second subject ending as well as beginning in E major. A similar case is seen in the first movement of Brahms's piano quartett in G minor, Op. 25, the second subject of which is in D major.

247. Raff, in his third symphony ('Im Walde'), has tried an experiment which has seldom, if ever, been repeated, and which certainly cannot be commended. The key of the symphony is F major, and in the first movement the second subject is in B flat—the subdominant. We have already shown (§ 241,) why this key has a disturbing effect upon the feeling of tonality, and a study of Raff's symphony certainly has not induced us to alter our unfavourable opinion of that selection of a key for the second subject. Raff has also employed the flat submediant and the flat mediant for his subjects—the former in the first movement of his 'Lenore' symphony in E major, which has the second subject in C, and the latter in the first movement of his sonata for piano and violoncello in D (Op. 183), which has the second subject in F major. In these cases, though their expediency is doubtful, the greater remoteness of the tonics renders the effect much less objectionable than when the second subject is in the subdominant.

248. We said above that the first subject of a sonata movement usually contains only one principal idea, or "theme"—to use a somewhat vague but convenient term; and that this generally consists of not more than two, or at most three sentences. The second subject, on the other hand, is in most cases far more extended. We often find as many as three or four different ideas

presented in succession, each complete in itself, and most frequently ending with a full cadence. This was why we said above (§ 239) that the term "group of second subjects" would be more strictly accurate, though not very convenient. We prefer to speak of the different themes introduced as "sections" of the second subject. The context will always prevent any confusion as to the meaning of the word "section," which we have employed in quite a different sense in *Musical Form* (§ 51).

249. In any but the smallest examples of the sonata form it is very rare to find a second subject containing less than two sections. Almost the only instances of this that we can cite from important works are the first movements of Beethoven's sonata in E minor, Op. 90, and of Schumann's symphony in C, in which they are certainly indivisible. These, however, are quite exceptional cases.

250. In modern compositions the second subject is mostly constructed of entirely different thematic material from the first; at the same time, the contrast must not be too violent; the second subject ought rather to be like *a continuation of the train of thought* of the first. The older composers frequently sought to obtain this by founding the first section of the second subject on a portion of the first subject presented in a new aspect. An extract from the finale of one of Haydn's quartetts will illustrate this. We first give the first subject—

HAYDN: Quartett, Op. 71, No. 1.

It will be seen that we have here a sentence extended to twelve bars by the addition of a second after-phrase. This sentence is repeated, *staccato* throughout and with varied harmony, completing the first subject.

251. A bridge-passage, 25 bars in length, commencing

and ending with a pause on the chord of the dominant seventh of G, leads to the second subject, which, as illustrating more than one point requiring notice, we quote in full.

HAYDN: Quartett, Op. 74, No. 1.

(2a)
(2b)
(4)
(4a)
(4b)
(6)
p
(8)
(2)
(4)
(6)
(8)
(2)
(4)
(6)
(8)
f
(8a)
(4)

This second subject has three sections. The first, containing 26 bars, consists of two extended sentences, and is founded chiefly upon the first two bars of the first subject, treated contrapuntally with a semiquaver accompaniment. The first sentence ends with an inverted cadence, and the second begins with the inversion of the theme and its counterpoint as seen at the commencement of our extract. A new continuation is given, which leads to a full close in G major at the 26th bar.

252. The second section of the subject is *piano* throughout, and presents a new theme. It commences with a sentence of six bars (the first and fifth being elided—see *Musical Form*, § 254). This sentence is repeated and prolonged by an additional after-phrase. The third section contains only one sentence of regular eight bar length, extended to fifteen bars by repetitions of the final cadence. It will be noticed that it is on a double pedal throughout. The entire second subject contains fifty-seven bars, as against twenty-four of the first subject. Of the double bar with the sign of repetition at the end of the subject we shall speak presently.

253. It will be seen that in the passage just examined all the sections of the second subject are in the same key, only a few transient modulations being introduced in the first section. This was the general, though not the invariable, practice of the older masters, and even with later composers the same method is frequently to be met with. As a striking instance of this, let the student examine the first movement of Beethoven's 'Eroica' symphony. We find here a very long exposition, of 148 bars. The second subject begins at bar 45, after a half-cadence in the key of B flat, with the following theme—

BEETHOVEN : 3rd Symphony.

At bar 65 there is a modulation for four bars to G minor, followed by one of two bars' length to C minor, after which a return is made to B flat, and the first section ends with a full close in that key at bar 83. The second section commences in the same key—

(We quote only enough to enable the student to identify the passage.) This section contains a transient modulation to D flat, and finishes in B flat at bar 109. The third and final section opens thus—we give the outer parts only—

This section, extending to bar 148, again contains none but transient modulations. Of the 104 bars of this very long second subject, scarcely more than a dozen are in any other key than B flat.

254. Many similar instances to the above might be quoted; it will suffice to refer to one. In Beethoven's piano sonata in E flat, Op. 7, the second subject contains five sections, all in B flat. They begin respectively at bars 41, 59, 93, 111 and 127. The second section is remarkable as containing an unusual modulation into the key of the supertonic (C major,) at bar 81; but with this exception the music hardly ever leaves the key of B flat.

255. On the other hand, we often find that the second subject begins in some different key from that in which it ends. To notice first a not very frequent case, we said above (§ 244), that in a *minor movement* the second subject could be either in the relative major or in the dominant minor key. Occasionally

the first part of the second subject is in one of these keys, and the continuation in the other. A very familiar example of this is seen in the first movement of Mendelssohn's trio in C minor. The second subject contains three sections, the first opening in E flat.

The second section begins with a fresh treatment in G minor of the first subject—a procedure very rarely to be met with; and a new continuation leads up to the third section, of which we quote the opening phrase—

The second subject ends in G minor. We can recall no other example of this use of the two keys for the second subject in the works of later composers; but similar instances are to be seen in the first movements of Clementi's sonatas in F sharp minor (Op. 26 No. 2,) and B minor (Op. 40 No. 2), and in the finale of Dussek's sonata, Op. 10 No. 3. It is worth noticing that in all the examples we have found the relative major key precedes the dominant minor.

256. Much more common than the case just noticed is that in which the first section of the second subject is in a different key from those that follow. Occasional instances of this are to be met with in Haydn. In the first movement of his quartett in A major, Op. 20 No. 6, the second subject begins in E minor, the key of E major not being introduced till the eleventh bar. The first two sentences of this second subject seem to hesitate between E minor and E major; and it is not till the closing

sentence that the major key is finally established. In another early quartett by Haydn (that in D major, Op. 17 No. 6), the second subject of the first movement begins in C major, and its first sentence ends with a half-cadence in A minor. To this succeeds the usual key of A major—the dominant being in the time of Haydn the invariable key for the second subject of a movement in a major key (§ 240).

257. The examples we have just referred to are quite exceptional in the works of Haydn, and we find no parallel instance in Mozart, who, as regards form, was less of an innovator than his older contemporary. It was Beethoven who was the first to employ this procedure with any frequency. The commonest case with him is the introduction of the second subject in the usual key, but with the *mode* changed—minor instead of major. In such cases the first section of the second subject generally modulates freely. We find examples of this method as early as the three sonatas (Op. 2,) dedicated to Haydn. In the first movement of the second sonata (in A major), the second subject begins at bar 58 in E minor; thence it modulates through G major and B flat major, and by a sequential passage of continually changing tonality (bars 69 to 75) to the chord of the dominant minor ninth of E; at bar 84 the key of E major is introduced, and continues to the close of the exposition, in bar 116. The third sonata of the same set shows a similar case. The second subject of the first movement begins at bar 27 in G minor, and does not reach G major till the commencement of its second section in bar 47. Another example of the same method is the first movement of the Sonata 'Pathétique.' Here the second subject, which is in the normal key of E flat, has a preliminary modulating section beginning in E flat *minor*.

258. Beethoven, however, does not always restrict himself to the same tonic for these preliminary sections. In his sonata in D, Op. 28 (first movement,) the second subject begins at bar 63 in F sharp minor, the normal key of A major not being established till later. The second subject of another sonata in D (Op. 10 No. 3) begins in B minor; the whole exposition is most instructive, and we shall proceed to give a short analysis of it.

259. The first subject, beginning in unison, extends to bar 16. It contains only one sentence; the fore-phrase ends on the pause in the fourth bar, and the after-phrase is extended to six bars; the after-phrase is then repeated in a varied form. The bridge-passage, which is founded upon the fore-phrase of the first subject, is only six bars long; it is in unison throughout, and ends with a pause on F sharp, in the 22nd bar. On the last crotchet of this bar the second subject enters; the first section begins in the key of B minor with an eight-bar sentence modulating to F sharp minor. The sonata is so familiar that it will be sufficient to quote the melody only.

BEETHOVEN : Sonata, Op. 10, No. 3.

(*a*)

From F sharp minor the music returns at bar 35 to A major, in which key (after a passing reference to the relative minor at bar 44) a full cadence concludes the first section of the second subject in bar 53. The second section commences in the same bar with an entirely new theme in A major—a seven-bar sentence, the first bar being elided.

(*b*)

On its repetition in A minor the passage breaks off suddenly on the G♯ in the sixth bar, and in the next bar continues thus—

(*c*)

Notice particularly the motive in the bass of the first bar—

Here we have the first four notes of the first subject; and from this germ all the rest of this second section is developed. We see it both direct and inverted in the latter part of the above extract, which is continued sequentially in the following bars; it is also present—though not so recognizable at first sight—in the descending scale passage of bars 85 to 91:

260. It is not very often that so much incidental modulation is to be met with in a second subject as that which is seen in the section we have just examined. A return having been made to the key of A, the third section, which began in bar 93, remains throughout in that key, excepting a transient suggestion of D in the first phrase. Like the final section in the movement by Haydn given in § 251, it is mostly built upon a tonic pedal, which here, contrary to general custom, is at first in the middle of the harmony. The melody commencing in bar 93

(*a*)

is obviously suggested by the commencement of the first subject,

(*b*)

especially in its rhythmic figure. It appears three times in different octaves; on its repetitions the pedal note takes its usual position as the lowest part of the harmony. The quiet passage which follows

(*c*)

may have been suggested by the commencement of the melody quoted at (*a*) above. If we substitute an ascending for a descending second as the first interval, and take the passage in augmentation

we see that the progression is identical. This may be intentional, but it may also be an accidental coincidence; in either case it gives unity to the music. The bars following our last extract form a *codetta;* we shall speak of this later in the chapter.

261. We have analyzed this exposition in considerable detail, because it affords an excellent illustration of a matter most difficult to explain except by illustration—how to obtain unity of style between the first and second subjects. We said in § 250 that the second subject, while different from the first, should be, as it were, a continuation of the same train of thought; the present movement shows admirably how this can be effected.

262. Occasionally the second subject begins in a key extremely remote from that in which it ends. In Beethoven's pianoforte concerto in E flat, it begins in B minor (the enharmonic of C flat minor); it then modulates to C flat major, whence it goes suddenly into B flat major, ending in that key. Somewhat similar is the second subject in Schubert's great sonata in B flat major. It commences in F sharp minor, and modulates through A major, B minor, and D minor, before it reaches F, the dominant of the original key. So much modulation is extremely rare.

263. It is worthy of notice that the commencing of the second subject in a key other than its principal key seems to be peculiar to movements in major keys. We have met with no examples of the same thing in a minor movement, excepting the alteration in the *mode* of the tonic (§ 257). The use in the minor key of both the relative major and the dominant minor, spoken of in § 255, is a different matter.

264. Quite exceptionally a second subject in a minor key ends in the minor mode after beginning in the major. The first movement of Beethoven's sonata in F minor, Op. 57, gives an example of this. The second subject begins at the end of bar 35 in the key of A flat major; at bar 42 it modulates to A flat minor, and all the rest of the subject, down to its close in bar 65, is in the latter key. We cannot find in Beethoven's works any other instance of this procedure, though there is some resemblance to it in the 'Kreutzer' sonata spoken of in § 246. There is, however, this difference—that in that case the minor key was the *normal* one; here it is the reverse. The same thing will be found in the first movement of Brahms's symphony in C minor, in which the second subject begins in E flat major and ends in E flat minor.

265. A point which often gives the student some trouble is, the determination of the limits of the second subject. This he will understand better after we have spoken in the next chapter of the recapitulation of a sonata movement; for the present it will suffice to say that in general the second subject reappears in the recapitulation in the tonic key; and if the student observes how much of that which in the exposition is in the dominant key (if the movement be major), or in the relative major or dominant minor (if it be minor), is found transposed into the tonic, he will generally be little at a loss to know where the second subject begins. If the second subject begins in a different key from that in which it ends, we shall most likely find the same relationship of keys in the recapitulation. For instance, the movement which we have just been analyzing (§ 259,) began in B minor and finished in A. In the recapitulation we find the keys to be E minor and D. Again, in Beethoven's sonata Op. 28, the second subject, which is mostly in A, commences in F sharp minor—its relative minor; in the recapitulation it begins in B, the relative minor of D, proceeding to that key at the same point where in the exposition the music modulated to A.

266. There is in general little difficulty in ascertaining where the second subject ends; because in the majority of cases the whole exposition is repeated, and the repeat shown by a double bar. In general there is here a full cadence in the key of the second subject, as in the example by Haydn given in § 251, where we have shown the repeat marks. Sometimes, however, the second subject ends a little earlier, and is followed by a few bars leading back to the first subject, or onwards to the second part of the movement. This is the case with Beethoven's sonata of which we gave the close of the second subject at § 260 (*c*). The last bar of that extract is continued as follows—

BEETHOVEN: Sonata, Op. 10, No. 3.

This passage, it will be seen, is founded on the opening notes of the first subject. (Compare § 259.) It leads back through the harmony of the dominant seventh to the tonic key. Such a passage we call a *codetta.* When it is present, the end of the second subject will be at the last full cadence in the key of that subject before the double bar.

267. The repetition of the exposition, though customary, especially with the older composers, is by no means obligatory. It is very rarely omitted by Haydn; but we find more than twenty symphonies by Mozart in which there is no repeat. Beethoven also frequently dispenses with it in his larger works—*e.g.* the Choral Symphony, the quartetts in F (Op. 59 No. 1,) and F minor (Op. 95), the sonata for piano and violin in C minor, Op. 30 No. 2, the piano sonatas, Op. 57 and Op. 90, &c. With later composers the omission is still more common. In order to ascertain in such a case where the second subject ends, observe its key, or if there be more than one key, the key of its final section. We shall learn in the next chapter that the second part of the movement (the development,) seldom begins in the same key in which the second subject ends, or, at any rate it will not have a full cadence in that key. In such cases therefore, as also when there is a codetta, the last full cadence in the key of the second subject shows the end of that subject, whether there be a repeat or not. The student who has carefully read this chapter ought to have no difficulty in deciding what the key of the second subject is.

268. We shall now conclude this chapter with a summary, giving as briefly as we can the points to be considered in writing the exposition of a movement in sonata form.

The exposition forms the first of the three parts of a sonata movement, and is itself divided into three parts, viz.: (i.) the first subject, (ii.) the bridge-passage, (iii.) the second subject.

269. (i.) The first subject, which is occasionally preceded by an introductory passage (§ 232), begins and ends in the key of the tonic, and seldom contains much modulation. It mostly consists of two or three sentences, sometimes of only one, and is not divisible into sections, like the second subject. In the large majority of cases it ends either on the tonic or dominant chord of the tonic key.

270. (ii.) The bridge-passage is that portion of the movement which modulates from the tonic key towards the key in which the second subject is to be introduced. It varies greatly in length, consisting sometimes of only a few bars, and at other times being of considerable extent, and containing two or three sentences. It sometimes begins with a continuation of the first subject; at other times it is constructed of entirely new material. It usually ends on the dominant, or the dominant seventh, of the key in which the second subject is about to enter; but when the second subject is in the dominant key, it occasionally ends with a half

cadence on the tonic (§ 236); it may also end on the dominant of the relative minor of the new key (§ 238).

271. (iii.) The second subject comprises all that follows the bridge-passage, as far as the end of the exposition. Whereas the first subject hardly ever contains more than one principal theme (though this may be extended or repeated,) the second subject—at all events in modern music—almost invariably has at least two parts, which we call 'sections' separated from one another by full cadences; and it is not unusual to find as many as four or five. These sections, while differing from one another, and from the first subject, should still be in keeping with it; in other words, the contrast should not be too strong.

272. The keys available for the second subject are: For a major movement (1) the dominant—the most usual key, (2) the mediant (major or minor), (3) the submediant major, (4) the relative minor (rare), (5) the flat submediant major, and (6) the flat mediant major. Both these are very rare and hardly to be recommended. For a minor movement the second subject may be in (1) the relative major, (2) the dominant minor, (3) the dominant major, (4) the submediant major.

273. In addition to the keys just named, the minor modes of the various major keys are also available; but these are very rarely used for the *final* section of the second subject. It is not necessary that all the sections should be in the same key; but, with rare exceptions, the final section is in a nearly related key to the original tonic.

274. The second subject, and with it the exposition, generally ends with a full cadence, followed by a repeat of the whole first part of the movement. Sometimes a few bars of codetta are added, to lead back to the first subject. In many cases, especially in modern compositions, there is no repeat of the exposition; but it is followed immediately by the second part of the movement.

CHAPTER VIII.

THE SONATA FORM (CONTINUED): THE DEVELOPMENT AND RECAPITULATION.

275. In the preceding chapter we have treated of the first of the three parts of which a sonata movement is composed—the exposition, and we have seen that while its details are in many respects subject to modification, its general outline remains the same in all cases. We always find two principal subjects connected by a bridge-passage, which effects the modulation from the key of the tonic, in which the first subject invariably appears, to the key (whatever that may be,) in which the second subject commences. But in the second part of the movement—the development, and, to a less degree in the third—the recapitulation, there is far greater variety. So much is this the case with the development, that it is absolutely impossible to give any rules as to what the composer should do, though, as we shall see presently, several general principles may be laid down to guide him as to what he should *not* do.

276. It is no doubt because of the impossibility of formulating any regular rules for the construction of this part of the movement that it is frequently described in English text-books as the "Free Fantasia,"—that is, the portion of the movement in which the composer is left free to follow his own fancy. In Germany it is termed '*Durchführung*,' *i.e.* 'development'; and we shall use both names indifferently; "development" is the more strictly accurate, but "free fantasia" is frequently more convenient.

277. When speaking in the last chapter (§ 224,) of the sonata form as a modification of the ternary, we said that the developments of which we have now to speak took the place occupied in the regular ternary form by the episode. Students will be aware that the object of episode is to furnish relief and contrast to the principal subjects. In the same way, the developments which precede the repetition of the principal subjects in the recapitulation have to furnish relief and (to a certain extent) contrast; but there is an important difference between the two forms. In the ternary form, as also in the Rondo form described in Chapter VI. of this volume, the contrast is secured by the introduction of entirely new material; here, on the other hand, while (as will be

seen later) episodical matter is not wholly excluded, we obtain the contrast chiefly by *the presentation of the material of the exposition under new aspects.* This is because the essential characteristic of the sonata form is unity; in other words it is a "movement of continuity" (§ 216).

278. It is in the developments of this second part that the composer's genius has the fullest scope; and it is here that the chief difference is seen between first-class and second-class workmanship. There are many composers who can find beautiful themes for their first and second subjects, who seem, whether from insufficient study, or from want of the necessary attention and self-criticism, to fail more or less completely in this part of the movement. It is here that the supremacy of Beethoven as an instrumental composer shows itself so conspicuously. In his developments there is nothing rambling, nothing incoherent; he has an inexhaustible faculty for presenting his ideas in fresh aspects, yet always logically connected with one another, each growing naturally out of the preceding, and leading as naturally into what follows. In this respect he has never been equalled; and for this reason we shall take most of our illustrations of development from his works.

279. The first example that we give is from his well-known sonata in E flat, Op. 7. It will be hardly necessary to say that we never find *the whole* material of an exposition treated in the second part. This would be impossible without extending the movement to enormous length. The composer is free to choose whichever of his subjects he prefers for treatment. In the present case, Beethoven has selected three short fragments from the exposition, which we here quote—

The passage at (*a*) is the opening of the first subject; (*b*) is the beginning of the bridge-passage; and (*c*) is the commencement of the last section of the second subject. The exposition ends at bar 136 with a full cadence in the key of B flat.

280. We now give the whole development ("free fantasia") of this movement, to show how Beethoven treats these three subjects.

Beethoven: Sonata, Op. 7.

sf
sf
sf
sf
sf
sf
sf
ff
p
decres.
pp
ff
ff
p

A very bold effect is obtained at the commencement by altering the harmony of the first notes of the subject. The passage at (*a*) of the last section here appears as the dominant seventh of C minor, instead of as the tonic of E flat. In this key follows at the fifth bar the scale passage from (*b*) imitated two bars later in the right hand, which is thus in contrary motion with the bass. These scales are continued in a free sequence through the keys of A flat and F minor; after which the bars quoted at (*c*) § 279 from the second subject are given, first in F minor, then a tone higher in G minor. After a half close in this key, and a sudden change from *ff* to *p*, an unexpected modulation (with an enharmonic change of E♭ to D♯,) brings the music into the key of A minor. Here the theme (*a*) is again presented in a varied form, *pp*, and followed by a new melody, the only episodical matter introduced, which appears to have been suggested by, rather than taken from, the passage at bar 91 of the exposition—

The whole passage is then repeated in D minor, and a beautiful modulation (analyzed in § 111 of *Musical Form*,) leads back at once to E flat, after the dominant seventh of which the first subject is introduced, and the recapitulation begins.

281. Now let us notice the course of the modulations. The keys passed through are the following: C minor, A flat major, F minor, G minor, A minor, D minor, this last being immediately followed by E flat. It would not be reasonable to draw conclusions from a single instance; for the present we merely ask the student to observe that no key is touched upon more than once, and that the two keys of the first and second subjects—E flat and B flat, the chief keys of the exposition—are avoided altogether.

282. For our next example we give the free fantasia of Haydn's symphony in G (No. 11 of Breitkopf and Härtel's edition), as an excellent illustration of the thematic development of a few simple subjects. As with our last example, we first quote the passages from the exposition which Haydn has chosen as the material for the developments.

HAYDN: Symphony in G.

(a)

(b)

At (*a*) is the opening of the first subject, which is preceded by a tolerably long introduction in slow time; (*b*) is the commencement of the second section of the second subject.

283. The middle part of this movement is quite different in the method of treatment from that in Beethoven's sonata just analyzed. The exposition ends with a full cadence in the key of D major. As Haydn intends to commence his free fantasia in the key of B flat, he prefixes two bars' rest (not quoted) to the beginning of his second part, no doubt, to render the sudden modulation less abrupt.

HAYDN: Symphony in G.

dim.
(a)
f
sf
p
pp
f
sf

sf
sf
sf
sf
sf
sf
sf
ff
p
f

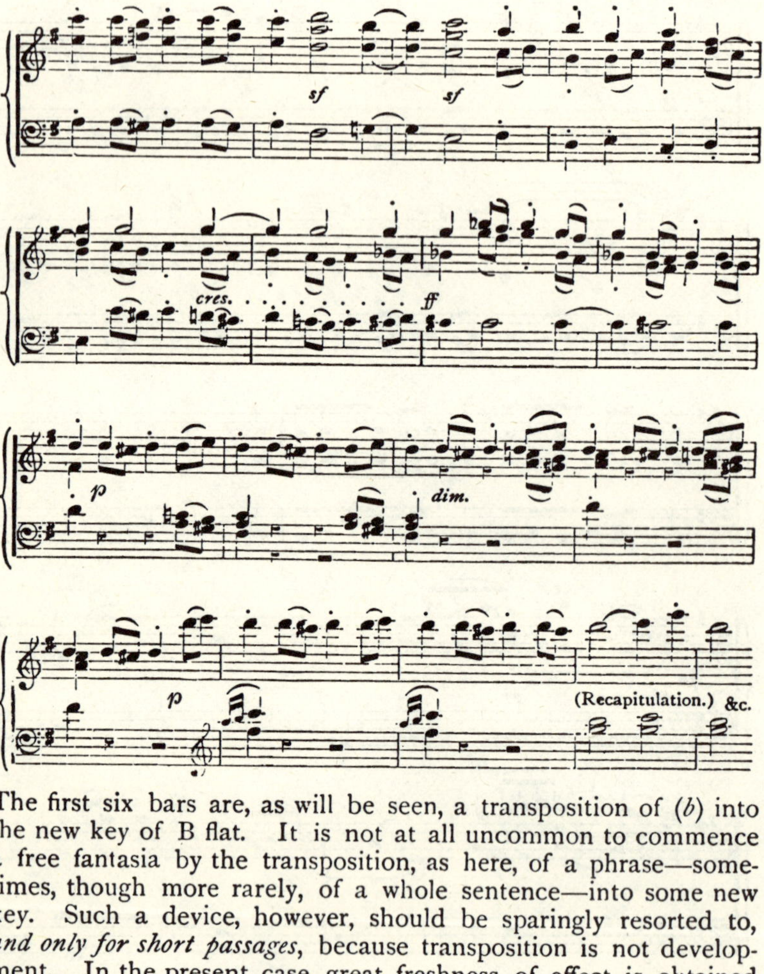

The first six bars are, as will be seen, a transposition of (*b*) into the new key of B flat. It is not at all uncommon to commence a free fantasia by the transposition, as here, of a phrase—sometimes, though more rarely, of a whole sentence—into some new key. Such a device, however, should be sparingly resorted to, *and only for short passages*, because transposition is not development. In the present case, great freshness of effect is obtained by the unexpected modulation to a key in the second degree of relationship. Immediately on the conclusion of this phrase, Haydn begins his thematic development. This is founded almost entirely on the first three notes of the passage taken from the second subject,

for it will be seen that the quaver passage at (*a*) is merely a slight alteration of the same figure by adding G as an auxiliary note between the two Fs.

284. From B flat Haydn first modulates to C minor, and thence, by means of the chord of the augmented sixth, to D

minor. A powerful unison passage, founded upon the figure quoted above, leads to a half cadence on the dominant of that key. The whole passage is then repeated a tone higher than before, but considerably extended toward its close by the unexpected introduction of the key of F major, delaying the half cadence in E minor. This is reached at the *ff*, and prolonged for four bars. The passage which follows is evidently a modification of the beginning of the first subject. We have it first in E minor, then in succession in D major, A minor, and G major.

285. We have now returned to the tonic key, and we know therefore that we are near the end of the developments; for except incidentally, in modulating between other keys, the tonic key should not be employed in the free fantasia. We shall see the reason for this later. In the movement we are now examining there is no further modulation, excepting slight passing references to C major and A minor (both nearly related keys to G); but the music continues in G and the free fantasia ends on the first inversion of the chord of the dominant seventh, continued for six bars, with the same persistent figure that we have seen nearly throughout the developments. The student will not fail to notice what perfect unity of style is secured by this method of treatment. Observe, before we leave this movement, the course of modulation;—B flat, C minor, D minor, E minor, F (incidentally), E minor again, D major, A minor and G.

286. The thematic development illustrated by our last example was first systematically employed by Haydn, though something similar is to be found in many of the episodes of Bach's fugues. But, as applied to the sonata form, Haydn may be fairly credited with the invention; and his skill in this direction has been equalled by few, and only surpassed by one—Beethoven. The varieties of thematic treatment are literally numberless, and their management can only be taught in one way,—by example. It is impossible within the limits of such a volume as this to give many lengthy extracts. We must content ourselves with referring our readers to the works of the great masters, and confine our quotations to short passages which will render our remarks intelligible. The two examples we have already given will help to show how the free fantasia is to be made into a homogeneous whole.

287. Our last extract, from Haydn's symphony, showed a free fantasia developed almost entirely from one small germ. We will now analyze the same portion of the first movement of Beethoven's Pastoral Symphony, where we shall find similar treatment of two or three different motives. We give the opening of the symphony, from the first subject of which the developments are almost entirely constructed.

BEETHOVEN : Pastoral Symphony.

The exposition of this movement ends in the key of C with a prolonged close on the tonic during twenty bars, and is continued by a codetta (§ 266,) of four bars, founded upon the first bar of the above quotation.

288. We now give the codetta, and the opening bars of the free fantasia.

After treating the first bar by itself in the codetta, Beethoven begins his development with working a two-bar section, consisting of the first and second bars of the subject. A repetition a fourth higher of the preceding eight bars brings the music into the key of B flat; and the second bar of the first subject is now worked by itself. With a boldness justified by the result, Beethoven dares to repeat this figure twelve times on the chord of B flat, and then twenty-four times on the chord of D major. The passage ends thus

289. Beethoven next takes the last two notes of the above figure and repeats them for four bars. The first phrase of the first subject is then given in the key of G major, with a new counterpoint above the last two bars.

It will be seen that the inversion of the two bars follows immediately, and is succeeded by a repetition in G of the passage previously heard in B flat, of which we quoted the commencement at the end of our extract in § 288. As before, the figure is heard for twelve bars on the chord of G, and then for twenty-four bars on the chord of E major, leading to a repetition of our last quotation a tone higher than before.

290. Probably the composer by this continued reiteration of the same figure intended to depict the impression produced by the sameness, without monotony, of the sounds of nature. No doubt he now felt that he had treated this one figure sufficiently; at the end of the passage of which we are now speaking, he therefore introduces a different part of the first subject. Our next quotation begins at the transposition of the fourth bar from the end of our last extract.

The theme now heard will be seen in the last four bars of our example § 287. It is given in succession in A major, D major, G minor, C major, and finally F major, with an inverted dominant pedal, leading back by means of a plagal cadence to the recapitulation, as seen in the last bars of the above passage.

291. The working of small fragments of his themes was a favourite procedure with Beethoven. One method, to which he was especially partial will be best explained by an illustration. In § 229 we gave the first subject of his 'Waldstein' sonata, Op. 53; we now give the commencement of the second part of the same movement. To save space we give the melody only.

BEETHOVEN : Sonata, Op. 53.

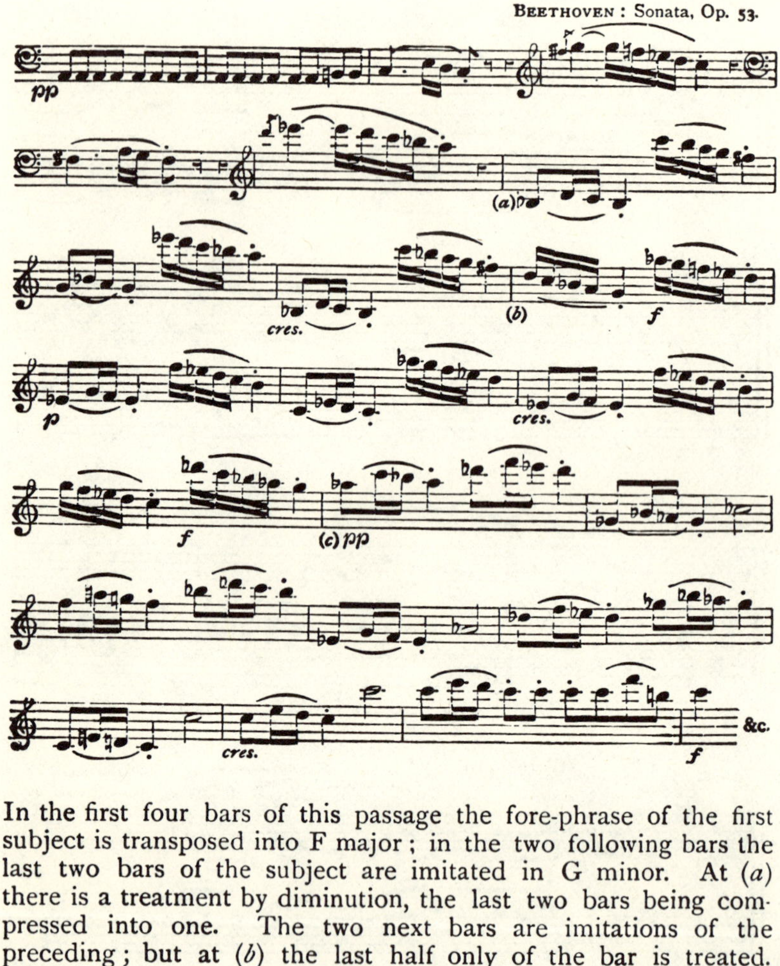

In the first four bars of this passage the fore-phrase of the first subject is transposed into F major; in the two following bars the last two bars of the subject are imitated in G minor. At (*a*) there is a treatment by diminution, the last two bars being compressed into one. The two next bars are imitations of the preceding; but at (*b*) the last half only of the bar is treated. Four bars later, at (*c*) the first half of the bar is developed separately, till a half cadence in F minor is reached at the end of our extract. In the passage which immediately follows our quotation the second section of the second subject is similarly treated. Beethoven takes first a four-bar phrase, then the second half of it, and lastly its final bar, and develops these portions in turn. This chopping of his subjects up into small pieces, and (if the expression may be allowed,) squeezing the last drop of juice out of them, is one of the striking characteristics of Beethoven's developments. Another excellent example will be seen in the sonata in D, Op. 28.*

* Whenever in this chapter a work is spoken of without any part being specially indicated, it is always the *first movement* that is being referred to.

292. Sometimes the developments will be more contrapuntal in style than in the examples we have hitherto been examining. Many good specimens of this kind of free fantasia will be found in Haydn's quartetts. As we cannot quote them here, we refer students who have access to the scores to such movements as the *vivace* of the quartett in C, Op. 50 No. 2.

and the *allegro spiritoso* of the quartett in F, Op. 74 No. 2.

In both these movements the subjects are treated by imitation in the free fugal style. The same thing will be seen in Beethoven's later sonatas—in Op. 106 and Op. 111, and in the finale of Op. 101. The last named movement has an extended, though somewhat free *fugato*, which occupies the whole of the free fantasia. It will suffice to quote the opening bars.

BEETHOVEN : Sonata, Op. 101.

The interval of entry of the second voice shows, of course, that we have here a *fugato*, not a fugue (*Fugue*, § 358). Mozart's sonata in D, beginning

may also be examined with advantage, because of the passages of canonic imitation to be found in the free fantasia.

293. There is one very important question in connection with the free fantasia on which we have not yet touched. This is, the introduction of episodical matter. Those examples of development which we have hitherto been analyzing have been entirely founded upon the material of the exposition. But this is by no means the invariable practice of composers. In many works we find a large amount of new matter introduced in the course of

the developments, and occasionally the whole second part of a sonata movement consists of episode. It is impossible to lay down any rules as to when, or how much episodical matter should be introduced. In this the composer's feeling must be his guide; but it is important to remember that the new material must always be *in keeping with* the character of the movement. The nature of the episodes will be best understood from examples.

294. Our first illustration will show the introduction of episodical matter as a new counterpoint to the chief subject of a movement. The first subject of the allegro of Beethoven's fourth symphony begins

(a) **Beethoven: 4th Symphony.**

In the first part of the free fantasia of this movement the first and second bars of the above extract are developed at some length in the keys of F major and D minor, the dominant chord of the latter key being at last followed by the tonic *major*. In this key our last quotation is repeated exactly—a major third higher—and followed by

(b)

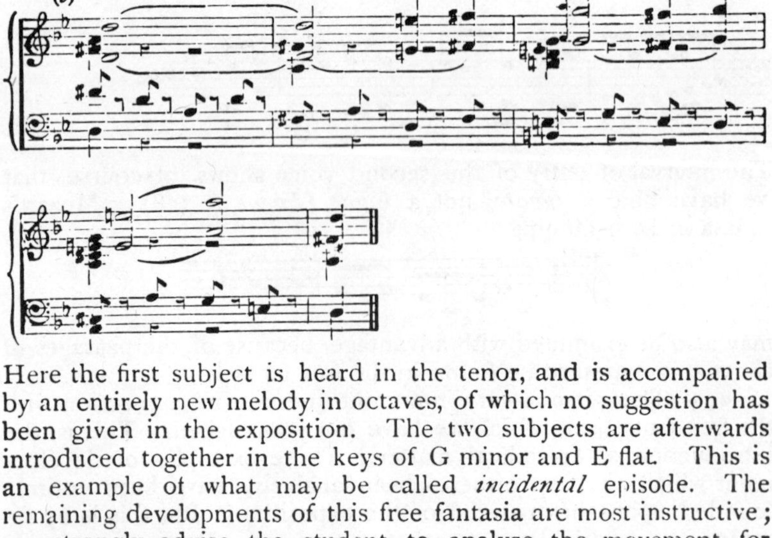

Here the first subject is heard in the tenor, and is accompanied by an entirely new melody in octaves, of which no suggestion has been given in the exposition. The two subjects are afterwards introduced together in the keys of G minor and E flat. This is an example of what may be called *incidental* episode. The remaining developments of this free fantasia are most instructive; we strongly advise the student to analyze the movement for himself.

295. More frequently the episodes are entirely independent of the themes of the exposition. As striking examples of this kind may be mentioned the episodes in the 'Eroica' symphony, and in Mendelssohn's 'Italian' symphony in A major. Both works are so well known that it will be sufficient to quote the melodies of the passages to which we refer.

BEETHOVEN: 3rd Symphony, Op. 55.

(a)

MENDELSSOHN: 4th Symphony.

(b)

In both these movements considerable use is made later of these episodes in the codas, of which we shall speak presently.

296. Sometimes the material of the exposition is but little employed in the developments; and the greater part of the free fantasia is made from episodical matter. This is the case in Beethoven's sonata in E major, Op. 14 No. 1, as will be seen by a short extract.

BEETHOVEN: Sonata, Op. 14, No. 1.

This passage, which is the opening of the free fantasia, begins with a suggestion in the first two bars of the commencement of the first subject. A new continuation (bars 3 and 4) introduces an episodical theme on which all the rest of the developments are founded until the music returns to the dominant of E minor. The first notes of the first subject are then heard (over a dominant pedal) in the tenor and treble part of the harmony alternately, till at the end of the pedal point the recapitulation begins with the return of the first subject. Another example of extensive use of episodical matter will be seen in Beethoven's sonata in F, Op. 10 No. 2.

297. Occasionally, the second part of a sonata movement consists entirely of episode, there being absolutely no development of the material of the exposition. We find an instance of this in the first movement of Mozart's sonata in D beginning

Another example will be seen in the finale of his sonata in C, No. 10. The movement will be identified by its opening bars.

This movement is in regular sonata form, including the repeat of the whole exposition; but the second part is not only entirely episodical, but (what is still more unusual,) contains hardly any modulation, being all in the keys of G major, and of C minor and major. This movement is referred to here, not as a model, but as an exception. With Mozart's sonata movements in general more episode and less thematic treatment will mostly be found in the free fantasia than with either Haydn or Beethoven; though numerous works might be named in which his thematic developments are fully equal in interest to those of his great contemporaries, showing clearly that it was choice, not inability, that caused him in so many instances to prefer the more episodical style of treatment.

298. When the first movement of a sonata is preceded by a slow introduction, this is occasionally introduced—sometimes in a varied form—at the beginning or in the course of the free fantasia. A very familiar example of this is furnished by Beethoven's Sonate Pathétique, which is too well known to need

quotation. At the end of the exposition, the opening bars of the *Grave* are introduced, leading, by means of a beautiful enharmonic modulation to the key of E minor, in which the free fantasia begins. Let the student notice that the fourth and fifth bars of the free fantasia are a development, or rather a modification, of the first bar of the introduction, with the omission of the first note.

A similar case is seen in Beethoven's quartett in E flat, Op. 127, in which the short *Maestoso* which opens the work is repeated at the close of the exposition, and again near the end of the free fantasia.

299. Another very fine, though much less generally known instance of the same procedure will be found in Clementi's sonata in G minor, Op. 34 No. 2. Here, however, the first subject of the allegro is itself developed from the short introduction, as will be seen from a quotation of the commencement of the sonata.

(a) *Largo e sostenuto.* **Clementi: Sonata, Op. 34, No. 2.**

The exposition of this movement, which is quite regular, extends to 73 bars, and ends in the key of B flat, the relative major, which, as we already know, is the usual key for the second subject of a minor movement. The free fantasia begins in C minor, and, after various modulations, ultimately reaches the dominant of A minor through a passage too long to quote, but which is founded upon the last four bars of the *Largo*. At the 43rd bar, the common time of the introduction is resumed, and a remarkable metamorphosis of the opening theme appears in C major.

This *Largo* continues for nine bars, and is followed by a return to the Allegro ($\frac{3}{4}$) which seven bars later introduces the recapitulation.

300. A somewhat similar, though not exactly parallel case will be found in the finale of Beethoven's string quintett in C, Op. 29. The movement is a Presto ($\frac{6}{8}$) in C major. Toward the end of the free fantasia there is a half close in A minor, leading to an *Andante con moto e scherzoso* in A major, eighteen bars in length, entirely episodical, and which is repeated in C major in the course of the coda which ends the movement.

301. It would require, not a part of a chapter, but an entire volume to deal fully with the possibilities of thematic development, as shown in the works of the great masters. From the various examples we have quoted and referred to, it is hoped that the student will have a fair idea of the general line he should adopt in trying to write developments for himself. Before proceeding to speak of the third part of a sonata movement—the recapitulation—we will give a few general principles for his guidance. It has been already said that strict rules cannot be laid down for this part of the composition ; but the principles we are now about to give are deduced from the actual practice of the great composers.

302. The first, and one of the most important rules to be borne in mind is, that the chief keys of the exposition—that is, the tonic of the movement and the key in which the second

subject appears—should be avoided as much as possible in the free fantasia, or, at most, only employed incidentally, that is, in the course of modulation between other keys. The only exception to this rule is that it is not uncommon to *begin* the free fantasia in the key in which the exposition ended; but as soon as this key has been left and the modulation has begun, it should not be returned to in the course of the further developments.

303. The reason for the rule just given is that, as the second subject is generally of considerable extent, sometimes (as we saw in the last chapter,) containing three or four sections, which in the majority of cases are all in the same key, there would be too much monotony of tonality were the key of the second subject to be much used during the second part of the movement. The same consideration renders the employment of the tonic key objectionable. True, we hear but little of it in the exposition; for the first subject is generally short, and the modulation begins at once in the bridge-passage; but we shall see presently that a great part of the recapitulation has to be in the tonic key, and it would therefore be most unadvisable to use the same key to any great extent for the developments.

304. Any other key than the two just named may be freely employed at the discretion of the student for the free fantasia; but there are one or two cautions to be given him in this matter. In the first place, it is not good to continue too long in any one new key, lest the mental impression of a fresh tonic be produced on the hearer. Especially is this the case with regard to the subdominant key. It would be most unwise to write the last part of a free fantasia in this key; because the tonic, returning immediately afterwards, would certainly have the effect of being a dominant of the key just quitted. The final return to the tonic key is almost always made from a key on its sharp side—at all events in a major movement.

305. Another point which it is important to remember is, that after a modulation has been made to any key, *and that key has been quitted*, it is not good to introduce it again, except transitionally, that is, for the sake of passing conveniently between other keys, as in a compound modulation. We know already that in a smaller composition it is not good generally to make the same modulation twice; and this principle holds good also of the free fantasia.

306. The material of the second part of a sonata movement should consist chiefly of *developments*. For this reason, a mere repetition or exact transposition of matter from the exposition is weak, if it be continued without modification for more than a few bars. Among the principal means of development are (1) the repetition of a subject with varied harmonies; (2) the separate working of small fragments of a subject, as in the 'Pastoral Symphony' analyzed in §§ 288–290; (3) the addition

of new counterpoints to the subjects; (4) the contrapuntal treatment of the subjects themselves, whether by fugal, canonic, or free imitation. Which of these methods (and the list is not exhaustive,) the composer may select is left entirely to his own taste and judgment. He is also quite free as to the choice of the subjects he may propose to treat.

307. The introduction of episodical matter is another point as to which no rules can be given. The only advice we can offer is, that such matter should be not so different in character from the rest of the movement as to produce an effect of incongruity. The amount of episode to be introduced is quite optional; in general it will be best to keep on the safe side, and rather use too little than too much.

308. The free fantasia must always end in such a way as to lead back to the key in which the recapitulation begins. This is mostly, though, as will be seen later, not invariably, the tonic. In the majority of cases the close of the free fantasia is on the dominant, or dominant seventh chord; not infrequently a dominant pedal is introduced. Examples of this procedure are too common to need quotation; they are to be met with everywhere. Less frequently other methods are adopted. In the first movement of Beethoven's symphony in C minor, and in the finale of the sonata in the same key, Op. 10 No. 1, the return is made through the chord of the diminished seventh on the leading note—another position of dominant harmony. In the 'Pastoral Symphony' we see (§ 290,) the recapitulation reached by means of a plagal cadence.

309. Some interesting examples are met with in the works of the great masters of a return to the first subject in a major key through the dominant of a nearly related minor key. In Haydn's quartett in E major, Op. 54 No. 3, the free fantasia ends with a dominant pedal, eight bars long, in C sharp minor, the first subject following at once in E major.

HAYDN: Quartett, Op. 54, No. 3.

310. Our next illustration, also from Haydn, shows a somewhat different modulation.

Here the free fantasia ends in F sharp minor; the dominant seventh in that key is resolved at the seventh bar of our extract on the submediant chord of the same key, which is quitted as the tonic of D major, and followed at once by the first subject in that key.

311. A differently managed modulation between the same two keys will be seen at the return of the first subject in Beethoven's second symphony. Here the free fantasia ends with a half cadence in F sharp minor.

At the third bar there is a sudden *piano* on the dominant. The addition of the A in the fifth bar changes the C sharp from the root to the third of the chord, and leads back at once to the key of D, and the resumption of the first subject.

312. We had noted several other passages for quotation, but must content ourselves with referring our readers to such examples as the return to the first subject in Beethoven's symphony

in B flat, No. 4, and in his sonatas in E flat, Op. 31 No. 3, E minor, Op. 90, and B flat, Op. 106. For our last illustration of the return to the first subject, we give an interesting passage by Mozart in which free sequential imitation is employed.

Mozart: Piano Quartett in G mincr.

It is difficult to show the part-writing of this passage clearly on two staves; it consists chiefly of a dialogue between the piano and the strings, the scale passages being allotted to the former, and the responding harmonies to the latter. In the last three bars before the re-entry of the first subject the strings and piano imitate each other.

313. The third part of a sonata movement is termed the *Recapitulation;* in this the material of the exposition is repeated, with more or less important modification. A moment's thought will show the student that it would be impossible to repeat the exposition as the third part of the movement without modification, for the

very simple reason that it never ends in the key of the tonic. In a regularly constructed recapitulation, therefore, the second subject, as well as the first, is introduced in the tonic key, and either the first bridge-passage is modified, so as to lead to the dominant of the tonic key, instead of to the dominant of the key in which the second subject appeared in the exposition, or else an entirely new bridge-passage is written. Exceptionally, as we shall see later, the bridge-passage is altogether omitted in the recapitulation.

314. There is far more variation to be met with in the recapitulation than is generally supposed. Before dealing with the numerous irregularities to be found in this part of the movement, it will be well to speak of the usual form, as we find it in the great majority of sonata movements in the works of the great masters.

315. In a regularly constructed recapitulation, the close of the free fantasia is immediately followed by the reappearance of the first subject in the tonic key. In many cases, perhaps in most, the subject reappears in its original form—possibly with a little more ornamentation (as, for instance, in Beethoven's sonata in D, Op. 28), but practically unaltered, though it is by no means uncommon to find it accompanied by a new counterpoint. As an illustration of this we give the beginning of the first subject of the allegro of Haydn's quartett in G. Op. 76 No. 1.

HAYDN: Quartett, Op. 76, No. 1.

This passage is then repeated in simple two-part harmony. In the recapitulation it is treated in the following manner—

The first four bars have a counterpoint in quavers above them, and the opening of the subject is then given to the first violin, and answered in canon at the octave and tenth below by the second violin and viola. More familiar examples of the addition of a new counterpoint to the first subject in the recapitulation will be seen in the first movement of Mendelssohn's symphony in A minor, and in the slow movement of Beethoven's Pastoral Symphony.

316. In the majority of cases, the bridge-passage in the recapitulation is constructed from the same material as in the exposition; but it is frequently shortened, and the course of modulation is usually varied, so as to end on the dominant of the key in which the second subject is now to appear. In general this will be the tonic key; the exceptions will be discussed presently. If the bridge-passage in the exposition ends with a half cadence in the tonic key, it is possible, though rare, for the bridge-passage in the recapitulation to be identical with that in the exposition. An example of this will be found in Haydn's sonata in B flat, referred to in § 236.

317. Occasionally in the recapitulation the bridge-passage is altogether dispensed with, and the second subject follows immediately on the close of the first. This is the case in the first movement of Beethoven's sonata in F, Op. 10 No. 2, and in the finale of his sonata in C sharp minor, Op. 27 No. 2. In the first movement of Weber's sonata in E minor, Op. 70, the second subject in the recapitulation follows the first immediately, but the bridge-passage is repeated almost note for note as the beginning of the coda.

318. If, in the exposition of a movement in a major key, the second subject has been in the dominant, it will in the recapitulation be in the key of the tonic. This rule may be taken as invariable; in several hundreds of movements that we have examined we have not found a single exception to it. If in the first part the second subject has been in some other key than the dominant, there is less regularity. For example, in Beethoven's sonata in C, Op. 53, the second subject is in the exposition in the key of the mediant, major and minor; in the recapitulation, it begins in the submediant (A major), and modulates through A minor to C major. The last part of the subject, which in the exposition was in E minor, is repeated in C minor, the return to the major key being reserved for the coda.

319. In two other movements in which Beethoven has put his second subject in the mediant—the first movement of the sonata in G, Op. 31 No. 1, and the finale of the piano trio in E flat, Op. 70 No. 2—the second subject in the recapitulation is first given in the key of the submediant major, and then repeated in the key of the tonic. Observe in all these cases, that as the submediant is a perfect fifth below the mediant, the tonal relation of these two appearances of the second subject is the same as if the keys had been, as usual, dominant and tonic. In the rare cases in which the second subject begins in the mediant minor (§ 242), it is found in the recapitulation in the tonic key. When the second subject is in the submediant in the exposition (§ 243), it is also Beethoven's practice to introduce it in the tonic in the recapitulation.

320. When the different sections of the second subject are not all in the same key (§ 256,) we usually find that their relation to one another in the recapitulation will be the same as in the exposition. If the second subject at first began in the dominant minor, and then proceeded to the dominant major (as in Beethoven's sonatas in A major and C major, Op. 2, Nos. 2 and 3), we shall find it in the recapitulation in the *tonic* minor and major. If, on the other hand, it began with a different tonic from that with which it ended—in which case the last key will always be the dominant—we shall almost invariably find that the first section of the second subject will, in the recapitulation, be in a key bearing the same relation to the tonic which the key in the exposition bore to the dominant.

321. A few examples will make this perfectly clear. We will take the same movements which we referred to in the last chapter (§§ 256, 258). In Haydn's quartett in D, Op. 17 No. 6, the second subject in the exposition begins in C major and ends in A major; the first of these keys is a minor third higher than the second. In the recapitulation, that part of the second subject which was in C appears in F—a minor third higher than D—and that which was in A is transposed to D. In Beethoven's sonata in D, Op. 28, the second subject begins in F sharp minor, and proceeds to A major; in the recapitulation the keys are B minor and D major. Again in the same composer's sonata in D, Op. 10 No. 3, the second subject begins in B minor before going to A major, the former key being the supertonic minor of the latter. In the recapitulation, the second subject begins in E minor, the supertonic minor of D. As all these three movements happen to be in the key of D, it is very easy for the student to notice that the same method is carried out in each case.

322. In movements in a minor key, if the second subject is in the dominant minor (§§ 244, 245,) the transposition in the recapitulation is simply to the tonic minor. But in the more frequent cases in which the second subject is at first in the relative major, there are two courses open to the composer. The plan

most frequently adopted by the older masters was to introduce the second subject in the tonic *minor* key. This, of course, necessitated some alteration both of its melody and harmony. As an example, we give the beginning of the second subject in the first movement of Mozart's symphony in G minor. In the exposition it is in B flat major.

MOZART: Symphony in G minor.

In the recapitulation we find it in G minor.

It is evident that the whole character of the subject is altered by this change to the minor mode.

323. In order to avoid the change of character just spoken of, the older masters sometimes, and modern composers more frequently, transpose the second subject in the recapitulation into the key of the tonic *major*. This procedure is more common with Haydn than with Mozart, who, as we have already had occasion to remark, was not much given to innovation in matters of form.

With Beethoven, we mostly find the tonic minor for the second subject in his earlier works, while in the later the tonic major is often to be met with. When the second subject in the recapitulation is in the tonic major key, the movement can either end in that key, or return to the minor mode for the coda. Examples of both are common.

324. Occasionally in a minor movement if the first subject be at first in the relative major, it is in the submediant in the recapitulation. This is the case in the first movement of Mendelssohn's symphony in C minor. The obvious reason is to preserve the usual tonal relation of the two entries of the second subject. (Compare § 319). In such cases a return is, of course, subsequently made to the tonic key.

325. If the second subject in a minor movement be in the submediant major, it will generally in the recapitulation be in the tonic major. This is the practice of Beethoven. Schubert, however, in two cases where he has his second subject in the submediant—in the first movements of the 'Tragic' symphony, and of the unfinished symphony in B minor—uses the relative major for his second subjects in the recapitulation, returning later to the tonic key; and the effect, though unusual, is certainly not bad.

326. If the second subject of a minor movement be in two keys, the relationship of the two will generally, though not invariably, be preserved in the recapitulation. (Compare § 320). Thus, in Clementi's sonata in B minor, Op. 40 No. 2, the second subject in the exposition has its first part in D major, and the second in F sharp minor; in the recapitulation the keys are G major and B minor. In Beethoven's sonata in F minor, Op. 57, the second subject begins in A flat major and ends in A flat minor. In the recapitulation it begins in F major and ends in F minor. An exception to this general rule will be seen in Mendelssohn's trio in C minor. The second subject, part of which we quoted in § 254, begins in E flat and ends in G minor. In the recapitulation the theme that was in E flat major appears, not in A flat, but in C major, and the last part of the subject is transposed to C minor.

327. Hitherto we have spoken only of those recapitulations which are tolerably regular in their form; but it must be added that such regularity is by no means invariable. It is quite impossible to enumerate all the variations to be met with in this part of the movement; we must confine ourselves to the more important, and to those which may be regarded as to some extent typical.

328. The first thing to be noticed is, that it is possible for the recapitulation to commence with the first subject, not in the key of the tonic, but in that of the subdominant. It is a very curious thing that examples of this are almost exclusively found in the works of two composers, utterly unlike in almost every respect—

Clementi and Schubert. We meet with it in at least three of Clementi's sonatas; viz.: those in E flat, Op. 10 No. 3, in B flat, Op. 14 No. 1, and in B flat, Op. 25 No. 3. Schubert does the same in his second and fifth symphonies, in his piano quintett in A, Op. 114, and in his piano sonatas in B major, Op. 147, and A minor, Op. 164. The only other instances of this procedure that we have found are in Mozart's sonata in C, No. 15, and in Hummel's trio in E flat, Op. 96. The object evidently is, that the key relationship of first and second subjects in the recapitulation may be the same as in the exposition; but the expediency appears to be at least doubtful, as the effect of beginning the recapitulation in another key than the tonic is hardly satisfactory. In the ternary form, of which we have already seen that the sonata form is a variation, the return of the tonic key is one of the chief characteristics of the third part of the movement.

329. Sometimes, though comparatively seldom, we find in the recapitulation that the re-entry of the second subject precedes that of the first. This is the case in the first movement of Mozart's sonata in D beginning

and also of his great sonata in the same key for piano and violin. Other examples may be seen in some of Haydn's symphonies, in Spohr's octett, Op. 32 (first movement,) and double quartett, Op. 65 (finale,) and in the first movement of Dvořák's piano quartett in E flat, Op. 87.

330. It is not very unusual to find considerable abridgment of the subjects in the recapitulation. For instance, in Schubert's piano quintett in A, Op. 114, not only does the recapitulation begin in the subdominant key (§ 328), but the first twenty-four bars are omitted altogether. A similar thing is seen in the first movement of Mendelssohn's string quartett in F minor, Op. 80, where only the final sentence of the first subject appears in the recapitulation. In a few cases, the first subject is entirely omitted. Examples of this will be seen in the first movement of Clementi's sonata in G, Op. 39 No. 2, and in the finale of Dussek's sonata in B flat, Op. 35 No. 1.

331. On the other hand, we occasionally find the first subject extended in the recapitulation. Beethoven's sonata in F, Op. 10 No. 2, affords a good illustration of this. The free fantasia ends on the dominant of D; and the first subject (which we quoted in § 225,) is given in its complete form in that key. It is then continued as follows; to show the connexion we quote the last chord of the full cadence in D.

BEETHOVEN: Sonata, Op. 10. No. 2.

The last eight bars of the first subject are then repeated in the key of F as before. The whole first subject now contains 27 bars, instead of twelve, as in the exposition.

332. It is unusual to find the first subject beginning, as here, in a different key from that in which it ends; another interesting example will be found in the recapitulation of Weber's sonata in C, Op. 24. The passage is too long to quote; the student who examines the movement will see that in the exposition the first subject consists of two perfectly regular eight-bar sentences, the first ending on the dominant, and the second with a full cadence on the tonic. In the recapitulation the first subject is introduced in E flat; the first six bars are almost unaltered, except in their key; but there is a new continuation, modulating through F minor and C minor back to C major. Instead of two sentences as before, there is now only one long sentence extended to seventeen bars.

333. The alteration of the second subject in the recapitulation is much more frequent than that of the first. Sometimes part of it is omitted, as in Haydn's quartett in G, Op. 77 No. 1, in which the flowing melody with which the second subject opens,

is not heard at all in the recapitulation, most probably because Haydn has used it so extensively in the free fantasia. Again, in the finale of Dussek's sonata, Op. 10 No. 3, the second subject, as already mentioned (§ 255,) is in two keys, the first section being in G major, and the second and third in B minor. In the recapitulation the first section does not reappear at all.

334. Sometimes considerable variation will be found in the recapitulation of the second subject. In Beethoven's sonata in F, of which we were speaking just now (§ 331), the second subject begins in F major, but has a new continuation, passing through

F minor and A flat before returning to the tonic key. At other times the general outline remains the same but the details are much altered. A good example of this is seen in the finale of Dussek's sonata in G minor, Op. 10 No. 2. In the exposition, the second subject commences thus—

DUSSEK: Sonata, Op. 10, No. 2.

In the recapitulation the passage is modified as follows—

335. Occasionally the second subject is so far altered in the recapitulation as to be almost a new subject, though constructed on the same lines as before. A very interesting example of this (far too long, unfortunately for quotation,) is seen in the first movement of Haydn's quartett in B flat, Op. 76 No. 4, which the student should examine. We give another illustration of the same point, from Mozart's little known quintett for horn and strings. We quote the melody only of the second subject, giving it first as in the exposition,

and then as it appears in the recapitulation.

If these two subjects are compared, it will be seen that there is a strong "family likeness" between them, especially in their rhythmic figures, but that the melodies are entirely different.*

336. An exceptional choice of key for the second subject by Beethoven deserves to be mentioned. In the finale of his sonata in E flat, Op. 31 No. 3, the second subject, which in the exposition is in B flat, appears in G flat major, the final sentence being repeated in E flat minor, and the coda being approached through the dominant of that key.

337. Occasionally in a minor movement, the entire recapitulation is in the tonic major key, the first subject being altered in the same way which we saw with the second subject in § 322. We have only met with two instances of this—in the first movements of Spohr's second symphony, in D minor, and of Weber's sonata in D minor, Op. 49. The latter movement ends in the major key; Spohr returns to D minor for the coda.

338. One very irregular kind of recapitulation has still to be noticed—if, indeed, it can be called by that name. In a few movements which we cannot but consider as being in sonata form, neither the first nor the second subject is repeated after the free fantasia; but a long *coda*, made of entirely new material,

* The explanation of the difference is that the passages quoted are written for the horn; and the technique of that instrument is such that an exact transposition of the first passage would have been extremely difficult. Mozart therefore modified it, and thus made it not only easier, but more effective, and better adapted to the nature of the instrument.

takes its place. A comparatively early example of this will be found in the finale of Hummel's sonata in F minor, Op. 20; while Schumann does the same thing in the first movement of his symphony in D minor, and in the finale of his symphony in C. Though in all these cases the end justifies the means, the plan is not to be recommended; for it unquestionably detracts from the unity that ought to characterize this form.

339. With the close of the recapitulation, a sonata movement may, and frequently does end; but it may also be followed by a *coda*. In the majority of the sonatas of Haydn and Mozart the coda is not to be found; it is also wanting in some of the earlier works of Beethoven—*e.g.* in the sonatas, Op. 2 No. 2, Op. 10 Nos. 1 and 2, and Op. 22. But with modern composers we usually find, especially in works laid out on a large scale, a coda of more or less extent and importance. As in the case of the free fantasia, it is impossible to give any rules as to what the coda should contain; this is entirely at the composer's discretion. Sometimes it is quite short, as in Beethoven's sonata in F minor, Op. 2 No. 1, in which the coda is nothing but an extension of the last sentence of the second subject. In other cases it is of considerable length; and it is then not unusual to find development of some of the themes which had not been treated in the free fantasia.

340. As an illustration of this, we will take the coda in Beethoven's sonata, Op. 7, which we select because in § 280 we quoted the whole of the free fantasia. The second subject of this sonata contains five sections (§ 254); but of these only a part of the fifth was employed in the free fantasia. One of the most important—the second, which begins at bar 59 thus—

BEETHOVEN: Sonata, Op. 7.

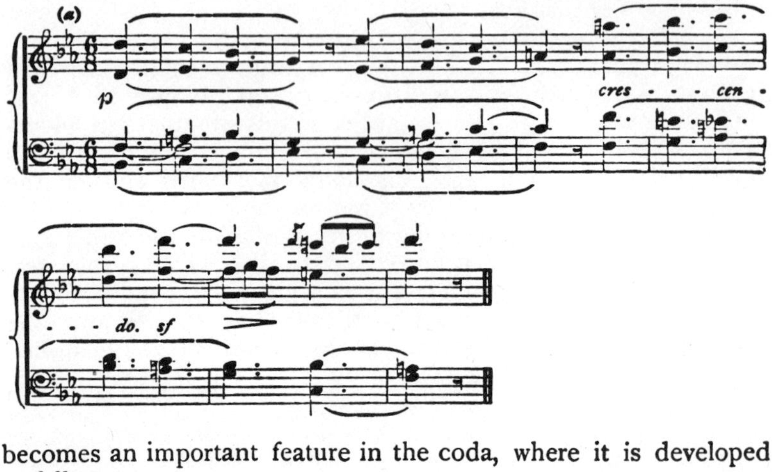

becomes an important feature in the coda, where it is developed as follows—

(*b*)

The end of this extract is followed by further developments of the themes given as (*c*) and (*a*) in § 279, bringing the movement to a close.

341. Sometimes, though not very frequently, the coda brings forward an entirely new theme. A good example is found in the first movement of Schumann's symphony in B flat, of which we gave the first subject in § 227. The coda begins with a quicken ing of the time (*Animato*), and thematic treatment of the first subject for more than fifty bars. At bar 57 of the coda, the following new idea is presented.

SCHUMANN: 1st Symphony.

These bars are then repeated, and the train of thought continued for some little time before the return of the commencement of the first subject, which is given in augmentation.

342. Another beautiful example of the introduction of new matter in the coda is seen in the finale of Mendelssohn's sonata in D for piano and violoncello. As the work is tolerably well known, it will suffice to quote the opening bars of the passage to which we refer.

MENDELSSOHN: Sonata in D, Op. 58.

343. When the final movement of a cyclic work, such as a sonata or symphony, is in sonata form, we almost always, at least in modern compositions, find a coda appended, in order to give more importance to the conclusion of the work. In such cases we sometimes find an alteration (which is generally a quickening,) of the *tempo*. As examples of this may be named the finales of Beethoven's symphony in C minor, and sonata in F minor, Op. 57. The same thing is also sometimes found in a first movement, as in the sonata just referred to, and in Schubert's great symphony in C, No. 7.

344. The form we have been discussing in this and the preceding chapter is so infinitely rich in its varied possibilities, that it has been impossible to treat it exhaustively; it is hoped that enough has been said to enable the student to make further investigations for himself. Once more we repeat what we have so often said before,—that more will be learned from analyzing the works of the great masters than in any other way. The student will best master the subject by carefully examining all the sonatas, trios, quartetts, or symphonies within his reach and noticing their structural peculiarities, resemblances and differences. The best models of form are Haydn, Mozart, Beethoven, and Mendelssohn.

CHAPTER IX.

MODIFIED SONATA FORMS.

345. In the Sonata Form which we have been discussing in the last two chapters we have seen that, while there was room for very considerable variety in the details of treatment, the essential outlines of the form remained the same in every case. But we frequently meet with movements evidently closely allied to the form of which we have been speaking, which nevertheless present points of difference sufficient to prevent our regarding them as regular sonata movements. Such may be termed *modified* sonata forms. The most important of these—the later Rondo form—will be discussed by itself in the next chapter; in the present one we shall speak of others, which more nearly approximate to the normal form already described.

346. The first of these is that which we name the Abridged Sonata Form. We know (§ 224,) that the regular sonata form contains three parts—the exposition, the development, and the recapitulation. Of these the development is sometimes quite short; in other cases it is the longest of the three sections of the movement. In the abridged sonata form of which we are now speaking, the middle part of the movement (the "free fantasia,") is entirely wanting. At the end of the exposition the music returns at once to the tonic key, and the recapitulation commences.

347. It will be obvious that the effect of this compression is to reduce the movement from a ternary to a binary form; and it would seem at a first glance as if it were merely reverting to the old sonata form described and illustrated in §§ 217–220. There is, however, one important difference between the two. In the older sonata form, the first subject was introduced at the beginning of the second part in the same key in which the second subject had been given in the first part of the movement. In the abridged sonata form, on the other hand, the first subject reappears in the tonic key, exactly as it would do in a fully developed sonata movement, and the whole of the second part, with possible occasional transitions to related keys, will be, like an ordinary recapitulation, in the tonic key.

348. The abridged sonata form is most frequently, though by no means exclusively, employed for the slow movements of cyclic

works (sonatas, &c.); and a short analysis of two or three movements written in this form will be sufficient to illustrate its special features. We will first take the *Adagio molto* of Beethoven's sonata in C minor, Op. 10 No. 1, as a particularly clear and perfect example. The movement contains 112 bars, of which forty-five belong to the first part.

349. The first subject, beginning

Adagio molto. BEETHOVEN: Sonata, Op. 10, No. 1.

contains two perfectly regular sentences of eight bars each, of which the first ends with a half cadence, and the second with a full cadence in the tonic key. At bar 17 begins the bridge-passage, which is only seven bars long, and which leads through the dominant seventh of E flat to the second subject in that key.

350. This second subject consists of one extended sentence twenty-one bars in length; if the student will analyze it, he will see that both the fore-phrase and the after-phrase are repeated in a varied form, and that the after-phrase is prolonged by cadential extensions and repetitions. It ends at bar 44 with a full cadence in E flat. A single chord of the dominant seventh, *ff*, reintroduces

the original key and the first subject. We quote the passage, beginning with the last three bars of the second subject.

351. The first subject is now repeated with more ornamentation, both of melody and harmony, and is followed at bar 62 by the second bridge-passage. This is constructed of the same material as the first one, the first part being absolutely identical; but it is now extended to nine bars, and the latter part is varied, so as to end on the dominant seventh of A flat, instead of on that of E flat, as before. The second subject is then introduced in the tonic key, with only very slight modifications, and at bar 91 it is followed by a coda, twenty-two bars long, founded upon the commencement of the first subject with a new and very beautiful continuation.

352. This Adagio illustrates two points frequently seen when the sonata form, whether complete or (as here) abridged, is used for a slow movement. Note, in the first place, that the second subject is not divisible into sections. We said in § 248 that in most cases the second subject could be so divided, but we were then speaking of the sonata form as usually found in *allegro* movements. In slow movements, on the other hand, the second subject is generally much shorter—sometimes, as we shall see directly, even shorter than the first.

353. The other point to be noticed is that in slow movements the subjects (more especially the first subject,) are generally varied, or perhaps it will be better to say ornamented, in the recapitulation. We saw in the last chapter (§ 315,) that this was occasionally done even in an allegro; but with an adagio or andante it is rather the rule than the exception. The student will no doubt remember that the same thing is very frequently to be seen in the simple ternary form (*Musical Form*, § 359).

354. For our next illustration we select the Adagio of Beethoven's sonata in D minor, Op. 31 No. 2. The movement

is too well known to need quotation; it will suffice to refer to the numbers of the bars. As in the example last analyzed, the first subject contains two sentences, and ends with a full cadence in the tonic at bar 17. The bridge-passage commences in the same bar. The reason we do not consider the four following bars as a prolongation of the final cadence of the first subject—for the modulation does not begin till bar 22—will be clear to the student, if he compares the corresponding passage in the second part of the movement (bars 60 to 63). The bridge-passage ends in bar 30 with a half cadence in F, and the second subject consists of only one eight-bar sentence, ending in bar 38. The return to the first subject, instead of consisting, as in our last example, of only a single chord, is a "link" (*Musical Form*, § 368,) five bars long, formed of the chord of the dominant minor ninth. The first subject is then repeated, its second sentence being accompanied by elaborate ornamental passages for the left hand. A modification of the first bridge-passage leads to the second subject in the tonic key; and a coda of twenty-three bars, chiefly founded upon the "link" and the first subject, concludes the movement, which, it will be seen, furnishes further illustration of both the points mentioned in §§ 352, 353.

355. The Adagio of Mozart's sonata in F (No. 12) shows much resemblance to the movements last examined, but has one or two points of difference that deserve notice. The movement commences thus—

MOZART: Sonata in F, No. 12.

Though the first subject *as printed* contains only eight bars, yet an examination of the music shows that we have here quadruple time with two accents in the bar, and that these eight bars are really equivalent to sixteen (see *Musical Form*, § 36). This first subject therefore, like the two by Beethoven examined above, contains two sentences, the first ending with a half cadence (feminine ending,) in bar 4. The fore-phrase of the second sentence (bars 5 and 6) is the same as that of the first sentence, but in the minor mode; and the after-phrase modulates to F minor (the dominant minor of B flat minor) and ends with a full cadence in that key, but with a major third (Tierce de Picardie), to lead back to the dominant of the original key.

356. It is unusual, we might almost say exceptional, for the first subject to end in the key of the dominant; but Mozart's doing so in this case renders a bridge passage superfluous;

consequently the second subject follows immediately on the final cadence of the first.

The second subject, excepting a momentary transition to G minor, is in the key of F major throughout, and ends with a short tonic pedal, after which the return is made at once, as in our example, § 350, through one bar of the chord of the dominant seventh, to the tonic key and the first subject.

The first subject is ornamented, as usual, and on its close is followed immediately by the second subject, now in B flat. This is also much ornamented. The movement contains no coda; on the close of the second subject there is only a final cadence over a tonic pedal. We quote the last two bars of the movement.

357. A very good example of this form in an allegro will be seen in Mendelssohn's 'Andante cantabile e Presto agitato' in B major and minor. The Andante, in B major, is a very regular and complete simple binary form; the Presto which follows has an exposition like that of a fully developed sonata movement.

After four bars of introduction the first subject begins thus—we give the melody only.

(*a*) MENDELSSOHN: Presto Agitato.

The first subject contains two sentences, the latter extended by the repetition of the last two bars of the after-phrase. The bridge-passage

(*b*)

leads to the key of A major in which the second subject commences.

(*c*)

The first part of the second subject modulates from A to D major, and thence to F sharp minor, in which key the latter half of the subject is given. Its second section begins

(*d*)

358. The second subject ends in F sharp minor, and thus furnishes an example similar to those which we have already seen (§ 255,) of a second subject of a minor movement in more than one key. At the close, the tonic, F sharp, is treated as a dominant, and the return is made at once to B minor by an inverted pedal.

The first subject then reappears unaltered; we have said above that ornamentation is most frequent in the repetition of the subjects in slow movements. The bridge-passage is modified as usual, and the second subject is then given in the keys of D major, G major, and B minor—in each case the fifth below the key in which the corresponding part appeared in the exposition. A long coda concludes the movement.

359. It should be noticed that in this abridged sonata form of which we are now speaking, the repetition of the exposition, which is so common a feature of the complete sonata form, is never met with. The reason is evident; there would be too great monotony if the subjects were heard three times in succession without the relief afforded by the free fantasia. It is true that in the old sonata form, which also had no developments, both parts were frequently repeated; but in these variety was obtained by the introduction of the first subject in a different key in the second part.

360. A species of composition in which the abridged sonata form is often met with is the OVERTURE. The form of the overture varies so much that it is impossible to classify it definitely; the present will be as appropriate a place as any to say a few words about it.

361. The name 'Overture' (*Fr.* 'Ouverture' = an opening,) was originally applied to the instrumental piece, of one or more movements, played at the commencement of an opera, or oratorio. It is also several times used by Bach as the title of the first movement of a Suite or Partita. The overtures of Bach, Handel, and their contemporaries are mostly in the form of a prelude and fugue, the former in slow and the latter in quick time. The fugue is not seldom followed by one (sometimes by more than one) dance movement, the minuet being that most commonly selected. The name 'Overture' would appear at this time to have been restricted to the form we are describing; for we find that in Handel's oratorios 'Athalia,' and 'Saul,' in which the instrumental introduction is not in the form of a prelude and fugue, the composer calls the movement not 'Overture' but 'Sinfonia.'

362. The development by Emanuel Bach and Haydn of the sonata form soon led to its introduction in the overture. We find it,—sometimes the old sonata form (§ 217), sometimes the modern, more or less complete, in several of the overtures to Mozart's early operas; while in French opera a good example,

dating from the last century, of a full sonata movement will be seen in Sacchini's overture to 'Œdipe à Colone' (1786).

363. In the overtures of Mozart and Beethoven the sonata form is mostly employed, sometimes with and sometimes without modification. Mozart's youthful operas are in some cases preceded by a short symphony in three movements, but in his later and better known works the sonata form is always used for the overtures. In those to 'Don Juan,' 'Der Schauspieldirektor' and 'Così fan tutte,' we find the form complete, and the structure quite regular; the overture to 'Titus' is also a fully developed sonata movement, in which, however, the second subject in the recapitulation precedes the first (§ 329). In the overtures to 'Figaro' and 'Idomeneo' the close of the exposition is followed by a short passage leading back at once to the recapitulation; these movements are therefore in the abridged sonata form of which we have already spoken in this chapter. The overture to 'Idomeneo' is further irregular, inasmuch as the second subject does not appear in the recapitulation. The overture to 'Die Zauberflöte' is often spoken of as a fugue; it is in reality a sonata movement of which the first subject is in fugal form. An example of a genuine fugued overture will be seen in Beethoven's Concert Overture in C, Op. 124, generally known as 'Die Weihe des Hauses.'

364. Sometimes the place of the free fantasia of an overture otherwise in sonata form is taken by an incidental slow movement. Examples of this will be found in Mozart's overture to 'Die Entführung aus dem Serail' ('Il Seraglio,') and Beethoven's first overture (Op. 138,) to 'Leonora.' In Mozart's overture (as also in that to 'Don Juan,') the recapitulation is not completed, as the movement in each case leads without a break into the first number of the opera.

365. The majority of Beethoven's overtures are in full sonata form. In addition to the two (Ops. 124 and 138,) of which we have just spoken the only exceptions are the overtures to 'Prometheus,' which is in condensed sonata form, and to the 'Ruins of Athens,' which is so irregular as to be in reality a fantasia for orchestra. In all the other overtures the sonata form is clearly to be traced.

366. A slow introduction, as in Mozart's overtures to 'Don Juan,' 'Così fan tutte,' and the 'Zauberflöte,' and in Beethoven's to 'Egmont,' 'Leonora,' 'Namensfeier,' and others, is far more common in overtures than in either symphonies or sonatas. It is hardly necessary to say that in speaking of the sonata form of the overtures we are referring to the allegro movements which follow such introductions where they exist.

367. It is not our purpose here to write a history of the overture, or to trace its development; we are concerned simply with its form. The overtures of Weber, Spohr, Cherubini, and

Mendelssohn mostly follow the lines laid down by Mozart and Beethoven. In the overtures to 'St. Paul' and 'Elijah' Mendelssohn has adopted the fugue form, combining it in the former case with a choral. The same composer's overture to 'Athalie' deserves a word of mention on account of a peculiarity in its structure. The introduction to this overture is in the key of F major, while the allegro that follows begins in D minor and ends in D major, the overture thus closing with a different tonic from that with which it commenced. Such a procedure is extremely rare,* and is certainly not to be recommended for imitation.

368. An important point to be noticed with regard to the use of the sonata form in overtures is, that the exposition should never be repeated, as is so often done in a sonata or symphony. The only case that we have met with in which there is a repeat of the first part is Mendelssohn's Overture for a Military Band, Op. 24. As this piece was the work of a boy of fifteen, it should be regarded as an exception, rather than as a precedent.

369. Many modern opera overtures are constructed on themes taken from the work which they precede. The first to do this systematically was Weber, in his overtures to 'Der Freischütz,' 'Euryanthe' and 'Oberon'; but he did it while carefully preserving the sonata form. Some more recent composers, however, merely string together themes from their work, sometimes with the addition of fresh material, in an incoherent manner; the result being that, however effective, such overtures are practically formless. An example of this kind will be seen in Hérold's popular overture to 'Zampa,' which cannot be classified under any known form. Another excellent illustration of the same kind is Rossini's overture to 'Guillaume Tell,' the subjects of which are not taken from the opera itself. We are not condemning these, and similar pieces, as music; we are simply pointing out to the student the existence of a certain class of overture the form of which cannot be strictly defined.

370. A very important modification of the sonata form is that to be seen in the first movement of the CONCERTO, as treated by Mozart, Beethoven, and their contemporaries and immediate successors. In its modern sense the word 'Concerto' is employed to describe a work written for a solo instrument with orchestral accompaniment; but in the last century it was also applied to pieces written for orchestra without special solo parts.† For

* A somewhat similar case may be seen in Weber's overture to 'Preciosa,' in which the introduction is in A minor, while the two following movements are in C major, in which key the piece ends.

† Bach, in his cantatas "Bringet dem Herrn Ehre seines Namens," "Es wartet Alles auf dich," "Nimm was dein ist und gehe hin," and "Siehe zu, dass deine Gottesfurcht nicht Heuchelei sei," has entitled the opening choruses 'Concerto'; and at the beginning of the cantata "Mein Gott, wie lang' ach lange," he uses the same word to describe an accompanied recitative. Evidently he thought of it in its original meaning—a concert, or combination of instruments and voices.

example, of Bach's six so-called 'Brandenburg Concertos,' four have parts for one or more solo instruments, while the other two (Nos. 3 and 6,) have no such parts. The same is the case with some of Handel's Oboe Concertos, which, as regards the composition of the orchestra (though not as regards the form,) more nearly resemble the symphony. The modern form of the concerto was fixed by Mozart, in whose works nearly fifty examples for various instruments are to be found. This form was also adopted by Beethoven, Weber, Spohr, and (with some modifications, to be mentioned presently,) by later composers.

371. In the concertos of Mozart and Beethoven, the first movement is always in a modified sonata form, and we have now to explain the nature of the modifications. Of these the most important is the *double exposition.* We have already seen (§§ 266, 267,) that in the regular sonata form the repetition of the exposition is very common. In the concerto form, as fixed by Mozart and adopted by Beethoven, we find instead of this, two different expositions, the first for the orchestra alone, and the second for the solo instrument accompanied by the orchestra. If we examine the entire series of Mozart's concertos, we shall find that this form did not spring full grown out of his brain, like Minerva from the head of Jupiter, but that it was gradually evolved. The earlier concertos contain only a short orchestral introduction, in which little more than the first subject of the movement appears; but in all the later examples we find the double exposition of which we are now speaking.

372. It is not to be supposed, however, that the two expositions in a concerto are identical; far from it. In the first place, the first exposition, for orchestra alone, differs from the exposition of a sonata in the fact that it always ends in the key of the tonic—in the majority of cases, with a full cadence in that key. The object of this is, to lead to the entry of the solo instrument, generally with the first subject, less abruptly than if the orchestra had ended in some other key. This first exposition therefore in its form more nearly resembles the recapitulation than the exposition of a sonata; and this resemblance is increased by the fact that the second subject, when it appears in the first exposition, is almost invariably in the key of the tonic, and not in that of the dominant, or (with a minor movement,) in the relative major.

373. We have just said "the second subject, when it appears in the first exposition"; and this brings us to the next point of importance. The first exposition rarely contains all the material to be found in the second. Sometimes the difference in length between the two is very slight; for example, in Mozart's concerto in A major (No. 23) the first exposition contains 66 bars, and the second 71, while in Beethoven's concerto in C minor, Op. 37, the respective lengths of the two expositions are 111 and 116 bars. On the other hand, it is not uncommon to find the second

exposition far longer than the first. In Beethoven's violin concerto the first exposition is 88 bars long and the second 136, while in Mozart's piano concerto in C minor, the disproportion is greater still, the second exposition containing 166 bars, as compared with 99 in the first.

374. There is a curious and interesting difference to be noticed between the practice of Mozart and Beethoven in the treatment of this double exposition. When the second exposition is considerably longer than the first, as in the examples referred to above, (and others might be given,) this generally arises with Mozart from the introduction into the second exposition of new themes, which had not been heard at all in the first one. In the concerto in C minor, for instance, the second subject (if it can be so called) of the first exposition begins thus—

MOZART: Concerto in C minor, No. 24.

(a)

Neither this theme nor its continuation (for which we must refer the student to the work itself,) is to be found in the second exposition, though both are used in the recapitulation. On the other hand, the second exposition contains two important themes in its second subject, beginning

(b)

and

(c)

neither of which is seen in the first exposition.

375. Somewhat similar cases are found in other concertos of Mozart. In the piano concerto in G (No. 17,) the first theme of the second subject

does not appear in the first exposition at all, though the second theme is found in both; in this movement the first exposition has 74 bars and the second 97. Again, in the last of the four concertos for piano in C which Mozart wrote, beginning

the two expositions have quite different second subjects, and that of the first exposition furnishes the material for nearly the whole of the free fantasia, which, as in a sonata or symphony, forms the second part of the movement.

376. In Beethoven's concertos, on the other hand, the greater length of the second exposition mostly arises, not from the introduction of new subjects, but from the larger development of those that have already been heard in the first exposition. A very good example of this will be found in his violin concerto. The work is so accessible * that it is needless to make quotations; an examination of the movement will well repay the student.

377. As a concerto is a piece written for the display of a solo instrument, (occasionally of more than one,) the second exposition will always be more florid than the first. In general the subjects are given in a more varied and ornamented form by the solo instrument (whether alone or accompanied,) than on their first presentation by the orchestra.

378. We said above that the first exposition usually ended with a full cadence in the tonic key. Occasionally, however, it leads more directly into the second, without a full close. This is seldom found in Mozart, as in his piano concerto in C, No. 21, where the solo instrument enters on dominant harmony; but Beethoven in all his later concertos (in G, Op. 58, in E flat, Op. 73, and in the violin concerto,) introduces the solo instrument on a chord of the dominant seventh, evidently to obtain greater continuity in the music.

* The score is published in the Peters edition.

379. When speaking in § 371 of the double exposition, it was remarked that the first exposition was for orchestra alone. In general the solo instrument does not enter till the second exposition. It is often stated that the introduction of the piano at the beginning of his concertos in G and E flat was an innovation of Beethoven's; but the same thing had been already done by Mozart in a very fine, though little known, concerto in E flat, of which we give the opening bars.

MOZART: Concerto in E flat, No. 9.

Neither in this case, nor in those by Beethoven just named, does the solo instrument reappear till the second exposition.

380. The second and third parts of the first movement of a concerto are devoted, as in the sonata, to the development and recapitulation. The commencement of each part is given to the orchestra alone, the solo instrument having always a rest at this point. In Czerny's 'School of Practical Composition' (almost the only theoretical work, by the way, that gives a detailed account of the concerto form,) the author speaks of the first movement as consisting of a *tutti* for the orchestra, followed by the first, second, and third solos for the pianist, the solos being divided from one another by shorter *tuttis* than the first. It will be readily seen that Czerny's first "*tutti*" corresponds to what we have here described as the first exposition, while the three solos are the second exposition, development, and recapitulation.

381. A specialty of this form to which we have not yet referred is the introduction of a *Cadenza* towards the close of the movement. It was the custom of Mozart and Beethoven to introduce in the last orchestral *tutti* of the recapitulation a pause, always on the second inversion of the tonic chord, to allow of a brilliant improvisation on the part of the soloist. Such an improvisation was called a 'Cadenza,' and in it the performer was expected not only to show his technical skill, but his ability in treating material taken from the movement itself. Mozart has left us 35 cadenzas

written for his own concertos—sometimes two or three for the same work; and Beethoven also wrote cadenzas for his concertos. He seems to have felt, however, that there was danger of an extemporized cadenza being out of keeping with the character of the rest of the movement; and in his last piano concerto (in E flat, Op. 73,) after the customary pause for the orchestra on the $\frac{6}{4}$ chord, he writes out in full the cadenza that he wishes played, adding a note "Non si fa una Cadenza, ma s'attacca subito il seguente," *i.e.* "Do not make a cadenza, but go on at once to the following." In more recent concertos, the cadenza is either dispensed with altogether (as in Mendelssohn's two piano concertos and in Brahms's concerto in D minor,) or written out in full by the composer himself, as in Mendelssohn's violin concerto, and the piano concertos of Schumann, Raff, and Rheinberger. It should further be remarked that the cadenza is sometimes introduced after a chord of the dominant seventh, instead of a $\frac{6}{4}$ chord, and that Mendelssohn in his violin concerto has placed it between the free fantasia and the recapitulation, instead of, as usual, toward the close of the latter.*

382. A very important innovation in the concerto form was made by Mendelssohn. He dispensed altogether with the double exposition, and introduced the solo instrument at the commencement of the movement. With this alteration the concerto becomes in all essentials identical with the sonata form. The example of Mendelssohn has been followed by Schumann, and by most later composers, though Brahms in his first piano concerto, Op. 15, has adhered to the older form, and given a complete double exposition. The two piano concertos by Liszt are so irregular in their form that they are in reality more like rhapsodies or fantasias than concertos of the kind we have been describing.

383. One more modification of the sonata form has still to be spoken of—the SONATINA. The name is the Italian diminutive of 'Sonata,' and means literally 'a small sonata,' but it is often somewhat loosely applied. We find it once in the clavier works of Handel, as No. 10 in the Third Collection. This 'Sonatina' is nothing more than a small piece for harpsichord, 19 bars long, and in simple binary form (*Musical Form*, Chap. IX.); it is not therefore a sonatina in the modern sense of the term. The same may be said of the only piece entitled 'Sonatina' in Bach's works—the short instrumental introduction to the cantata "Gottes Zeit ist die allerbeste Zeit."

384. The Sonatina properly so called is a sonata on a very small scale. In many cases both first and second subjects are extremely short, the bridge passage is wanting altogether, and

* A cadenza similar to that here described will occasionally be found in pianoforte sonatas. Examples may be seen in the first movements of Clementi's sonatas in C, Op. 36, No. 3; B flat, Op. 46, and A major, Op. 50 No. 1, and of Beethoven's sonata in C major, Op. 2 No. 3.

there is little or no free fantasia. The general outline of the sonata form is preserved, and that is all. As an example we give the first movement of a very short sonatina by Kuhlau.

Kuhlau : Sonatina in G, Op. 55, No. 2.

O

The first subject contains only one eight-bar sentence, ending with a half cadence ; the second subject, in the dominant, follows at once without a bridge-passage. This subject also consists of only one sentence, extended to twelve bars by prolongations of the cadence. Instead of a free fantasia, a single eight-bar sentence leads back at once to the return of the first subject, now varied and extended, which is followed by the second subject in the tonic key. There is no coda.

385. It must not be supposed that all sonatinas are as concise in their form as that which we have just given. To save space we selected one of the shortest we could find. It is in fact impossible to lay down any absolute line of demarcation between the Sonatina and the Sonata. For example, Clementi's sonatas, Ops. 37 and 38, are in some editions called sonatinas; while Beethoven's sonatina in G, Op. 79, the first movement of which is 201 bars in length, is more extended in its developments than either of the two sonatas, Op. 49, which in all respects are more really sonatinas than Op. 79. The same is still more the case with the same composer's 'Two Easy Sonatas' in G major and F major, which are strictly sonatinas, and not properly sonatas at all.

386. In some examples of the sonatina, the sonata form is altogether abandoned. In the six sonatinas, Op. 20, by Dussek, in Nos. 1, 2, and 5, the first movement is in simple binary form, and is followed by a short movement in the older rondo form. In two other examples by the same composer (Op. 28, Nos. 2 and 5,) both the movements are in simple binary form. In such cases the name 'Sonatina' ceases to be strictly applicable. The same remark will apply to the two easy sonatas by Beethoven of which we spoke just now, the first of which, at all events, is a sonata only in name.

CHAPTER X.

THE MODERN RONDO (RONDO-SONATA) FORM.

387. IN Chapter VI. of this volume we dealt with the older Rondo form, and we remarked (§ 180,) that there was another kind of Rondo, differing altogether from the one there treated of, and which was a modification of the sonata form. We have now to explain the construction of the more modern rondo.

388. As in the older rondo, so in that now under consideration, the opening subject is almost invariably a simple binary form of two sentences, ending with a full cadence in the tonic key. If we compare in any of Beethoven's sonatas the first subject of the first movement with that of the rondo, we can hardly fail to be struck with the greater simplicity of the rhythmic construction in the latter. It is very rare for the opening of a rondo to be in any but perfectly regular four- and eight-bar rhythm. The only exception to this that we can recall is in the rondo of Haydn's Piano Sonata in C, No. 16, the first subject of which was quoted in § 230 of *Musical Form*, as an example of six-bar rhythm. It is rather curious that the later rondo form is extremely rare in Haydn's works, though common enough in those of Mozart and Beethoven.

389. The rhythmic regularity of which we have just spoken generally gives a song-like character to the opening of a rondo, which further helps to distinguish it from a movement in sonata form. This will be clearly seen if we quote the commencement of a few rondos by various composers. To save space, we give the melody only of the first sentences.

(*a*) *Allegretto grazioso.* MOZART: Sonata in B flat, No. 13.

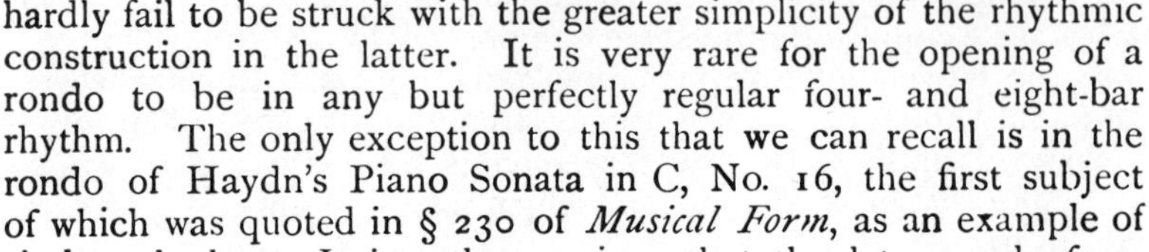

MOZART: Sonata in E flat, for Piano and Violin.

(*b*) *Allegro.*

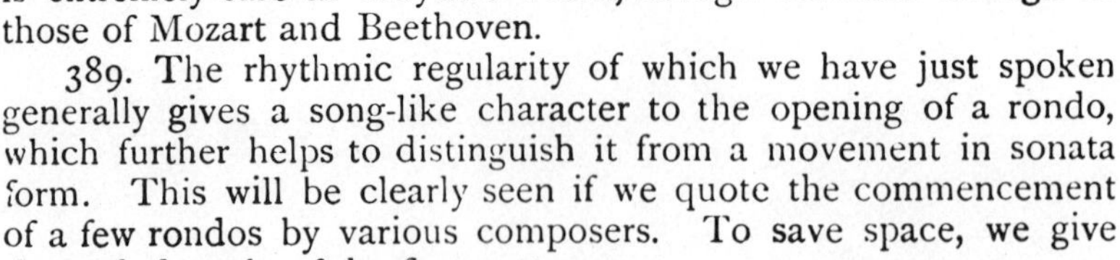

(*c*) *Poco Allegretto e grazioso.* BEETHOVEN : Sonata, Op. 7.

(*d*) *Allegretto.* BEETHOVEN : Sonata, Op. 31, No. 1.

(*e*) *Allegretto.* SCHUBERT : Sonata in A.

The student will do well to compare the first movements of the works from which we have quoted with the themes here given. He will at once perceive the difference in character of which we are speaking.

390. The opening of a modern Rondo form so closely follows the plan of a sonata movement that it can be appropriately described as the 'Rondo-Sonata' form—the name which we give in our heading as the second title. The first subject is followed, not (as in the older rondo) by an episode, but by a bridge-passage, leading in a major movement to the key of the dominant, and in a minor movement to that of the relative major, to introduce the second subject, which here follows the same rules with regard to its tonality as in a sonata movement. It is worth noticing that Beethoven, who made many innovations as to the key of the second subjects in his sonata movements (see §§ 241–246), never tried similar experiments in his rondos. In these the second subject is always in the dominant or the relative major, according as the movement is in a major or a minor key. *

391. Here the student may very naturally ask, Why not call this theme, in the dominant or the relative major, as the case may be, the first episode? for we read in the sixth chapter that a rondo contains one principal theme, interspersed with episodes. This question has been not infrequently put to the author by his own pupils; and, as the distinction is not always understood, it is as

* The second subject of the rondo in the sonata, Op. 49, No. 1, is an apparent exception to this rule: but the movement is irregular in form, as we shall show later in this chapter

well to make it clear. An episode never appears more than once in the course of a movement, though it may be referred to later in the coda; but we shall see presently that what we are now speaking of as 'second subject' will be heard subsequently in the tonic key, just as in a sonata movement. Any subject which is heard twice in different keys, the second being the tonic, can never in a regularly constructed movement be regarded as episode.

392. The second subject in a modern rondo is generally shorter than the corresponding portion of a movement in sonata form, seldom containing more than two sections, and not infrequently only one. This second subject always ends on the dominant, or dominant seventh of the tonic key. In the somewhat rare cases in which the form is used for a movement in a minor key,* the second subject ends in the relative major, but is followed by a *codetta* modulating back to the tonic key, and ending on its dominant harmony.

393. We now come to the first important respect in which this form differs from the true sonata form. We have already learned that in a movement in sonata form, either the whole exposition is repeated, or the free fantasia follows the second subject—possibly with a codetta between the two (§§ 266, 267). But in the rondo-sonata form *the whole exposition is never repeated, while the first subject invariably is so.* Here is a rule which will enable the student to distinguish without fail between the two forms. This additional appearance of the first subject gives, as we shall see presently, the three entries which are alike distinctive of the older (§ 188,) and of the modern rondo forms. With this re-entry of the first subject the first part of the movement concludes —always, be it observed, in the tonic key.

394. In the second part of a rondo-sonata movement is seen the other fundamental distinction between it and the sonata form. In the latter, the second part consists chiefly of development of the material of the subjects announced in the exposition, and, though the introduction of episodical matter is not infrequent, episode generally occupies only a subordinate position. In the rondo-sonata, on the other hand, we find exactly the converse; the second part of the movement begins with an entirely new episodical subject, in a different key from those of the first and second subjects. The keys generally chosen for the episode are, in major movements, either the subdominant major, the relative minor, or the tonic minor; in his minor movements Beethoven puts his episode into the submediant major, while Schubert, in the rondo of his sonata in A minor, Op. 42, has the episode in the tonic major, as has also Mozart in the rondo of his sonata

* In the entire collection of Beethoven's works, only three minor movements are written in the Rondo-sonata form. Curiously enough, all three are in C minor; they are the finales of the Sonata Pathétique, of the sonata for piano and violin, Op. 30, No. 2, and of the piano concerto in C minor, Op. 37

in the same key. Occasionally a major key in the second degree of relationship is selected for the episode. Thus Beethoven in his Rondo in G, Op. 51 No. 2, has the episode in E major. This piece also furnishes a somewhat rare example of a change of *tempo* for the episode, the Rondo being in $\frac{2}{4}$ time (*Andante cantabile e grazioso*), and the episode in $\frac{6}{8}$ (*Allegretto*).

395. The end of the episode, in whatever key it may appear, is so contrived as to modulate back to the dominant harmony of the tonic key, exactly as is the case with the close of the free fantasia in a sonata form. The recapitulation which succeeds follows exactly the lines of the corresponding portion of a sonata movement, but with this difference, that the first subject is more frequently (though not invariably) ornamented on its reappearance. A bridge passage leads in due course to the second subject, now almost always in the tonic key, and the movement concludes with a coda, in which the first subject is frequently introduced for the fourth time.

396. Before analyzing a few examples of this form, it will be well to summarize it in a few words. It will be seen from our description that we have here, as in the sonata, another variety of ternary form. Its three parts are the following :—

PART I. First subject. Bridge passage. Second subject, followed by codetta, leading back to dominant of the tonic key. Repetition of first subject.

PART II. Episode, ending on dominant harmony of tonic key.

PART III. First subject. Bridge passage. Second subject (in tonic key). Coda.

397. The movements now to be analyzed will not only illustrate the general outline above given, but will also show some points that we have not yet had opportunity to refer to. As a short and simple example, we first take the rondo of Beethoven's sonata in E major, Op. 14 No. 1. The student is advised to number the bars of his copy tor reference. In our own numbering we do not include the half bar with which the movement begins, as it contains no strong accent.

398. The first subject of the rondo begins with a simple sentence of eight bars—

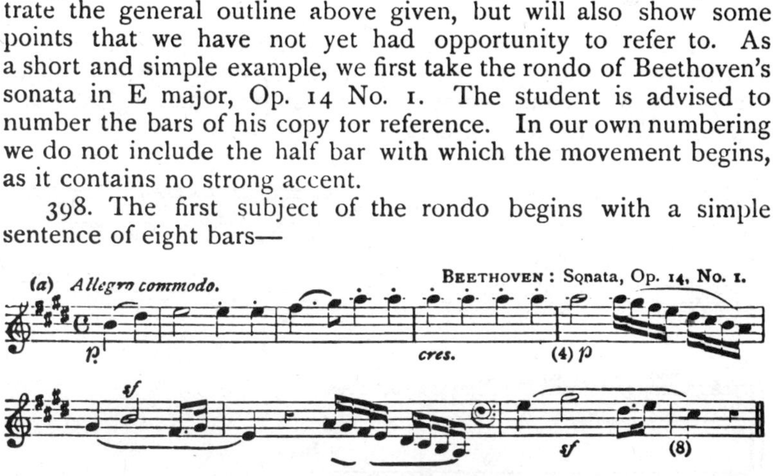

(It is sufficient to quote only the melody.) This subject is then repeated as far as the sixth bar, and the bridge passage begins with imitative treatment of the descending scale in the first subject.

(*b*)

The bridge is only seven bars long, and at bar 21 the second subject follows.

(*c*)

This subject is unusually concise; it consists of only one sentence, the after-phrase being a slightly varied repetition of the fore-phrase. The last two chords of the above extract form a "link" which leads at once to the repetition of the first subject, now in a complete form.

399. A codetta, formed from the material of the first subject, leads to the episode, which begins at bar 47 in the key of G major —a key in the second degree of relationship to the original tonic (§ 394). We give the first bars.

(*a*)

This episode modulates through A minor and B minor back to G major (bar 60), and thence to E minor (bar 64), concluding with a half cadence on the dominant of that key (bar 83). We then reach the recapitulation. The first subject is given unchanged in E major, and the bridge-passage is transposed a tone lower than before, and is now in A major, instead of B major. The introduction of the second subject in the key of the subdominant at bar 98 is most unusual, and the modification of the after-phrase, with the return through F major to the tonic key, is as beautiful as it is unexpected and original.

(*b*)

The coda, which immediately follows the pause, is mostly constructed from the first subject. We see it with syncopations in the upper part (bar 108,) and in the bass (bar 112), while at bar 121 the melody is modified by the introduction of passing notes and rests; and the coda ends with a portion of the bridge-passage transposed into E, and with the final cadence modified.

400. For our next example we take the Rondo of Beethoven's sonata in B flat, Op. 22. The form here is the same as in the movement just analyzed, but it is on a larger scale, the present rondo containing 199 bars as against 131 of the rondo in E. The first subject, beginning

(*a*) *Allegretto.* BEETHOVEN: Sonata, Op. 22.

contains two sentences; the first, eight bars long, ends with a full cadence in the dominant key, and the second, which, by a cadential repetition, is extended to ten bars, ends in bar 18 with a full cadence in B flat. The bridge-passage, six bars in length, modulates to the dominant key; it will be recognized by its commencement.

(*b*)

The second subject consists of one eight-bar sentence, of which we quote the fore-phrase—

(c)

The after-phrase is a varied repetition of the fore-phrase, and ends with a full cadence in F. On the last note of this cadence begins a codetta, the first eight bars of which consist of arpeggios modulating to B flat minor, and ending at bar 40 on the dominant of that key. Passages of imitation, founded on the beginning of the first subject, lead back at bar 49 to the return of that subject, given complete and without any alteration.

401. At bar 67 the episode begins in B flat minor, with a modification of the bridge-passage (bar 18). The proper subject of the episode appears a little later, at bar 72.

(a)

This passage, in three-bar rhythm, is repeated an octave higher, and the cadence is prolonged by two bars. At bar 80 the first bars of the episode are treated contrapuntally,

(*b*)

till bar 95, when the subject before given in F minor is repeated in B flat minor. At bar 103 begins the return to the first subject. The first two bars of this subject appear in the bass in G flat major, then a tone higher in A flat minor, and a continuation of the music through B flat minor leads back to the first subject, now in the middle part of the harmony.

(*c*)

In the second sentence the melody appears again in the upper part, but the octaves are now broken. The bridge-passage, beginning at bar 129, is extended by two bars, and introduces the second subject at bar 137—now in the key of B flat.

402. The coda of this movement is of considerable extent—54 bars. It begins with the first bars of the codetta (bar 32) now transposed to the tonic key, and with a new continuation, leading to the key of E flat. In this key the fore-phrase of the first subject is heard, and continued with thematic developments through C minor back to B flat. The whole of the first subject is now repeated, with a new variation in triplets.

Though it is very common to find a reference to the first subject in a coda, it is rather rare to find it repeated (as here,) in its entirety. It will be seen that we have in this movement four complete appearances of the first subject, of which the third and fourth are varied. At bar 182, a new theme, evidently suggested by the bridge passage, is heard, and the movement concludes with a last reference (bar 194,) to its opening bars.

403. It will be seen that in the rondo we have just analyzed there is much more thematic development than in that in E. In some cases thematic development takes the place of episode,—or perhaps it would be more strictly accurate to say that the episodical matter, if it can be so called, is developed from the first subject of the movement. This is the case in the finale of Beethoven's Sonata quasi Fantasia in E flat, Op. 27, No. 1, which, though not entitled 'Rondo' is really in the form now under notice. The first subject begins

BEETHOVEN: Sonata, Op. 27, No. 1.

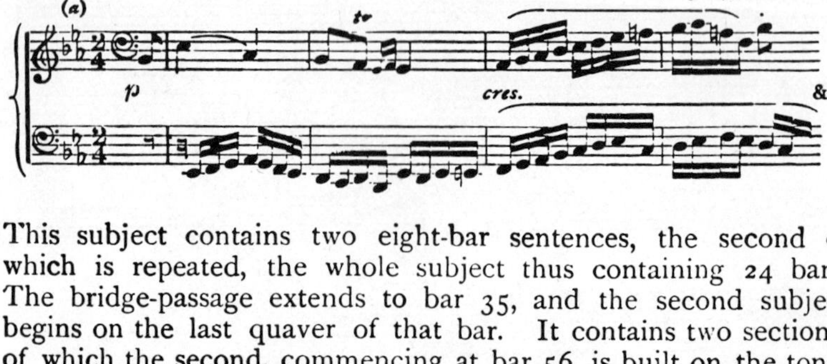

This subject contains two eight-bar sentences, the second of which is repeated, the whole subject thus containing 24 bars. The bridge-passage extends to bar 35, and the second subject begins on the last quaver of that bar. It contains two sections, of which the second, commencing at bar 56, is built on the tonic pedal of B flat. At bar 72, A flat is added to the tonic chord of B flat, thus converting it to the dominant seventh of E flat (§ 392), to lead back to the return of the first subject at bar 82.

The first sixteen bars appear unchanged; but the second sentence is modified on its repetition (bar 98), and modulates to E flat minor, and thence to G flat, in which key the following theme appears at bar 106.

It will be seen that both the subject in the bass and the counterpoint in semiquavers are suggested by the opening bars of the movement quoted at (*a*) above. Properly speaking, there is no real episode in the movement. Similar examples, and perhaps even more pronounced, will be seen in the Rondos of Beethoven's sonatas in G, Op. 31 No. 1, and E minor, Op. 90, and of his sonata in C minor, Op. 30, No. 2, for piano and violin.

404. As the examples hitherto analyzed have all been taken from sonatas, we give as our next illustration one which forms a complete piece by itself—Schubert's Rondo in A, Op. 107, for piano duet—a work of the utmost interest from its intrinsic beauty, as well as a characteristic specimen of this form. The first subject, commencing with the following melodious theme,

SCHUBERT: Rondo, Op. 107.

consists of four eight-bar sentences, of which the third is a repetition of the second, and the fourth an ornamented version of the first. The bridge-passage begins in F sharp minor,

and modulates to the key of the dominant, ending, not (as usual,) with a half cadence, but with a full cadence in that key.

405. The second subject contains two sections; the first opening thus—

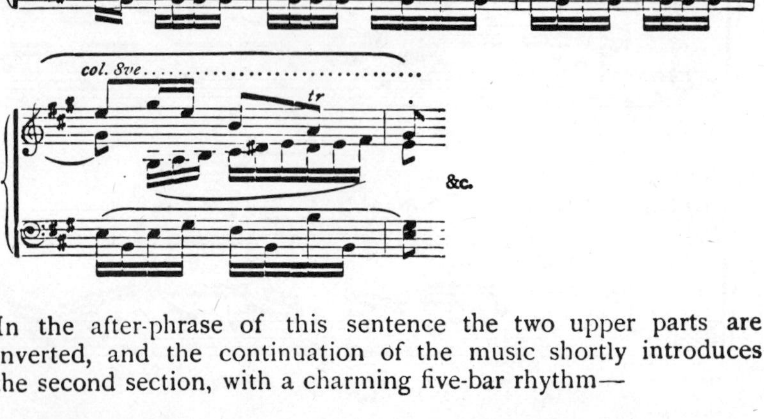

In the after-phrase of this sentence the two upper parts are inverted, and the continuation of the music shortly introduces the second section, with a charming five-bar rhythm—

(b)

A full cadence in the key of E is repeated and prolonged over a tonic pedal, after which the return to the first subject is made through the following graceful passage—

(c)

The first subject is then repeated in its entirety, and is followed by the episode, which begins in C major, with the following vigorous theme in the bass accompanied by arpeggio triplet semiquavers in the upper parts.

(d)

406. The episodical portion of this movement is comparatively short—37 bars,—and it is interesting as showing a combination of the two methods that we have noticed in previous examples. The first fourteen bars are constructed from new material; but from the fifteenth bar, the second section of the second subject (§ 405 (*b*),) is introduced with a new accompaniment of triplets, first in B flat, then, by a remarkable enharmonic change, in B major, next through D minor, and so back to C, and A minor, after which the recapitulation begins with the first subject in A major.

407. This recapitulation, which is quite regular, is followed by a long and very beautiful coda. At the end of the second subject, on a tonic pedal, as before, an interrupted cadence leads at once to F major, and the subject, § 405 (*b*) is heard in the tenor.

A modulation back through A minor introduces the passage of which we quoted the opening at § 405 (*c*), at the end of which the first subject appears for the last time, now in the tenor, and with a counterpoint in semiquavers above it.

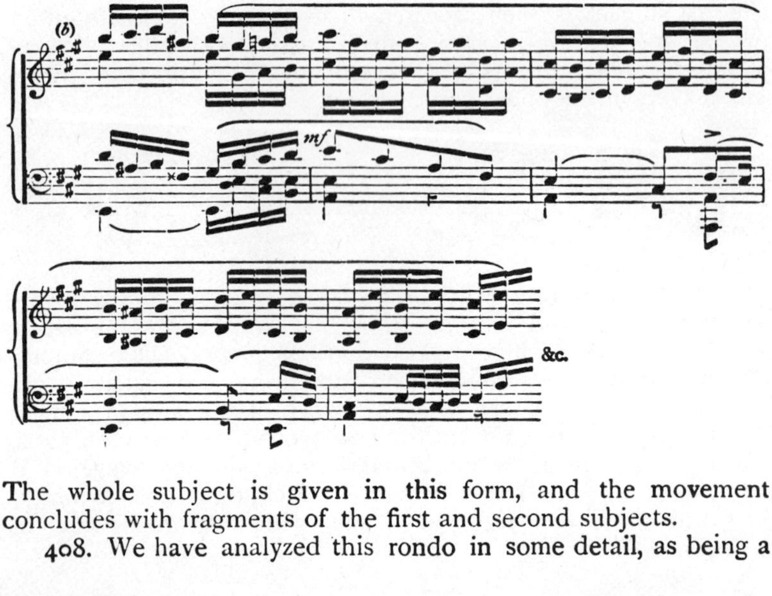

The whole subject is given in this form, and the movement concludes with fragments of the first and second subjects.

408. We have analyzed this rondo in some detail, as being a

particularly good example of the form we are now treating; and we advise the student to procure the piece for himself, and examine it thoroughly. It is one of the ripest and most characteristic of Schubert's works, and he will certainly not regret making its acquaintance.

409. It is very seldom that much irregularity is met with in this form, of which the variations are mostly much less important than those of the sonata form. Occasionally, however, we find a movement which it is impossible to consider other than a rondo, but which departs somewhat widely from the outline we have given. Such a case is seen in the Rondo of Beethoven's little sonata in G minor, Op. 49 No. 1, to which we referred in the foot-note of § 390. It begins with a first subject of two perfectly regular eight-bar sentences, both ending with a full cadence in G major, the tonic key. The music then modulates at once to G minor, and after four (unison) bars of "bridge," a new theme is introduced in the tonic minor. This cannot be considered a second subject, for it does not afterwards reappear in a different key: neither can it be regarded as episode, because we find it again in the same key at bar 68. It can only be called a prolongation of the bridge-passage. It is of irregular rhythmic construction, the fore-phrase containing three bars with a feminine ending, and the after-phrase five, which are extended to seven by the repetition of the cadence. The after-phrase modulates to B flat major, in which unusual key the second subject makes its appearance at bar 32. This second subject contains two sections, each of which is composed of two eight-bar sentences. At the end of the subject (bar 64) the unison passage (bars 16 to 20,) is repeated, and is followed by the prolongation of the bridge-passage. This has its after-phrase varied so as to end in G minor, and to lead back through the chord of the dominant seventh to the first subject, in G major as before. This is immediately succeeded by the second subject, now also in G major, after which a coda, developed from the first subject, concludes the movement.

410. It will be seen that the keys in which the second subject is introduced are those which would be usual if the key of the piece were G minor, instead of G major; but it is altogether exceptional to find a second subject of a major movement in the major key of the flat mediant (§ 247). The explanation is that the whole movement, as we have seen, is irregular in form; and it is for that reason that we have analyzed it.

411. It is worthy of notice that the rondo-sonata form is always met with either as an independent piece, as in Beethoven's Rondo in G, Op. 51 No. 2, or the Rondo by Schubert analyzed above, or as the finale of a cyclic form, such as a sonata or quartett. If a rondo is found, as is not uncommon, in a middle movement, or even a first movement of a large work, it is

always in the older rondo form described in Chapter VI. Though the examples analyzed in this chapter have all been taken from pianoforte music, the form is frequently used also for symphonies, quartetts, &c.; but in the majority of instances it will be found that in such cases, there is very little or no episode, but that the middle section of the movement mostly consists of thematic development, as in the sonatas referred to in § 403. Such a movement evidently differs from a sonata movement only in the additional entry of the first subject at the end of the exposition, the third appearance of this subject making the movement into a Rondo.

CHAPTER XI.

MIXED AND INDEFINITE FORMS.

412. IN the preceding chapters of this volume we have dealt, as fully as our space permitted, with the principal forms to be met with in the instrumental works of both older and more recent composers. Many pieces are, however, to be found which cannot be properly classified under any of the divisions of which we have treated, but which either partake of the characteristics of more than one, or are so vague in their form and outline as to refuse to be brought under any. It is of these we have now to say a few words; the former we call MIXED, and the latter INDEFINITE FORMS. We shall speak first of the mixed forms.

413. The available combinations of the different forms with which we are already acquainted are so numerous that it is quite impossible to treat them exhaustively. The plan we shall adopt will be to take various examples of mixed forms from the works of the great composers, and to show in what their peculiarities consist. When the student understands how they are constructed, he will probably find little difficulty in analyzing for himself such others as he may meet with.

414. Hardly less difficult than the exhaustive treatment of these mixed forms is their systematic classification. In many cases, indeed it is almost impossible to decide with certainty whether the amount of variation from a normal form is sufficient to entitle a movement to be classed among the mixed forms or not. Take, for instance, the finale of Weber's sonata in D minor. The composer himself calls it 'Rondo,' but an examination of the movement shows that it differs widely, both from the old Rondo form treated of in Chapter VI., and from the Rondo-sonata form examined in the last chapter. The first subject will be recognized—

This sentence is followed by a second, extended to twelve bars, and ending at bar 20 with a full close in the tonic key. The long passage that succeeds (bars 21 to 84,) is difficult to characterize. It cannot be called an episode, for it scarcely leaves the key of D, neither is it a bridge-passage, for it leads, not to an episode or a second subject, but to a return of the chief subject at bar 84. The first real episode begins in G major at bar 129.

(*b*)

This is extended at considerable length, and ends in bar 196. A long codetta, founded upon the first subject, leads back to a second return of that subject at bar 229. The close is now modified, so that the music modulates to B minor, and thence to A minor.

415. After a half close in A minor, a new episode commencing

is introduced in the key of A major. This, both in tonality and character, resembles a second subject, and, as will be seen directly, it appears again, later in the movement, in the tonic key. With all respect to Weber, it must be remarked that this rondo is very faulty in its form. The almost universal practice of the great composers is to make the first important modulation, for a piece in a major key, to the dominant side, so as to preserve the supremacy of the tonic key. It would have been unquestionably better had Weber introduced this subject in A before that in G. So far as we can see, nothing is gained by departing from the usual method. A long passage, mostly founded on the opening bars of our last quotation, leads back to the third appearance (bar 358,) of the first subject. This is followed at bar 392 by the repetition of the entire first episode—see § 414 (*b*)—now transposed into A major. The irregularity in the form of the movement is now strikingly apparent. We have called this theme in G major "episode," for want of another word; but the fact of its appearing a second time prevents its being really an episode (§ 391). If, on the other hand, we call it a second subject, it is most unadvisable that it should first appear in the subdominant key and subsequently in the dominant. It is immediately succeeded by the theme which was before heard in A, and which is now transposed into D (bar 459). The movement ends with a coda, in which the first subject is heard for the last time. The whole must be regarded as an irregular combination of the older and the modern rondo forms, and therefore a mixed form. From its peculiarities of construction, we do not recommend it for imitation.

416. The *Andante con moto* of the same sonata furnishes another example of a mixed form—here, however, much easier to account for and justify. It is a simple combination of the variation and older rondo forms. After an introduction four bars long, the theme is announced. It is in simple binary form, consisting of two sentences, each eight bars in length. It will suffice to quote the fore-phrase of the first sentence.

WEBER: Sonata in D minor, Op. 49.

This theme is twice varied, after which comes an episode, mostly in G minor, but with incidental modulations to other keys. Though its commencement is founded upon the theme,

its continuation is quite different. It is thirty-one bars long, and is followed by the third variation. To this succeeds a second episode in E flat,

only twelve bars long, after which a codetta of four bars, which is nothing but a repetition of the fore-phrase of the second sentence of the theme, leads to the final variation. A coda of eleven bars concludes the movement.

417. The finale of Mozart's piano sonata in D ($\frac{6}{8}$,) shows a not unusual compromise between sonata and rondo forms. The first subject begins

(a) *Allegretto.* **MOZART:** Sonata in D, No. 17.

The second subject contains three short themes of which we quote the commencements, that the student may be able to identify them.

The first, as is not uncommon with Haydn and Mozart, is developed from the first subject. At the end of the sentence the first two bars of which are seen at No. 3, the exposition is completed, and a codetta of six bars leads back to the return of the first subject.

418. Thus far the movement is in the regular Rondo-sonata form described in the last chapter; but from this point it more resembles a sonata movement. It contains nothing that can be called episode; all that follows, down to the recapitulation,

is thematic development. We know already (§ 403,) that cases of this kind are not uncommon in the modern rondo form; but the peculiarity here is, that the first subject does not appear at all at the beginning of the recapitulation—perhaps because it has been almost continuously present in the developments. The recapitulation commences with the *second* subject, and the first is not heard again till the coda. It would be possible to regard this as one of those cases in which the second subject precedes the first in the recapitulation (§ 329); but this assumption will not make the form a regular sonata form, as we still have the additional entry of the first subject at the end of the exposition. It is in fact a mixed form, partaking of the characteristics of both rondo and sonata forms, with more of the former than the latter.

419. The converse case will be seen in the finale of Beethoven's sonata in F minor, Op. 2 No. 1. This movement as a whole must be regarded as in sonata form; for the entire exposition is repeated, which is never the case in a rondo. But the middle section of the movement, instead of free fantasia, contains an episode of a character strongly contrasted with the principal subjects.

BEETHOVEN: Sonata, Op. 2, No. 1.

This feature of the movement prevents our considering it a regular sonata form; it is another mixed form—a sonata movement with a rondo-like episode in place of the usual free fantasia.

420. The adagio of the third sonata in Beethoven's Op. 2 shows yet another mixed form. This is a combination of ternary with irregular sonata form. The chief subject is in E major; at bar 11 the key changes to E minor, and the music modulates to G. In this key what may be described as a second subject appears at bar 19. Note that G would not be a suitable key were the movement in regular sonata form. It would be more appropriate as the key for an episode in either ternary or older rondo form; but this is not an episode, as it is introduced later (bar 59,) in the tonic key of E major. The movement therefore resembles a sonata form in the double appearance of the second

subject; while the key in which that subject first appears, and the absence of anything like development render it possible also to regard the movement as an irregular ternary, with an unusually long coda (beginning at bar 53,) in the course of which a great part of the episode, as well as the whole first subject, is repeated in the tonic key. The third repetition of the first subject (bar 67,) might induce us to consider this as a rondo were it not that there is no new episode, but only a modified repetition of the first one, after the second appearance of the first subject.

421. A somewhat, though not altogether, parallel case to that just noticed will be seen in the first movement of Beethoven's sonata in F, Op. 54. Here we have a combination of the simple ternary and older rondo forms. It commences with a subject, twenty-four bars long, but consisting of only one sentence extended by repetitions. We give the fore-phrase :—

In tempo d'un Menuetto. BEETHOVEN: Sonata, Op. 54.

The fore-phrase is repeated, and the after-phrase prolonged by a double repetition of its first section. Like the fore-phrase, the after-phrase is given twice. It is followed by a new idea, beginning in octaves with both hands.

Though episodical in character, this can hardly be called a regular episode, for it is still in the tonic key. It modulates to the key of the dominant, and is then repeated, with some modification, in the key of A flat. From this key modulations are made through F minor and D flat back to the dominant of F. The first subject is then repeated with some embellishments, after which a few bars only of the octave passage quoted at (*b*) above are heard, and the first subject is given for the third time, with a more florid variation than before. A coda, as usual, concludes the movement. It will be seen that we have here the three appearances of the chief subject characterizing the rondo form, but that, instead of a second episode, there is only a partial repetition of the first one. The movement is, as we said above, a combination of the ternary with the older rondo form.

422. Another example of a mixed form will be seen in the finale of Beethoven's sonata in F sharp, Op. 78. This is a movement which is very difficult to analyze with certainty, by reason of the indefiniteness of its form. The first subject, which is a large binary form, extends to bar 47, and ends in the tonic key, F sharp major. At bar 57 a new theme is presented, in D sharp major and minor. As this theme appears subsequently (bar 116,) in the tonic key, it must be considered a second subject, not an episode (§ 391). The movement can be therefore neither in ternary nor in older rondo form. But it is certainly not in rondo-sonata form; for in this the second subject would appear in the dominant key, and would be followed, as we saw in Chapter X., first by the return of the first subject in the tonic key, and then either by an episode or by developments. As a matter of fact it leads back at bar 89 to the first subject in the subdominant key. At bar 116 the second subject, as just now mentioned, appears in the tonic key, and at bar 150 the first subject is heard for the last time, with a new prolongation serving as coda. The whole movement is very irregular, and is a kind of cross-breed between sonata and rondo forms.

423. Schubert's well-known Impromptu in F minor, Op. 142 No. 1, shows a mixed form of another kind. It begins like a sonata movement, the first subject

ending in F minor at bar 13. A long and very interesting bridge-passage introduces at bar 45 the second subject in the normal key of the relative major.

To this subject is appended at bar 69 an entirely new theme, beginning in A flat minor and modulating freely.

It at last returns to A flat major (bar 111,) the passage last quoted being repeated in the major mode, and with a new continuation. At bar 130 a return is made to the first subject.

424. It might be imagined that we had here a modification of the regular sonata form by the substitution of an episode

for the free fantasia. But the subsequent repetition (beginning at bar 197,) in the keys of F minor and major of the whole of this portion of the movement negatives this hypothesis. After the first subject has been repeated, a modification of the bridge-passage leads to the resumption of the second subject, now in F major, followed, as we have just said, by the whole of what, for want of a better name, we may call the intermediate section of the piece. It would be, of course, *possible* to regard the whole of this section as a continuation of the second subject. In this case the movement would be in the abridged sonata form described in Chapter IX. ; but the whole passage beginning with our last quotation is so episodical in character that it is better to consider the movement as irregular.

425. Another irregular movement by Schubert must next be noticed. This is the finale of his piano quintett in A, Op. 114. The form is probably absolutely unique—at least in modern music. The movement contains 472 bars, and is divided into two exactly equal parts of 236 bars each. The first part is like the exposition of a sonata movement, but with the second subject, beginning at bar 84, in the key of D major—the subdominant. The whole first part is marked to be repeated. The curious point about the movement is, that the second part is, with the exception of a few slight changes in the distribution of the stringed instruments, an exact transposition of the first. All which in the exposition was in A is now in E, and all that was in D is now in A. There is not a single bar of coda. We have in this finale a fusion of the old sonata form, described in §§ 217–221, with the more modern form. From the older form is borrowed the parallelism of the two halves of the movement (compare the sonata by Scarlatti in § 217), while the preservation of the relation of the keys of the first and second subjects in both parts of the movement is a feature of the modern sonata form to be found when the first subject in the recapitulation is in the key of the subdominant (§ 328).

426. Another curious point about this movement is the presentation of the second subject, and the close of the exposition in the subdominant key. This is as unusual as it is mostly unadvisable (§ 241). In the present case, however, the bad effect is neutralized by the introduction of the first subject immediately afterwards in the *dominant* key—a key, be it noticed, exactly as far on the sharp side of the tonic as the subdominant is on the flat side; so that between the two the equilibrium is maintained. The student need hardly be reminded that the more usual course of modulation is the converse,—first to the dominant key, and later to the subdominant.

427. Space will not allow of our analyzing several other examples of mixed forms which we had noted; the varieties are so many that it would in any case have been impossible to

exhaust the subject. We now proceed to say a few words about the indefinite forms. There are some names which are so variously applied as to render accurate definition an impossibility; and it is of these that we have now to speak.

428. A few words may first be said as to the INTRODUCTION. This differs from all the other forms we are considering in the fact that it is never complete, but always leads into the following movement. It is invariably in slow time, and ends mostly with a half cadence on the dominant of the key of the following movement,* which will have the same tonic as the introduction itself, though the mode is sometimes changed from major to minor, and *vice versâ.* The material of the introduction is mostly quite different from that of the movement into which it leads, though sometimes, as in Beethoven's Sonata Pathétique, and in his Sonata Op. 81, the subject is reintroduced in the following allegro. It is mostly met with at the commencement of a work in cyclic form, such as a symphony, quartett, or sonata; but it is also sometimes to be found before other movements than the first. In Beethoven's Septett, Op. 20, the finale is preceded by a short introduction, as also is the fugue in his great sonata, Op. 106. In the 'Waldstein' sonata (Op. 53,) an introduction to the rondo takes the place of the slow movement.

429. The introduction is also not infrequent before variations and rondos, when these form independent pieces. Examples of the former will be seen in Beethoven's variations, Op. 35, and in Chopin's Variations on 'La ci darem,' Op. 2, and of the latter in Hummel's Rondo in A, Op. 56, and Schubert's Introduction and Rondo, Op. 145. The form and style of these and other Introductions differ so widely that no rules can be given to the student as to how they should be written. He will best learn how to set to work by examining for himself as many specimens as possible.

430. The TOCCATA derives its name from the Italian verb *toccare*, to touch—that is, to play a keyboard instrument. In the seventeenth century the word was used, according to Michael Praetorius (*Syntagma Musicum*,) to describe "a prelude which an organist improvises out of his own head, before a motett or fugue, with mere single chords and flourishes (*Colorature*)." Many of the Toccatas of Bach, both for clavier and organ, correspond to this description, though Bach frequently includes the fugues that follow such preludes under the same name, as in the Toccatas for clavier in C minor, F sharp minor, and D minor. At other times he restricts the name Toccata to the showy and florid prelude, as in the organ Toccatas in F major and D minor. Marx in his 'Composition' (Vol. III. p. 42,) speaks of the Toccata as a higher kind of Etude, devoted to something more than a merely technical end. All authorities are agreed that the

* In the introduction of Mendelssohn's Capriccio in A minor, Op. 33 No. 1, the close is made on the chord of the diminished seventh.

name is used so loosely that it is impossible to distinguish it from a prelude or a fantasia.

431. In some cases a Toccata is a free improvisation on one particular figure. For example, the second movement of Beethoven's sonata in F, Op. 54, which is founded almost entirely on the figure of the commencement

is best described as a Toccata, though the composer has not given it that name. Schumann's Toccata for the piano (Op. 7,) is in reality a study in double notes, written in regular sonata form. Beyond these generalizations it is not possible for us to go.

432. No less variable are the forms to be met with under the name of Capriccio, or Caprice. Like the Fantasia, to be spoken of later, the name of the piece implies that the composer is free to follow his own whims. It is found three times in the clavier works of Bach, and the pieces bearing it are absolutely different in form. The Capriccio in B flat ('On the departure of his beloved brother') is a descriptive fantasia in six movements; that in E major is a free fugue; while the Capriccio which forms the finale of the Partita in C minor is a contrapuntal movement in binary form. Of the two Capriccios in Handel's 'Suites de Pièces' that in G minor is a free two-part fugue, and that in F major is in the old ternary form, with a *Da Capo*.

433. In more recent compositions we find the name applied to works of very various forms. The Caprices of August Eberhard Müller are really elaborate Etudes written in sonata form. Weber's Capriccio in B flat ('Momento Capriccioso,' Op. 12,) belongs to the mixed forms, being a compound of the ternary and the older rondo form. Of the various examples to be seen in Mendelssohn's works, the Capriccio in B minor, Op. 22, for piano and orchestra, consists of an introduction and an allegro in sonata form; the three Capriccios, Op. 33, for piano solo are similarly constructed, excepting that the second has no introduction; while the Capriccio in F sharp minor, Op. 5, and the 'Scherzo a Capriccio' in the same key are in ternary form. Stephen Heller applies the name 'Caprice' to several of his transcriptions of songs by Schubert and others. These examples will sufficiently show the vagueness with which the term is used.

434. Another of these indefinite forms is the Intermezzo. The name signifies an intermediate movement of some large work, and it is frequently used in this sense. Schumann several times employs it instead of 'Trio'; *e.g.* in his sonata in F sharp minor,

Op. 11, the third movement of which he entitles 'Scherzo e Intermezzo,' and in his Romance in B major, Op. 28 No. 3, where the two trios (for such they undoubtedly are,) are called 'Intermezzo 1, 2.' In the well-known Novelletten, Op. 21, it is even more clearly seen that Schumann considered the two terms convertible; for in Nos. 2 and 3 the middle part of the movement is called 'Intermezzo,' while in No. 8 a similar part is called 'Trio.'

435. It is not only to a middle *section* of a movement that the name is applied; we often find it given to a middle movement of a cyclic work. The third movements of Mendelssohn's piano quartett in F minor, Op. 2, and string quartett in A minor, Op. 13, and the third movement of his quintett in A, Op. 18, are all called 'Intermezzo'; and so are the fourth movement of Schumann's 'Faschingsschwank,' Op. 26, and the second movement of his piano concerto. An examination of these works, in some of which the Intermezzo replaces the scherzo and in others the slow movement, will clearly show the student why we include this among the "indefinite" forms. Sometimes the name is given to quite independent pieces, as in Schumann's 'Six Intermezzi,' Op. 4, the fourth of which is a small binary, while the other five are all in ternary form.

436. The last form of which we have to speak is the **FANTASIA**—one of the most indefinite and varied of them all. The name originally meant an improvisation, in which the composer followed his own fantasy; and many, especially of the older fantasias have no distinct form which it is possible to describe. Bach mostly employs the word in the same sense as 'Prelude,' as, for example, in the Chromatic Fantasia and Fugue in D minor, or the Fantasia and Fugue in A minor; but he sometimes also treats the Fantasia as an independent form. Curiously enough, the only Fantasia by Handel, (which is to be found in the third set of his 'Suites de Pièces,') is a very regularly constructed movement in old sonata form. The fantasias of more recent composers generally consist of a series of movements following one another without a break, in various keys, not always even ending with the same tonic with which they begin. For example, Hummel's Fantasia in E flat, Op. 18, begins in that key, and ends in G minor, while Beethoven's Fantasia in G minor, Op. 77, has the last movement in B major. These, however, may be regarded as exceptional cases; in the majority we find the usual law of tonality, about which we shall have something to say in our next chapter, adhered to.

437. Occasionally a Fantasia is in one movement and one *tempo* throughout. This is the case in Mozart's Fantasia in C minor—not the one usually prefixed to the sonata in the same key, but a smaller work beginning

MOZART: Fantasia in C minor.

which is, moreover, far more regular in its form than the majority of such movements, being in fact a sonata movement with episodical matter in place of the free fantasia. The second and third of Mendelssohn's three Fantasias, Op. 16, are also single movements, the second being a very condensed and rather irregular sonata form, while the third is a simple binary. It is worth noticing, as illustrating the indefinite meaning attached to the names, that Mendelssohn has entitled these three pieces 'Fantasias or Caprices.'

438. Composers often endeavour to give a certain unity to the fantasia by reintroducing the first subject near the end of the piece. Mozart does this in his larger Fantasia in C minor, with which most readers will probably be acquainted, and in the fine Fantasia in F minor, written for a mechanical organ, but best known in its arrangement as a piano duet. This work is in three movements, each leading into the following. The first is an introduction and fugue in F minor; then comes an Andante in A flat major, and the final movement is a second fugue, on the same subject as the first, but with new countersubjects and more elaboration. Similar treatment will be found in Schubert's magnificent Fantasia in F minor, Op. 103, for piano duet, in which the first allegro is followed by a Largo, and this by a Scherzo and trio, both of these movements being in F sharp minor; after which we find a finale founded upon the subjects of the first movement.

439. Though the different movements of a Fantasia are, as was said above, often connected with one another, we sometimes meet with examples in which such a piece contains detached movements, like a sonata or a quartett. Such is the case in Schumann's great Fantasia in C, Op. 17. The first movement, in C major, is an irregularly constructed ternary form, the episode being in C minor; the second movement is a March in E flat

with a trio in A flat; and the finale is a slow movement of irregular form, in C major. Mendelssohn's Fantasia in F sharp minor, Op. 28, has also three detached movements, the third of which is in regular sonata form—a rare thing in a fantasia.

440. The work just spoken of shows the transition to the *Sonata quasi Fantasia* of which Beethoven gives us two examples in his Opus 27. Mendelssohn's Fantasia is, in fact, built on the same lines as Beethoven's Sonata quasi Fantasia in C sharp minor. Beethoven's applies the term to sonatas of irregular form, and one or two of his other sonatas (*e.g.* Op. 54 and Op. 109,) might also have been called 'quasi Fantasia' with hardly less appropriateness than those to which he has given the name. Joachim Raff has also written a 'Fantasia-Sonata' (in D minor, Op. 168), in which not only are the movements continuous, but the subjects of the first movements reappear in a metamorphosed shape in the finale. What we mean by this will be seen by an example. After some preludial matter, the first subject of the opening allegro begins thus—

Raff: Fantasie-Sonate, Op. 168.

In the finale the same theme is given in the following shape—

The second subject is also similarly transformed. This process commonly known as the "metamorphosis of themes" is largely employed by Liszt in his 'Symphonic Poems,' which are in reality Fantasias for orchestra.

441. There is another kind of Fantasia, quite different from those of which we have been speaking. In this variety, the chief themes are not original, but are taken from the works of other composers. Such Fantasias are mostly founded on operas, sometimes on songs, in which case they are frequently called 'transcriptions.' They have no definite form, but usually contain an introduction and one or more themes with variations, interspersed with episodical matter. They are mostly intended for showy concert pieces. Thalberg, Liszt, Heller, Raff, and others have left us good specimens of fantasias of this kind, of which the artistic value is for the most part comparatively small.

CHAPTER XII.

CYCLIC FORMS.

442. WE have now, as far as our space would allow, treated separately the various forms to be found in the instrumental works of the great composers, and we have seen that they were mostly extensions or variations of the two typical forms, the binary and the ternary, which were explained in Chapters IX. and X. of *Musical Form.* But some of these forms, and more especially the Sonata Form, are mostly found, not as independent pieces, but as parts of a larger work consisting of two, three, four, or even more movements. The term *Cyclic Form* is applied to works in which two or more movements are combined to form a homogeneous whole.

443. We have more than once had occasion in this and the preceding volume to point out the gradual evolution of the larger art-forms from the smaller; we have seen how the ternary form is developed from the binary, and how the sonata form, the various rondos, and the fugue are developed as extensions of the simple ternary. The same process of development, though differently applied, may be seen in the construction of the larger art-works with which we have to deal in this chapter.

444. To make this clear, let the student remember what is the essence, as distinguished from the mere accidents of ternary form. It is the element of *contrast* produced by the insertion of an episode in a different, though related, key to that of the principal theme, sometimes also (*Musical Form*, §§ 398, 399,) in a different *tempo*, after which the chief subject is repeated, generally with some modification. Now suppose that, instead of these three parts of one movement, we have three different movements, the second contrasted in key and *tempo* with the first and third, and that this latter, instead of being a more or less varied repetition of the themes of the first, is constructed of new material, having the same tonic, and a character which is in keeping with the first movement; we then have the three-movement form which we may regard as the *typical* Cyclic Form. Of this the two-movement form is a contraction by the omission of the middle movement, while pieces in four and five movements are extensions, by the insertion of more than one middle movement.

445. We have just spoken of the last movement of a cyclic work having a character which is in keeping with the first. This unity of character is extremely difficult to define in words; but the student will understand our meaning if he will take two pieces in the same key and by the same composer, and observe how inappropriate the last movement of the one would be as a finale for the other. Take, for instance, Beethoven's two sonatas in C minor, Op. 10 No. 1, and the 'Pathétique,' and exchange their last movements. We select these two works because they both belong to the same period of the composer's production. It is impossible not to feel that the unity of both works would be destroyed if the exchange we are suggesting be made. That this unity of which we are speaking was really considered by the composer, is proved by an interesting fact. We know from Ries that Beethoven originally wrote the finale of his 'Kreutzer' sonata for the sonata in A major, Op. 30 No. 1, but that he found, on reflection, that it was too brilliant to be in keeping with the rest of that work, and that he subsequently replaced it by the variations which are published as the final movement.

446. The oldest of the cyclic forms were the Suite and the Overture—the latter, of course, only when it contained more than one movement, as in many of Handel's overtures. The Suite has been described in Chapter III. (§§ 46–48), and the Overture in Chapter IX. (§ 361). From the suite was developed the most important of the modern cyclic forms, that used for the sonata, trio, quartett, and other chamber music, and in the orchestra for the symphony and the now nearly obsolete serenade. As the different kinds of works we have enumerated are all constructed on the same plan, there will be no occasion to treat them separately. The form taken as a whole is often conveniently, though loosely, spoken of as "classical form," from its general adoption by all the great masters of instrumental music from Haydn onwards.

447. We will first speak of such cyclic works as are in three movements—this being, as we have said, the typical form of which others are variations. With modern composers this form is almost entirely confined to chamber music written for two, or at most three instruments; in quartetts and symphonies the four-movement form is almost always employed, though symphonies in three movements are to be met with among the earlier works of Haydn. Mozart also shows considerable partiality for this form, no fewer than nineteen of his symphonies, among them some of his finest, containing only three movements. With piano sonatas down to the time of Beethoven the four-movement form was very rare. Haydn only uses it once in 34 sonatas, and Clementi only once in 64, while not one of

Mozart's pianoforte sonatas has more than three movements.* Even Beethoven, though many of his sonatas have four movements, has given us twelve with three, while of his piano and violin sonatas only three out of ten have a fourth movement.

448. For a cyclic work in three movements, by far the most frequent order is, that the first movement shall be an allegro in sonata form, with or without an introduction; the second will be a slow movement of some kind (Andante, Larghetto, Largo, or Adagio), while the third and final movement will again be a quick movement, in the same key (or, at all events, with the same tonic,) as the first. There is in general far more variety in the form selected for the third than for the first movement. It may be in complete sonata form, in any of various rondo forms, in variation form, or even in ternary form. Which the composer may select will depend largely upon the character and form of the two preceding movements. To this general scheme numerous exceptions are to be found; of these we shall speak presently. We shall first notice the form most frequently to be met with.

449. We have spoken above of this three-movement form as a development of the principles on which the ternary form is constructed (§ 444). We know that the episode which constitutes the second part of a ternary form is always in a different key from the first part. Similarly, the second movement of a cyclic form is in the overwhelming majority of works in a different key from the first. The exceptions are so rare that even a musician so well read as A. B. Marx says in his 'Composition' (iii. 222,) that he does not know a single case. They are, nevertheless, to be found. In three of Clementi's sonatas, those in D, Op. 39 No. 3, in B minor, Op. 40 No. 2, and the 'Didone abbandonata' in G minor, Op. 50 No. 3, all the three movements are in the same key. Other examples are seen in Mozart's beautiful Concertante Quartett in E flat, for four wind instruments with orchestra, in his Serenades in D for strings and kettle-drums, and in E flat for wind instruments, and in his Notturno in D for four orchestras, all of which works are in three movements, each in the tonic key. In Schubert's string quartett in E flat, Op. 125 No. 1, all four movements are in the same key. These examples simply prove that the rule is not without exception.

450. The choice of key for the second movement of a cyclic

* The sonata in B flat in four movements contained in most editions of Mozart's sonatas, beginning

is not an original work, but an arrangement by some unknown editor of movements from other compositions.

form is guided by the same considerations which influence us in the selection of a key for the episode in a simple ternary form. In an enormous majority of cases this second movement will be in a related key to that of the first, and a nearly related key is more often met with than one in the second degree of relationship. If the work be in a major key, the subdominant is most frequently chosen for the middle movement, as in Beethoven's sonata in G, Op. 31, No. 1 (Adagio in C major), and Mozart's three sonatas in B flat, all of which have slow movements in E flat. The subdominant appears to be a preferable key, for the middle movement, to the dominant, because, if the work is regular in form, and the first movement has been in sonata form, the dominant will most likely have been chosen for the second subject of that movement, and will thus have had considerable prominence in the exposition. Nevertheless, many examples are to be found of a middle movement in the dominant key (Haydn, Sonata in E flat, No. 3, Beethoven, Sonata in D, Op. 12 No. 1, Piano Quintett in E flat, Op. 16, &c.).

451. Of the nearly related minor keys, the one most usually chosen for the second movement of a work in a major key is the relative minor, and this is much less common with later than with earlier composers. It is frequently to be found in the works of Haydn and Mozart, but less often in those of Beethoven, *e.g.* in the slow movements of the Eroica symphony, the pianoforte concerto in G, Op. 58, and of the quartetts in F, Op. 18 No. 1, and C, Op. 59 No. 3.* We meet with two instances in the works of Schubert (the trio in E flat, Op. 100, and the great symphony in C), one in Mendelssohn (quartett in D, Op. 44 No. 1), and two in Schumann (the quintett, Op. 44, and the Concertstück for four horns, Op. 86).

452. Much rarer is the employment of the mediant minor (the relative minor of the dominant). It is never once found in Beethoven, and only twice each in Mozart (fifth string quartett, and sonata in E flat for piano and violin), Schubert (sonata for four hands in B flat, and solo sonata in E flat, Op. 122), and Mendelssohn (quartett in E flat, Op. 12, and quintett in B flat, Op. 87). It is also once employed by Weber—for the slow movement of his sonata in A flat. Of the employment of the supertonic minor for a second movement we have found no instances, probably because its tonic would be dissonant to the tonic of the first movement.

453. It is by no means unusual to find the slow movement in a key which is in the second degree of relationship. Of

* These quartetts, like several other of the instances to be quoted directly, have four movements; but it will be seen later in this chapter that the principles guiding the selection of key for the slow movement are the same for works with four movements as for those with three.

these the tonic minor, as in Beethoven's sonata in A, Op. 12 No. 2, and his trio in D, Op. 70, No. 1, is probably the most common; for the tonic minor is the nearest to the tonic major of all the keys in the second degree of relationship (*Musical Form*, § 87). The minor subdominant is less frequent; an instance of its employment will be seen in the second movement of Mendelssohn's Italian symphony. The major keys of the major and minor mediant and submediant were all used by Haydn in his quartetts and symphonies, and many examples are to be seen in the works of Beethoven (*e.g.* in the piano sonatas Op. 2 No. 3, Op. 7, and the concertos in C major and E flat). With Mozart the employment of these keys was less frequent.

454. It is possible, though rarely advisable, to introduce the second movement in an unrelated key to the first. Probably the earliest instance of this is to be found in a sonata by C. P. E. Bach. The key is G, and the slow movement is in F sharp minor. Haydn's sonata in E flat (No. 1) has the second movement in E major, and the same relationship will be seen in Brahms's sonata in F, Op. 99, for piano and violoncello, in which the slow movement is in F sharp major. Among other examples may be named the adagio in F sharp minor of Beethoven's sonata in B flat, Op. 106, and the andante of Schubert's sonata in B flat, which is in C sharp minor.

455. If a cyclic work be in a minor key, the second movement will, with extremely rare exceptions be in a major. In many cases the relative major is the key selected, as in Mozart's piano quartett in G minor, Beethoven's piano trio in C minor, Mendelssohn's trio in the same key, and Schubert's sonata in A minor, Op. 42. The submediant major, the next most nearly related key (*Musical Form*, § 82), is also frequently to be met with, as in Mozart's sonata in A minor, and Beethoven's sonatas in C minor, Op. 10 No. 1, and F minor, Op. 57. The tonic major, though seldom if ever employed by Mozart, is found as the key of the slow movements in three of Haydn's quartetts—those in F minor, Op. 20 No. 5, B minor, Op. 64 No. 2, and D minor, Op. 76 No. 2. It is also frequently used by Beethoven (sonata in A minor, Op. 23, quartett in E minor, Op. 59, No. 2, &c.). Of the choice of the dominant major for the slow movement of a work in a minor key we can only recall one instance—Schubert's sonata in A minor, Op. 164, which has the second movement in E major.

456. As with works in major keys, so in those with minor, we occasionally find the second movement in an unrelated key. One of Emanuel Bach's sonatas in B minor has the slow movement in G minor. Haydn's quartett in G minor, Op. 74 No. 3, has the adagio in E major. The same relation of keys is noticeable in Mendelssohn's piano concerto in G minor, and in

Beethoven's quartett in F minor, Op. 95, the second movement of which is in D major. Another example from Beethoven is seen in his concerto in C minor, of which the slow movement is in E major. As with works in a major key, the cases we have just quoted must be regarded as exceptional.

457. In the choice of the form for the second movement considerable variety is offered to the composer. Sometimes a slow movement is in full sonata form, as in Beethoven's symphonies in D and B flat, and in the sonata, Op. 106. This form, however, is seldom used except for works laid out on a large scale, and in four movements, though an example of its employment in a work in three movements may be seen in Mozart's so-called 'Strinasacchi sonata' for piano and violin in B flat. More frequently however, the abridged sonata form is to be met with. This form was described in our ninth chapter, and we refer our readers to the analyses of slow movements which were there given (§§ 348–356). At other times the simple ternary form will be selected. Examples of such slow movements are given in Chapter X. of *Musical Form*. The variation form is also not infrequent for the middle movement (Mozart, Sonata in F for piano and violin, Beethoven, sonatas, Op. 14 No. 2, and Op. 57). Occasionally the older rondo form (Chapter VI.,) is met with, as in the slow movement of Dussek's very fine sonata in E flat, Op. 75, and in Mozart's sonata in the same key (No. 41) for piano and violin. Sometimes the middle movement consists merely of an introduction leading into the finale, as in Haydn's sonata in D, No. 7, and Beethoven's sonata, Op. 53.

458. We sometimes find the middle movement of a cyclic work in three movements in quick *tempo*, instead of slow. In Haydn's sonata in C sharp minor, No. 6, the second movement is an *allegro con brio* in A, and in six of his sonatas (Nos. 22, 23, 24, 28, 33, 34,) the place of the slow movement is taken by a minuet and trio. Similar examples will be seen in Beethoven's sonatas Op. 10 No. 2, and Op. 14 No. 1. It will mostly be found in such cases that the preceding movement is of a somewhat quiet character; but the composer must be guided by his feeling in the form that he may choose. This is a matter on which no definite rules are possible.

459. In the form of the finale of a work in three movements there is quite as much variety as in the middle movements. Perhaps on the whole either the older rondo or the rondo-sonata form is the most common, but the sonata form is often employed, as also is the variation form—*e.g.* in Mozart's sonata in D, No. 6, and Beethoven's sonata in A, Op. 30 No. 1. Haydn was very partial to the ternary form in his smaller works; it is to be found in several of his sonatas and trios.

460. Before proceeding to speak of cyclic forms in two and four movements, a few words should be said as to the irregularities

often to be met with in the arrangement of the movements. In the normal form the first movement will always be in regular sonata form, the second a slow movement of some kind, (or occasionally a minuet,) and the finale will be in one of the forms mentioned in the last paragraph. But to this regular plan many exceptions are to be found. Mozart's piano sonata in A major has the first movement in variation form, the second is a minuet and trio, and the finale is in ternary form (§ 212). The same composer's sonata in G for piano and violin (No. 35,) begins with a long introductory adagio, the first part of which has the form of an exposition of a sonata movement, while the second part is incomplete, and leads into an *allegro* in G minor in full sonata form; the finale is an air with variations in G major. Again, Mozart's trio in E flat for piano, clarinet, and viola, has for its first movement an *andante* in sonata form, but without repeat of the exposition. This is followed by a minuet and trio in B flat, and the work concludes with the rondo which we analyzed in Chapter VI., §§ 208, 209.

461. It would be impossible to speak of half the varieties to be met with in these irregular cyclic forms; we will conclude this part of our subject by referring to two well-known examples by Beethoven. The sonata in C sharp minor, Op. 27 No. 1 contains an *adagio*, an *allegretto* in the form of a minuet and trio, and a *presto* in complete sonata form. It thus resembles, as we shall see presently, a regular four-movement sonata, *with the first movement omitted.* Had it been preceded by a first movement, the adagio would have been in some other key than C sharp minor. The other example is the sonata in E major, Op. 109. The first movement is a mixed form, combined from ternary and older rondo; the second movement (*prestissimo,*) is an irregular sonata form, and the finale is in variation form.

462. The two-movement form, as was said above (§ 444) is a contraction of the typical form by the omission of the middle movement. This form was a favourite with the older piano composers,—Haydn, Clementi, and Dussek; curiously enough, Mozart never employed it for his sonatas for piano solo, though we find more than a dozen of his sonatas for piano and violin in only two movements. Beethoven also adopted it several times in his sonatas, some of his finest (*e.g.* Op. 90, in E minor, and Op. 111, in C minor,) being in this form. We have met with no example of a later date than Beethoven, unless we reckon as coming under this category Mendelssohn's 'Serenade and Allegro giojoso' Op. 43—in any case an exceedingly irregular piece, as the first movement is in B minor and the second in D major.

463. If a work be in two movements, it is mostly desirable that these should be contrasted in form. True, we sometimes find sonatas in which both movements are in regular sonata form,

as in two very fine examples by Dussek—the sonatas in D, Op. 9 No. 3, and E, Op. 10 No. 3; but far more frequently the forms are different. Thus, in Haydn's beautiful sonata in C, No. 16, the first movement is in double-variation form (§ 169), and the second is a rondo. In Dussek's sonata in G minor, Op. 10 No. 2, the first movement (*Grave*) is a large binary form of irregular construction, and the following *allegro* is in regular sonata form. In Clementi's sonata in E flat, Op. 35 No. 2, the first movement is in very condensed (not *abridged*) sonata form (*Lento*), without repeat of the exposition, and the second movement (*presto*) is a regular sonata movement. In Mozart's sonata in E minor, for piano and violin, the first movement is in sonata form, and the second is a minuet and trio. In Haydn's sonata in G, No. 13, the first movement is in double-variation, and the second in simple ternary form. In Dussek's sonatas in G, Op. 35 No. 2, B flat, Op. 39 No. 3, and A major, Op. 43, and in Beethoven's sonata in E minor, the first movement is in sonata form, and the second is a rondo. In Mozart's sonata in A (No. 29,) for piano and violin, and in Beethoven's sonata in C minor, Op. 111, the first movement is in sonata, and the second in variation form; while in Beethoven's sonata in F, Op. 54, the first movement is a mixed and the second an indefinite form, as we saw in the last chapter. These examples (and many more might be given,) will sufficiently show the student what variety is possible in the two-movement form, which, it should be added, is seldom, if ever, found, except in sonatas.

464. The four-movement form, the most important of all, is an extension of the typical three-movement form by the addition of a second middle movement. The older composers, Haydn, Mozart, and their contemporaries, restricted the use of this form almost entirely to orchestral music, or to chamber music for several instruments (quartetts, &c.). Beethoven was the first who frequently used it for solo sonatas, which, since his time, are quite as often written with four movements as with three.

465. In cyclic works (whether sonatas, trios, quartetts, or symphonies,) in four movements, if the form be regular, the two middle movements will almost invariably be a slow movement, and a minuet and trio, or scherzo. With extremely rare exceptions, the slow movement will be in a different key from the first allegro, while in the large majority of cases the minuet or scherzo will have the same tonic as the first and last movements. The first movement will be in sonata form, and the finale either in the same form (as in Beethoven's symphony in C minor), or, more commonly, in one of the rondo forms, the rondo-sonata form being more frequently adopted by modern composers. If the variation form has not been already employed for the slow movement, it is sometimes used for the finale, as in Beethoven's quartett in E flat, Op. 74. Beethoven sometimes writes a fugue

as the final movement of a cyclic work, as in his quartett in C, Op. 59 No. 3, his sonata for piano and violoncello in D, Op. 102 No. 2, and his solo sonatas, Ops. 106 and 110. Some of Haydn's quartetts, and Mozart's quartetts in F major (No. 8) and D minor (No. 13,) also conclude with a fugue. The last movement may also be in one of the mixed forms. An example of this will be found in the finale of the 'Eroica' symphony, which is a combination of the variation and the free fugue form.

466. It is entirely at the option of the composer whether the slow movement or the scherzo (or minuet) shall follow the first allegro. In most cases the slow movement precedes the scherzo, but we find several works in which this order is reversed. As examples may be mentioned Beethoven's quartett in F, Op. 59 No. 1, his trio in B flat, Op. 97, his sonatas Ops. 106 and 110, and the choral symphony, in all of which the scherzo is the second movement. An examination of these, and other similar cases, would seem to show that the scherzo is introduced immediately after the allegro when the latter is serious in style, as in all the examples we have referred to. Beethoven appears to have felt that in such cases a slow movement would not offer sufficient contrast to what had preceded.

467. In a few cases, which are mostly to be met with in Beethoven's works, neither of the middle movements is a *slow* movement, in the ordinary acceptation of that term. In the eighth symphony, in F, Op. 93, the second movement is the popular *allegretto scherzando*, in abridged sonata form (§ 346), and the third is a minuet (not *scherzo*,) and trio. In his pianoforte sonata in E flat, Op. 31 No. 3, the two middle movements are a scherzo and a minuet. The former is in duple time, and in regular sonata form, and the slow minuet that follows takes the place of the more usual andante or adagio. In the trio in E flat, Op. 70 No. 2, both the middle movements are marked *allegretto*. The former, which serves as slow movement, is, as we have already said (§ 170), the only example in Beethoven's works of the double variation form; the latter is a minuet and trio, with the repetitions described in § 76 as sometimes to be met with in movements of this form.

468. As with works in three movements, so with those in four, we often meet with instances in which the normal form is widely departed from. To mention first two familiar examples by Beethoven,—the sonata in A flat, Op. 26, has no movement in sonata form; the first is an air with variations, the second a scherzo, the third (the famous 'Funeral March') is in simple ternary, and the finale in modern rondo form. The Sonata quasi Fantasia in E flat, Op. 27 No. 1, has the first movement in ternary form, the second is a scherzo, the Adagio introducing the finale is in simple binary form, while the finale is in modern rondo form. In Haydn's quartett in F minor, Op. 55 No. 2, the slow

movement, which is in double-variation form, and of considerable dimensions (*Andante più tosto Allegretto*, $\frac{2}{4}$, 202 bars—not counting the repeats,) precedes the allegro in sonata form. In this work all four movements have the same tonic, the order being, Variations (F minor and major), Allegro, in sonata form (F minor), minuet (F major,) with trio (F minor), finale, again in sonata form (F major). Haydn frequently in his sonatas, trios, and quartetts, employs the variation form for the first movement, and a solitary instance of the same by Mozart may be seen in his quartett in C, No. 10.

469. Exceptionally, when the first allegro is preceded by a slow introduction, the allegro itself will not be in the same key as the introduction. An instance of this will be seen in Beethoven's sonata, Op. 102 No. 1, for piano and violoncello. The key of the work, as is proved both by its commencement and close, is C major; but after an introductory andante of 27 bars, the succeeding allegro is in A minor. Schumann's first string quartett (in A minor, Op. 41 No. 1,) has an introduction (*Andante espressivo*,) of 33 bars leading to an allegro in F major. A somewhat similar case is seen in Mendelssohn's quartett in E flat, Op. 12, but with this difference, that it is here the finale, instead of the first movement, which is not in the key of the tonic. The finale here is in C minor, but it is followed by a long coda in E flat, founded upon the first subject of the first allegro. In this way Mendelssohn gives unity to the work as a whole.

470. This unity of a cyclic work, to which we incidentally referred earlier in this chapter (§ 445), is a consideration which should never be left out of mind. Composers have sometimes sought to attain it by making each movement lead into the following without a break, as in C. P. E. Bach's symphonies, and some of his sonatas, in Haydn's sonata in A, No. 26, and in Mozart's symphony in D, No. 23. At other times express directions are given, if a movement has ended, as usual, with a full cadence, that there is to be no pause. Mendelssohn has done this in his symphony in A minor, as also has Schumann in his symphony in D minor, originally entitled 'Introduction, Allegro, Romanze, Scherzo, and Finale, *in one movement*.' But he has done more than this. The theme of the introduction appears again in the Romanze, and the first subject of the finale is identical with one of the most important episodes in the first allegro. In his symphony in C major, Schumann uses what we may term the "motto" of his introduction

at the end of the first allegro, of the scherzo, and of the finale, and further develops the second subject of his finale from the opening bars of his adagio.

471. In speaking just now (§ 469,) of Mendelssohn's quartett in E flat we referred to the reintroduction of the theme of the first allegro towards the end of the work. Other instances of the same manner of giving unity to the composition as a whole are to be seen in Beethoven's sonata in A, Op. 101, and in his sonata for piano and violoncello, in C, Op. 102 No. 1. In both these pieces the opening bars of the work recur just before the last allegro. In Mendelssohn's solo sonata for piano, in E, Op. 6, the theme of the first movement is heard, as in the quartett above spoken of, at the end, and not at the beginning, of the finale.

472. Another method of obtaining unity of style is, to write more than one movement on what is virtually the same subject, but in a modified form. Of this we saw an example in the last chapter in the Fantasie-Sonate of Raff (§ 440). One of the most interesting instances of this method is seen in Schubert's string quartett in E flat, Op. 125 No. 1. In this work, not only are all the four movements in the same key (§ 449), but all are made from the same material,—the ascending scale of E flat. This will be clearly seen from the first bars of each movement

(*a*) *Allegro moderato.* SCHUBERT: Quartett in E flat, Op. 125, No. 1.

(*b*) *Scherzo. Prestissimo.*

(*c*) *Adagio.*

(*d*) *Allegro.*

473. Sometimes, though comparatively seldom, a cyclic work will contain more than four movements. In Raff's first symphony, entitled, 'An das Vaterland,' there are five movements—an *allegro* in D major, a *scherzo* in D minor, a *larghetto* in B flat, an *allegro dramatico* in G minor, and a finale consisting of a *larghetto sostenuto* in D minor leading into an *allegro deciso trionfante* in D major. We find examples in Schumann's works of pieces in more than four movements. His third symphony (in E flat), has a second slow movement preceding the finale. His 'Faschingsschwank aus Wien,' Op. 26, consists of an Allegro, a Romanze,

Scherzino, Intermezzo, and Finale. The allegro offers a rare instance of the employment of the old rondo form for a first movement; the finale is in sonata form, and the three intermediate movements are in simple binary and ternary forms. A more recent example of a symphony in five movements is seen in Goldmark's 'Ländliche Hochzeit' ('Rustic Wedding'). The work, though entitled a symphony, has little in common with the regular symphonic form, the five movements of which it consists being the following: 1. Wedding March: Variations; 2. Bridal Song: Intermezzo; 3. Serenade: Scherzo; 4. 'In the Garden:' Andante; 5. Dance: Finale.

474. Another cyclic form in which more than four movements are sometimes met with is the *Modern Suite*. This differs widely from the older Suite treated of in Chapter III., inasmuch as it is not necessary that all the movements should be in the same key, nor that they should all be dance forms, though such forms are frequently to be met with in them. The word 'Suite' is, in fact, used very loosely by modern composers, and might be applied to almost any cyclic work other than a symphony or sonata. To show how different may be the component parts of two works both bearing the same name, we will give the list of movements in two examples. Bizet's 'Petite Suite d'Orchestre' ('Jeux d'Enfants,') contains a March, a Berceuse, an Impromptu, a Duo, and a Galop, all of which are written in binary form. On the other hand, the 'Nordische Suite' by the Danish composer Asger Hamerik, which has also five movements, consists of an Introduction and Scherzo, entitled 'Im Walde' (In the Forest), a Volkslied, a Springtanz, a Minuet, and a Bridal March. In its modern acceptation, the word 'Suite' is as indefinite as 'Capriccio.'

475. The string quartett may be said to have been invented by Haydn, and the four-movement form which he adopted has been the model for all composers who have succeeded him. But it is an interesting fact that of his first twelve quartetts, Ops. 1 and 2, no fewer than eleven have five movements, while the twelfth (Op. 1 No. 5,) has only three. The additional movement in every case is a second minuet, the two minuets being always the second and fourth of the five movements. This renders highly probable the inference that the quartett form was developed from that of the *Serenade*, about which it will now be needful to say a few words.

476. The SERENADE (*Ital.* = 'Serenata') was a somewhat indefinite cyclic form, which is described in detail in Jahn's 'Mozart' (Vol. I., pp. 306, sqq.). According to Jahn, it frequently commenced, and sometimes ended with a March; a well-known example of this will be found in Beethoven's Serenade-Trio for strings, Op. 8. But a more distinctive feature was, that in the majority of cases, a minuet was introduced between every

Andante and Allegro. Here will be seen the resemblance to the early quartetts of Haydn spoken of in the last paragraph. In general the first movement (with or without an introductory March,) was in sonata form; the last movement was an Allegro, or Presto; and frequently two slow movements of different character were introduced, separated from one another and from the Allegro by Minuets. The result is that we sometimes find a serenade containing as many as eight movements. For instance Mozart's large Serenade in D, known as the 'Haffner Serenade,' begins with an introductory *allegro maestoso*, leading into an *allegro molto*, in regular sonata form; to this succeeds an *andante* in G, with violin obligato; the third movement is a minuet in G minor, with a trio in G major. Next comes a long Rondo in G, of 453 bars. This, being a middle movement, is in the *older* rondo form; the rondo-sonata form is seldom if ever found except as a final movement. The fifth movement is another minuet and trio in D, major and minor, and the sixth an *andante* in A major. A third minuet, with two trios follows, and the finale consists of an introductory *adagio*, and an *allegro assai*, again in sonata form, and of large development, the movement containing 474 bars. Other similar examples might be given; but this one will suffice as an illustration.

477. The Cassation and Divertimento were similar in form to the Serenade, but differed from it in the fact that they were written for solo instruments, each string part being only played by one instrument, while the Serenade was for full orchestra. Beethoven's Trio in E flat, Op. 3, for violin, viola, and violoncello, with its two slow movements and two minuets, is in its form a Divertimento, as also are his Septett, Op. 20, and Schubert's Octett. The choice and order of movements, both in the Serenade and the Divertimento, is left largely to the discretion of the composer.

478. Another important cyclic form is that of the Concerto. We spoke in § 370 of the old meaning of the word; we are now using it in its modern sense, as a work written for one (occasionally more than one) solo instrument with accompaniments for the orchestra. From the time of Bach down to a comparatively recent date, the concerto was always written in the three-movement form which we have spoken of (§ 444,) as the typical cyclic form. All the concertos of Bach, Mozart, Beethoven, Mendelssohn and Schumann contain an allegro, a slow movement and a finale, which is mostly in rondo form. Of the double exposition of the first movement, as found in the works of Beethoven and Mozart, we spoke in detail in Chapter IX. (§§ 371–379). We have now to deal with the principal modifications of the concerto form introduced by modern composers.

479. It is rare to find a concerto with more than three movements. Perhaps the best known instance is Brahms's second

concerto for the piano, (in B flat, Op. 83,) which has been not inaptly described by an annotator as "a symphony with pianoforte *obbligato*," and which is quite symphonic in its form. Another example, though not quite parallel, will be seen in Scharwenka's concerto in B flat minor, Op. 32. The first *allegro* of this work has a regular exposition in sonata form, but an *adagio*, 71 bars in length, takes the place of the free fantasia, and is followed by the recapitulation of the *allegro*. The second movement is a scherzo, and the finale is in a somewhat free sonata form. Tschaikowsky's concerto in B flat minor, Op. 23, has also four movements, the first allegro being preceded by an introductory andante, 106 bars long, in large binary form, and in the key of D flat major, though the tonality of B flat minor is suggested by the first two bars. The three movements that follow are in the usual form, though rather free in treatment.

480. Much more frequent than the introduction of a fourth movement in a concerto, is the departure from the normal form described in § 478. Two of Max Bruch's violin concertos illustrate this. In his first (Op. 26 in G minor,) the first movement is simply a prelude (*Allegro moderato*,) resembling an incomplete sonata form, and leading into an extended and very beautiful adagio. The finale is in sonata form. The same composer's second violin concerto (in D minor, Op. 44,) begins with an *adagio ma non troppo*, in sonata form; but the second movement, entitled 'Recitative,' has no distinct form at all, and resembles a fantasia. The third movement begins in B flat, and ends in D major—a seeming irregularity, which, however, is justified on examination, as the first part of the movement, though in the same *tempo* as that which follows, is really only of the nature of an introduction, and connects the finale with the second movement, which ends with a half cadence in B flat. The proper first subject of this finale does not appear till the signature is changed to D major.

481. Even greater irregularities are to be met with in the piano concertos of Camille Saint-Saëns. The first (in D major,) is tolerably regular, though the preceding of the first allegro by an introduction is unusual; but the second, and best known of the four—that in G minor, Op. 22—is very free in construction. The first movement is an *andante sostenuto*, in large binary form; the second (*allegro scherzando*,) has the form of a sonata movement, and the character of a scherzo; while the final *presto* is in free sonata form with the rhythmic figures of a Tarantella.

482. Saint-Saëns' third Concerto (in E flat, Op. 29,) departs still more widely from the usual model in its first movement, which is a kind of free rhapsody on the opening subject—

a theme strongly suggestive of the commencement of Schubert's great symphony in C. The whole movement is most irregular in form, the *tempo* being changed at least six times. In his fourth Concerto (in C minor) further irregularities are to be seen. The first movement begins with a theme followed by two variations, and continues with an andante in A flat, in which key it ends. The concerto contains only two movements; but the second includes an *allegro vivace*, an *andante*, and another *allegro*. The whole form is most irregular, and the material of this movement is mostly made from transformations, or 'metamorphoses' of themes already heard in the preceding.

483. The concerto just spoken of appears to be modelled on those of Liszt, about which a few words must here be said. It is impossible to regard Liszt's works bearing that name as concertos in the ordinary acceptation of the term; they are rather brilliant rhapsodies for piano and orchestra in which one or two chief themes are ingeniously metamorphosed, and interspersed with episodical matter of more or less importance.

484. A few words may be said in concluding this chapter on a form of which Liszt has left us several examples—the *SYMPHONIC POEM*. These are a series of orchestral pieces written to illustrate a more or less definite programme. The order of their movements, &c., therefore depends upon the subject selected for illustration; and hardly two are identical in this respect. But Liszt has endeavoured to secure artistic unity by presenting his principal subjects under different aspects,—in fact by the "metamorphosis of themes" of which we have more than once spoken. As an illustration of his method, we quote the leading theme of the third Symphonic Poem, 'Les Préludes.' It first appears in the following simple form, in unison.

LISZT: 'Les Préludes.

(*a*) *Andante.*

Shortly after, the tempo is changed, and the theme is heard in the bass with arpeggios above it.

(*b*) *Andante maestoso.*

The two forms of the theme which we next find are somewhat more modified:

(*c*) *L'istesso tempo.*

(*d*) *L'istesso tempo.*

The programme of the work is given in an extract from Lamartine's 'Meditations Poétiques'; and the passages last quoted are evidently designed to illustrate the words "Love forms the enchanted aurora of all existence."

485. The "storm which interrupts the first pleasures of happiness" is depicted in the two metamorphoses of the theme which next succeed—

(*a*) *Allegro, ma non troppo.*

(*b*) *Allegro tempestuoso.*

The author next speaks of the calm of a life in the country, as a rest for the soul tossed by tempests. Liszt illustrates this by a new change in the form of the theme.

(*c*) *Un poco più moderato.*

The call of duty to the field of battle gives one more transformation of the subject.

(*d*) *Allegro marziale animato.*

These illustrations will sufficiently explain the composer's method, which may be best described as a free application and modification of the variation form treated of in Chapter V. of this volume.

CHAPTER XIII.

ORGAN MUSIC.

486. THOUGH no absolutely new forms are to be met with in organ music, it is of great importance that any one who attempts to write for the instrument should have some knowledge of its special peculiarities. It need hardly be added that for this purpose it is highly desirable that a composer thould have at least some practical acquaintance with the instrument; without this it is almost impossible that he should write in the most effective manner. But inasmuch as even organists themselves appear sometimes when writing to overlook points of importance in the treatment of the instrument, it will be advisable to say something on this matter before proceeding to speak of the forms of organ composition.

487. It would be beyond our scope, even had we the needful space, to enter into any detailed description of the mechanism of the organ. For such we must refer our readers to the standard works on the subject, *e.g.* the excellent volume by Hopkins and Rimbault. It will suffice to say here that the organ is an instrument with from one to four (or occasionally even five) keyboards, each of which, except as regards its compass, exactly resembles the keyboard of the piano. In modern organs the compass of each "manual" (as it is termed, because the keys are played by the hands), is from 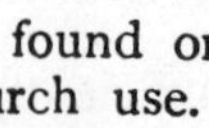 to 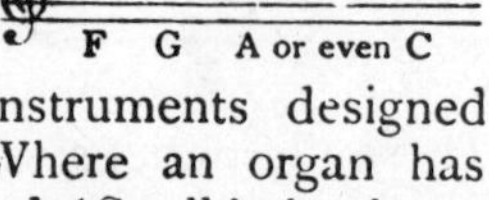

the last being rare, and mostly found on instruments designed for concert rather than for church use. Where an organ has two manuals, these will be the 'Great' and 'Swell,' the latter being so called because the pipes are enclosed in a box furnished with shutters which can be opened by a pedal moved by the foot of the player. If there are three manuals, the third is the 'Choir,'* while a fourth will be the 'Solo Organ'; this last is

* The word "third" here does not refer to the position of the manuals, of which the choir is the lowest, the great next, the swell the third, and the solo, when there is one, the fourth.

only met with on very large instruments. The most powerful 'stops' (§ 488,) are placed upon the great organ, though the solo organ, when present usually contains some powerful reeds. In the extremely rare cases in which there is a fifth manual, this will be the 'Echo Organ.'

488. While, however, the compass of the manuals is only from four-and-a-half to (at the utmost) five octaves, this by no means represents the actual compass of the organ itself. Whereas on the pianoforte each key when pressed down gives only one sound, a large number of sounds, differing both in quality and in pitch, may be produced by the pressing of a single key on the organ. Each row of keys is furnished with "registers" (in England more commonly called "stops"), each of which has one pipe* in connection with each key. Each stop therefore gives a complete chromatic scale, of approximately the same quality of tone, for every note on the manual.

489. It was said just now that the various stops differ in pitch. In some of these, and the most important, the sound produced corresponds to the notation. Thus, when the lowest key is pressed down, the note heard is , exactly as it would be on the piano. As an open pipe producing this sound is eight feet in length, any stop in which the notes produced are in unison with the notation is called an "eight-feet stop." If the pipes, instead of being open, are closed at the top, the effect of which is to lower their pitch by an octave, the C we have just given will be produced by a pipe only four feet in length; but as the pitch is the same as with an open pipe of eight feet, such a stop is said to be "of eight-feet tone." In other words, the term "eight-feet" is applied to all stops, whether the pipes be open or closed, which give sounds in unison with the notation.

490. The pitch of an organ pipe depends upon the length of the vibrating column of air within it. Every student of acoustics knows that if a string or air-column produce a certain sound, the half of that string or column will give a note an octave higher, the fourth two octaves higher, and so on. As the tone of the organ would be exceedingly dull were only unison stops employed, we always find, even in small instruments, stops of a higher pitch. An octave stop, that is, one in which every note sounds an octave higher than its notation, will evidently have its lowest pipe four feet long; it is therefore called a "four-feet stop"; while one that when the lowest key is pressed down gives the note  will, for a similar reason, be called a

* In the "mixture" stops to be presently described, there are often as many as four or five pipes to each key.

"two-feet stop." It should be said here that, except occasionally for special solo effects, such stops are never used without the unison stops; they are simply employed to give more brightness to the unison tone by the reinforcement of the upper-partials. The unison tone should always predominate.

491. On all large modern organs will also be found stops sounding an octave lower than the notation. This is the converse case to that just noted. If the lowest pipe of a unison stop is eight feet long, it is evident that a pipe an octave lower in pitch must be sixteen feet long. A stop of this kind, generally called in England a "double" stop, is described as a "16-feet stop," if the pipes be open, and as "of 16-feet tone" if they be stopped. All the stops hitherto described, giving the unison, or the octaves, higher or lower, of the key pressed down, are called "foundation" stops.

492. In addition to the class of stops we have described, there are two others to be mentioned—those known as "mutation" and "compound" stops. By "mutation" stops are meant those which give *some different note* from that shown by the key pressed down. If, for instance, such a stop is drawn, and when the lowest key is put down we hear the sound , which is a twelfth above the note sounded by the same key on the eight-feet stop, which is always taken as the standard from which others are reckoned, the stop is called the 'Twelfth,' and is a "mutation" stop. Such stops always give one of the upper partial tones of the unison (8-feet) stops,—generally the twelfth (the third note of the harmonic series), occasionally the major third (fifth note of the series). In large organs, when there is a 16-feet stop on the manual we sometimes find a Quint, or double-twelfth, giving the third upper partial of the 16-feet tone.

493. If two or more of these upper partial tones of the unison stops are acted upon by the same draw-stop, so that one cannot be sounded without the others, such a stop is called a "compound" stop. Unlike the mutation stops, the names of which generally indicate their pitch, the compound stops are mostly called by such indefinite names as Sesquialtera, Cornet, Mixture, Furniture, &c. It is extremely rare to find any but the *consonant* upper partials of the 8-feet tone (the major thirds, fifths, and octaves,) introduced in either mutation or compound stops. The object of both kinds of stops is to give additional brilliancy to the organ tone by the reinforcement of the various upper partials of the 16- and 8-feet tone; and it is the business of the organ-builder to voice these stops in such a manner as not to render these over-tones too prominent, otherwise the organ becomes what is known as 'screamy.'

494. There is another classification of organ stops, according to the manner in which their tone is produced. If the air in the pipe is set in vibration by blowing against a sharp edge, called the lip, the stop is said to be a "flue-stop"; if the sound is produced by blowing against an elastic tongue called a 'reed,' the stop is a "reed-stop."* The large majority of stops in all organs are flue-stops; but reeds are also to be found in all except very small instruments.

495. It was said in § 488 that the stops of an organ differed not only in pitch but in quality. The pitch of a note depends upon the length of the pipe, the quality upon its form. There is hardly any limit to the varieties of tone to be found in a very large organ; but this is a matter into which it is impossible to enter here. The student, if he has not a practical knowledge of the instrument, must consult some good book on the subject, such as Hopkins and Rimbault's work, above referred to.

496. A very important feature of the organ, not yet mentioned, is the *Pedal Organ*. The Pedals (as their name implies,) are keys to be played with the feet. They are arranged in the same way as the manual keys, but are much larger and broader, and, to avoid the risk of pressing two together by the foot, are separated from one another. On modern organs they have usually a compass of two octaves and a fourth, from  to ; but on many old organs, and on some modern continental ones, the upward limit of the pedal board is E, D, or even occasionally C. It must here be pointed out that the true pitch of the pedal organ is an octave lower than that noted, being really from  to . On the manuals, as has been already said, the 8-feet stops are the unison stops; on the pedals, on the other hand, 16-feet stops are the unison stops, and the 8-feet stops, where they are found, are reckoned as octave stops. A "double" stop on the pedal organ will be a 32-feet stop; this is only to be met with on the very largest instruments. It is very important that the composer should bear this difference of pitch between manuals and pedals in mind, when writing for the organ, and if he wishes the pedal part to be played on 8-feet stops alone, he must expressly indicate this, as Mendelssohn has done in the first variation of his sixth organ sonata.

497. Though the keys of the pedal board are arranged in the same way as those of the manuals, it will be evident that many rapid passages that would be perfectly easy for the hands would

* For an explanation of the production of the tone in flue-stops and reed-stops, *see* Sedley Taylor's "Sound and Music" (Macmillan & Co.).

be quite impossible for the feet. But, as two notes lying near one another can always be played with the same foot—one with the heel, and the other with the toe—more execution is possible, even on the pedals, than those unacquainted with the organ might imagine. The two following passages from Bach's organ works will show what is practicable.

(*a*) BACH : Organ Fugue in D major.

(*b*) BACH : Toccata in E.

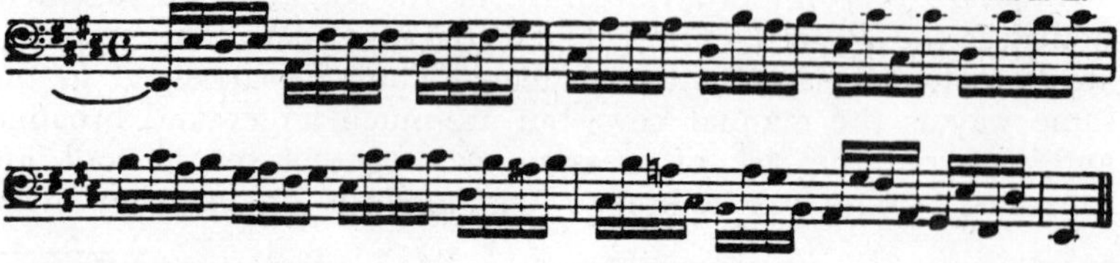

These passages illustrate both the alternate use of the two feet and the employment of the heel and toe of the same foot.

498. Music for the organ is generally written on three staves —one for each hand, as for the piano, and a third for the pedals. In old English organ music, where the part for the pedals was unimportant, mostly consisting of a few long holding notes, this part was often written on the left-hand staff, but in modern music a separate line is always given to it. Sometimes, for the sake of clearness, it is expedient to use more than three staves. The following passage from Mendelssohn's organ sonata in F minor will illustrate this point.

MENDELSSOHN : 1st Organ Sonata.

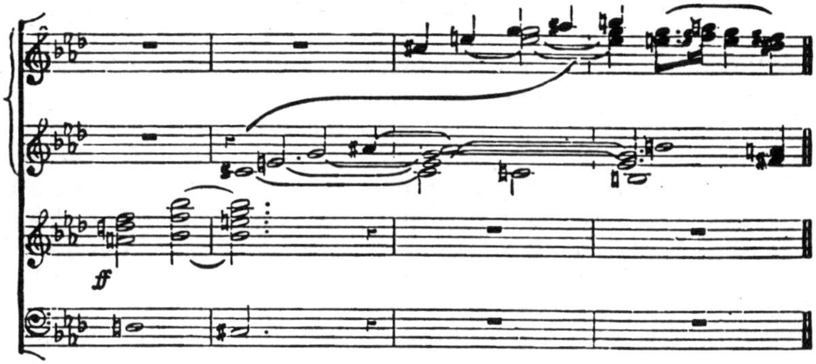

The 'Clav. I.,' 'Clav. II.' is the abbreviation for 'Clavier I., II.' the German equivalent of our word 'Manual.' The composer's intention is here plainer than it would have been had he compressed the manual parts on two staves.

499. The passage just given illustrates also another matter—the combination of the different manuals in organ music. In the above extract they are used alternately; but they are quite as frequently employed together, one hand playing on each, as in the following quotation from the adagio of the same sonata.

MENDELSSOHN: 1st Organ Sonata.

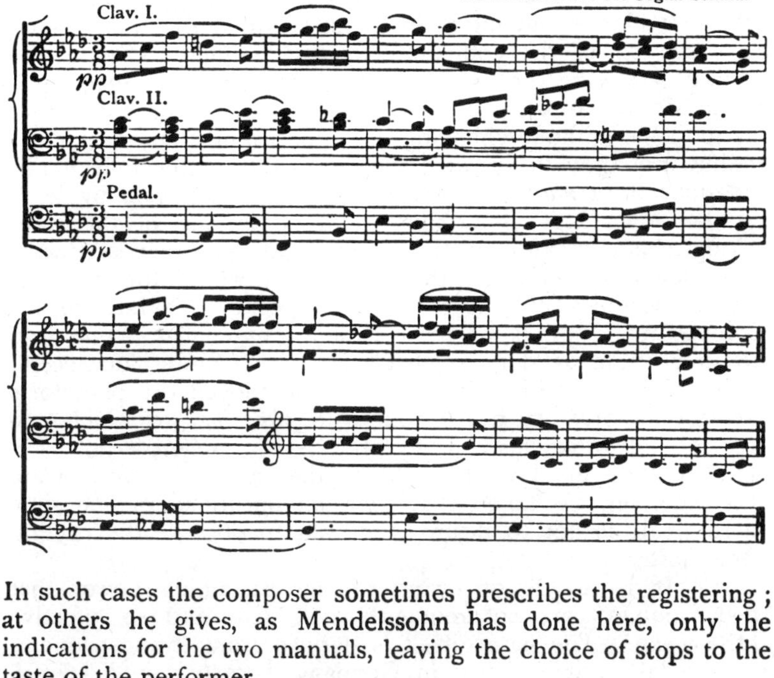

In such cases the composer sometimes prescribes the registering; at others he gives, as Mendelssohn has done here, only the indications for the two manuals, leaving the choice of stops to the taste of the performer.

500. In one important respect, which must always be borne in mind by the composer, the organ differs from all other instruments, excepting those which we may describe as its distant relatives, the Harmonium and American Organ. Owing to its construction, it is capable of sustaining the same sound, unchanged in quality and power, for any length of time that may be desired. In the piano the tone begins to diminish in intensity as soon as the note has been struck; while on both stringed and wind instruments there are limits to the duration of the sound, depending in the former case on the length of the bow, and in the latter on the capacity of the player's lungs. But on the organ there is no such restriction. A key pressed down either by finger or foot, admits the air to the pipe until that key is released, when the sound ceases instantaneously. Hence the necessity for the most perfect *legato* in organ playing. It is not intended to imply that the *staccato* is never admissible on the organ. It is sometimes employed, especially by modern writers; but its use is exceptional, and the *legato* style is certainly that which best befits the nature of the instrument.

501. Owing to the unvarying strength of every sustained tone, the organ must be regarded as, in a certain sense, the most expressionless of all instruments. Accentuation, in the sense in which that word may be applied to the piano or violin, does not exist upon the organ. No difference in the player's touch makes the slightest alteration in the strength of the tone. With the exception of the comparatively slight difference made by opening or closing the swell-box in which the pipes acted upon by one of the manuals are enclosed, any *crescendo* or *diminuendo* is impossible without changing the stops, which in most cases modifies not only the power, but the quality of the tone. The gradations from *piano* to *forte* are made, so to speak, by leaps and bounds. This immobility of tone is one of the most striking characteristics of the organ, and one that especially fits it for the service of the church, in which the personal element occupies only a subordinate position. Marx in his 'Composition' speaks of it as "the *dogmatic* instrument, firm and immovable as dogma itself." As a substitute for accent, in the sense in which that word is employed in pianoforte playing, the organist has recourse to *phrasing*, to which can often be advantageously added the *tempo rubato*,—that is a slight dwelling upon what would be the accented notes. Care must, however, be taken that such modifications of the time are so small as not to destroy, or even to obscure the rhythm of the music.

502. It is no doubt owing to this sustaining power that "pedal points" are so frequently met with and so effective on the organ. The name itself is derived from the instrument, and a pedal point is called in Germany "organ point" (*Orgel-*

punkt). Perhaps the most striking example of its employment is to be seen in Bach's great Toccata in F, which commences with a tonic pedal 54 bars long, followed shortly afterwards by a dominant pedal of the same length. Other fine specimens of pedal points, though less extended than those just referred to, will be found in Bach's Pastorale in F, of which nearly the whole first movement is constructed on pedals, and in several of Mendelssohn's organ sonatas.

503. Into the question of the varieties of organ tone we have not space to enter here. For the composer who practically understands the instrument, the information would be superfluous, and one who does not himself play the organ will do well to leave the registering to the performer, and merely to indicate generally the kind of effect that he desires. One or two general hints may nevertheless be given.

504. In addition to such general indications as *p*, *mf*, *f*, &c., it is sometimes desirable that the composer for the organ should prescribe more definitely the kind of tone that he wishes. For example, a *piano* passage might be marked 'Great, 8 feet,' 'Choir, 8 feet' (or '8 and 4 feet') 'Swell, with reeds, 8 ft.,' or in various other ways. Such a course is especially advisable when two manuals are being played simultaneously, as in our example to § 499. It is true that Mendelssohn has not here prescribed any special stops; but in a note at the beginning of the sonata he explains that this is because stops bearing the same name differ much in different instruments, and adds that the quality of tone of two manuals used together must always be contrasted. It may be well to add to what has just been said that if it is desired to thicken the tone by the 'doubles' (16-feet stops,) this had better be expressly marked, thus, '16 and 8 feet,' '16, 8, and 4 feet,' &c.

505. The changing of the quality of tone on any manual can be effected to a limited extent, that is, as regards a few of the most frequently used combinations, by means of what are called 'composition pedals.' These are mechanical contrivances acted upon by the player's foot, which throw in or out certain of the draw-stops. Sometimes 'composition-knobs' placed immediately under the key-boards, and pressed by the player's thumbs, answer the same purpose. Many French organs, and some English, have instead of these a system of 'ventils,' or valves, which cut off the wind from the pipes without acting upon the draw-stops. But, inasmuch as only a few combinations are possible by these means, and as the arrangement of the composition pedals differs very much in various instruments, it is well, if much changing of the stops be desired, to leave one hand at liberty for a moment, if possible, from time to time, to allow the player to make the desired alterations.

506. Though in general the bass of the harmony is given

to the pedals, it is not advisable that they should be used continuously. A very agreeable contrast is often obtainable by giving the bass to the manual, with 8-feet tone only. Mendelssohn has done this in the Adagio of his sonata in F minor quoted above. For the first forty bars the bass is played on the manuals alone, and the pedals enter for the first time, with the 16- and 8-feet tone, at the 41st bar—the beginning of our extract in § 499.

507. Bach, in a few of his arrangements of Chorals for the organ, has employed the pedals not for the bass of the harmony, but for giving out the melody of the choral. He has done this when the real bass was so florid that it would have been difficult to play with the feet. An interesting example of this method is seen in the choral 'Wo soll ich fliehen hin,' of which we quote a short extract, beginning at the sixth bar—

This is a trio for two manuals and pedal. The first manual (right hand,) gives the sounds as they appear in the notation.

The second manual (16 feet,) sounds an octave lower than written, while the pedal (4 ft.) instead of sounding, as usual, an octave lower than its notation, sounds an octave *higher*, the result being that in the third and fifth bars of this quotation, the melody in the pedal really lies above the right hand part of the manual, and is at the top of the harmony.* This passage also illustrates the possibility of obtaining three different qualities of tone on the organ simultaneously.

508. Owing to the necessity for a perfect *legato* in organ playing (§ 501), it is advisable in polyphonic writing, especially in fugues with florid subjects, not to write for too many independent parts; for this would render a clear performance very difficult, or even impossible. If we examine the organ fugues of Bach, which are the most perfect models of this style, we shall find that, though they are mostly for four parts, it is only in a comparatively small portion of the fugue that all are heard together. For example, the favourite fugue in G minor,

contains 115 bars; from these we exclude the first seventeen, which contain the exposition, as not bearing upon the point in question. Of the remaining 98 bars only 30 are in four parts, while 46 are in three, and the rest in only two-part harmony. Where the subject is less florid, and the motion less animated, a larger proportion of four-part harmony may be used; but even in such cases it will be well to have frequent rests in one or other of the parts. For an instance we refer to Bach's 'Dorian' fugue in D minor (see *Fugal Analysis*, Fugue No. 6). Here the subject is slow and stately, and no note shorter than a quaver is to be found throughout the whole piece. Nevertheless, about 75 bars, or more than one-third of the whole fugue, is in three-part harmony.

509. The forms of organ music are very varied, but, as they mostly belong to one or another of those with which the student is already acquainted, few of them will need detailed description. Take, as an illustration, one of the commonest of the organ forms —the Prelude and Fugue. The difference between the organ fugues of Bach and his numerous fugues for the harpsichord, such as the 'Forty-Eight' is not a difference in the form, but in the medium of its presentation. Granted that many of the

* It is extremely rare in England, though somewhat more common in Germany, to find a 4-feet stop on the pedal organ. To realize Bach's effect when that stop is wanting, three manuals would be required; and the pedals (with *no* stops of the pedal organ drawn) would have to be coupled to a 4-feet stop on that manual which was not being played on by either hand.

organ works are laid out on a larger scale than the majority of the clavier fugues, though this is not always the case, we still find, when we come to analyze them, that the framework is the same. We have already spoken of the form both of the Prelude and of the Fugue in Chapter IV. of this volume. The Fantasia, Toccata, Variation, Chaconne and Passacaglia are all forms with which the reader will be familiar from the earlier part of this book. But it will be well to say something of the *Organ Sonata*, as its form often differs considerably from the sonata form which we studied in Chapters VII., VIII. and XII.

510. Bach's six sonatas for the organ are in reality trios for two manuals and pedal, written strictly in three-part harmony throughout,* and in the imitative contrapuntal style. Each sonata contains three movements, all of which are either in simple binary or ternary form. The first and last movements are always in quick tempo (*allegro*, or *vivace*,) except in the third sonata, which has an *andante* for its first movement; while the middle movement, as usual in sonatas, is in every case slow (*adagio*, *largo*, &c.). The fourth sonata has an introductory *adagio* of four bars. The style of the music will appear from the following examples, which are the opening bars of the first and second movements of the second sonata.

(*a*) *Vivace.* BACH: Organ Sonata, No. 2, in C minor.

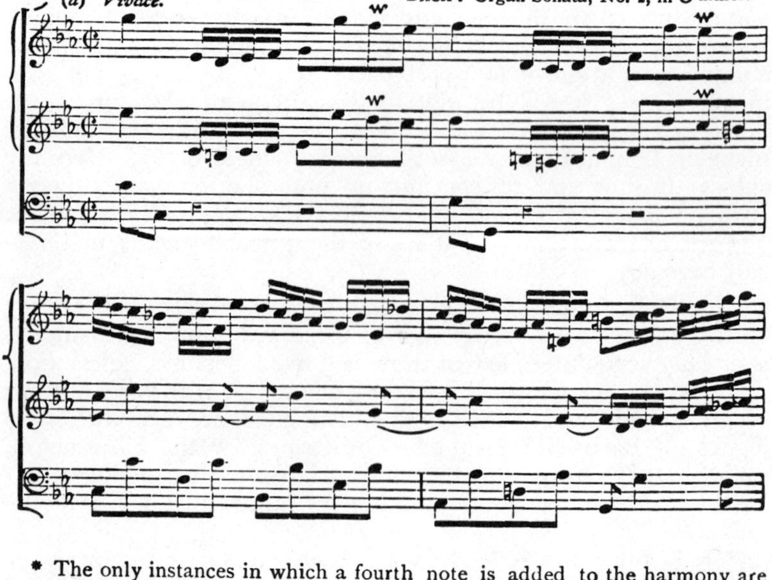

* The only instances in which a fourth note is added to the harmony are in the first movement of the second sonata—one of the passages being seen in the sixth bar of our extract (*a*) below—and at the end of the first movement of the sixth sonata. In all these cases an additional note is necessary as the resolution of a dissonance in the preceding chord.

&c.

(b) Largo.
&c.

511. The sonata form has been largely employed by modern writers for the organ since the example was set by Mendelssohn. It is a curious thing that in his six Organ Sonatas, Op. 65, there is only one movement (the first movement of the first sonata in F minor,) which is in what we know as the modern sonata form; and even here we find considerable freedom. The second movement of this sonata, from which we quoted in § 499, is in simple binary form; the third movement (*Andante, Recit.*) is simply an introduction to the finale, which is a mixed form, more resembling a toccata than anything else. A somewhat similar form is employed for the finale to the fifth sonata. The first movement of the fourth sonata (in B flat,) is a large ternary form; while the sixth sonata begins with a set of variations on the choral 'Vater unser in Himmelreich.' Nearly all the other movements in the sonatas are either simple binary forms or fugues, with or without introductions.

512. It is not easy to see why Mendelssohn should have (as it would appear,) so studiously avoided the sonata form in these works; for more modern writers have shown that it is by no means unsuited for the instrument. We find several movements written in this form in the organ sonatas of Merkel, Rheinberger, and others; but it is worth mentioning that we have met with no instances in these of the repetition of the exposition, so commonly found in sonatas for the piano.

513. There is in general much more variety to be found in the character and order of the different movements of an organ sonata than in those of a piano sonata. For example, no two of Mendelssohn's sonatas have the same arrangement of the movements. Nos. 3 and 6 end with a quiet *andante;* in the second and fourth, the finale is a fugue; while in the first and fifth the form of the last movement, as we said just now, is free, resembling the indefinite form of the toccata (§ 430). No less diversity is to be found in more modern sonatas. To give but two instances from the sixteen organ sonatas of Rheinberger,—his Pastoral Sonata in G, Op. 88, contains a Pastorale in binary form, an Intermezzo (*andante con moto,*) which is only an introduction leading into the third movement, and a Fugue. His tenth sonata (Op. 146, in B minor,) consists of a Prelude and Fugue, an Air with Variations, and a Fantasia (*adagio,*) leading into a finale in sonata form. The fugue, being particularly suitable to the character of the instrument, forms one of the movements of most organ sonatas; we find it in four out of Mendelssohn's six sonatas, and in nearly all of Rheinberger's. On the other hand, the scherzo is very seldom to be found, probably because of its being too light in character; the only example we have met with is in Rheinberger's eighth sonata. The only definite rule to be given to the composer as to his movements

is, that the first and last should, as in other cyclic works, have the same tonic.

514. Somewhat akin to the organ sonatas are the works which C. M. Widor (organist of the Church of St. Sulpice, Paris,) has published under the name of 'Symphonies for the Organ.' Each of these is a collection of pieces, sometimes as many as six in number, very various in form, in which the organ is treated in orchestral style. They are sometimes very free, not to say vague, in construction, but are full of inventive power, and admirably adapted to show off the resources of a large instrument; but it may be doubted whether such movements as the Scherzo in No. 2, or the Intermezzo in No. 6, however effective in its way, would not, by reason of their light staccato style, be far more effective on the orchestra than on the organ.

515. In addition to the more important forms of which we have spoken, smaller movements are often written for the organ, such as Andantes, Marches, 'Meditations,' &c. The form of such pieces will be mostly either the simple binary or the simple ternary. The 'Offertoire,' so often met with as the title of an organ piece, is a very vague and indefinite name. It means a piece written for performance during the offertory at Divine service; and the form may be whatever the composer may choose to select.

516. Occasionally organ music, like that for the piano, is written for two performers. In such a case, the music will be on six staves—three for each player, and there will be a double pedal part, the 'Secondo' player taking only the lower half of the pedal board and the 'Primo' the upper half, for obvious reasons.* A fine example of such a duet will be seen in Merkel's organ sonata for two players, Op. 30, in D minor.

517. There is a tendency among a certain school of organ writers to adopt what may be best described as a 'tawdry' style of composition, with clap-trap effects for *vox humana*, tremulant, &c. Against such a style an emphatic protest should be made. From its very nature the organ is the most dignified of all instruments, and it is as unbecoming to degrade it to cheap and showy display as it would be to compel an archbishop to dance a *pas seul*, or to sing a music-hall song. Let the student take for his model Bach (though he can never hope to equal him,) and Mendelssohn, rather than Batiste *et hoc genus omne.*

* Bach in his Choral Preludes occasionally writes a double pedal part (one for each foot,) for a single player, as in his preludes on "Aus tiefer Noth" and "An Wasserflüssen Babylon."

CHAPTER XIV.

VOCAL MUSIC.

518. HITHERTO we have treated only of the various forms of instrumental music; we have now to complete our subject by saying something about such music as is written for voices, either with or without instrumental accompaniment. Though there will be found to be little that is new in the *forms* of vocal music, these being for the most part nearly or quite identical with the instrumental forms with which the student may now be assumed to be familiar, there are several important considerations to be borne in mind in writing for voices, quite irrespective of the form of the music; and it will be well, before proceeding to speak of vocal forms, to give a few hints for the guidance of young composers on certain points which are too frequently overlooked or disregarded.

519. The human voice is the most perfect, and, when properly trained, and directed by artistic feeling on the part of the possessor, one of the most delightful of all musical instruments. It must, of course, be understood that we are using the word "instrument" here in its widest sense as equivalent to "tone producer." It is not only capable of the minutest shades of intonation, but is unsurpassed in its capabilities of expression. But this expressive power is closely connected with the fact that, with rare exceptions, to be presently noticed, all vocal music is associated with words. Instrumental music, not being so associated, is often spoken of as "absolute" music, and deals with ideas of a nature which is seldom capable of being translated into any words. It has been said that "where speech ends music (that is, *absolute* music) begins"; and from this point of view instrumental music would rank higher than vocal. On the other hand it cannot be denied that in countless instances the combination of music with words heightens the effect of both. As a familiar example may be named the air "He was despised" in the 'Messiah.' Beautiful as the music is in itself, it would lose a great part of its emotional power, were it not inseparably associated with the text which it so admirably illustrates.

520. One of the most important points to be considered in vocal composition is *the adaptation of the music to the words.* By this we do not mean merely that the music should illustrate the sense of the words, *e.g.* that grave and serious words should not

be set to lively music, and *vice versâ;* for this is a matter that will be self-evident to every thoughtful composer. Even in this matter, however, the great masters themselves are not always beyond reproach. Mendelssohn, in one of his charming letters, speaks of a mass of Haydn's which he had heard as being "scandalously merry"; and it must be admitted that much of the church music of the last century, and even of this, leaves much to desire on the score of appropriateness of sentiment. This, however, is not the point to which we are now referring. We are speaking now of the absolute necessity of making the accents of the music correspond with the accented syllables of the text. All teachers of composition know how common it is for pupils, when beginning to write songs, to put such unimportant words as articles or prepositions on the accented beats of the music. As an example of the kind of mistake to which we are referring, we give a passage from an old song called 'The Pilot' written by John Davy, an English composer of the early part of the present century.*

(*a*)

In the first bar of this extract, the word "of" is placed upon the second accent, and in the third bar "to" is on the strongest accent of the bar. Let anybody read the lines, emphasizing the words thus—

"The signals *of* distress he hears,
And *to* the found'ring vessel steers,"

and the absurdity becomes manifest at once. It would have been far more correct to have altered the music slightly, and written

(*b*)

521. Here it will be well to digress for a moment, to impress upon the student the importance of care in the selection of words for setting. Especially is this necessary in the case of songs which, like that from which we have just quoted, contain several stanzas, all set to the same music. A much greater freedom in the position of the accents is allowable in poetry than in music; and when (as in the above lines,) the accents of the words are at

* JOHN DAVY, (born 1765, died 1824,) was a composer of songs and incidental music to plays, much of which in its time enjoyed considerable popularity. He is now only remembered by one song, "The Bay of Biscay," which is still sometimes heard in our concert-rooms.

irregular intervals, it is advisable to modify the melody accordingly; this, indeed, is the practice of the great composers.

522. Another point, somewhat akin to that just noticed, is, that the cadences in the music must correspond in their position with the breaks in the sense of the words. Nothing produces a more absurd effect than the introduction of a cadence of any kind between words which should be closely connected. Davy's song, above referred to, gives a ludicrous example of this mistake also. In the third verse are found these lines—

"His steady orders all obey,
And now the vessel on her way
Pursues, the Pilot bent to save," &c.

Davy has set the second and third lines thus—

The second bar, it will be seen, introduces a full cadence in C major, and the next phrase begins on the last note of the bar. It is absurd enough to make a full close at "on her way," but the effect of the following line is still more ridiculous; for the quaver rest after "pursues" does not detach that word from what follows. The third and fourth bars form one phrase; and the words, *as here set*, if they have any meaning at all, mean that the vessel is pursuing the Pilot! Scarcely less comical is a well-known passage in Balfe's once very popular song, "Come into the garden, Maud," where Tennyson's

"Queen rose of the rosebud garden of girls"

is distorted into

"Queen of the rosebud,—garden of girls."

523. Even the great masters have not always been free from the fault of insufficient attention to the accentuation of the words. One example from the works of Handel will be sufficient to show this. In the song "Praise ye the Lord" in 'Solomon,' the composer has set iambic verses, in which the accent occurs on every second syllable, in slow triple time, with the accent on every third note, thus—

HANDEL: 'Solomon.'

Here the accented notes of the third, fifth, and ninth bars are set to what are evidently the unimportant words of the text, as will be felt at once, if the student will read the text without reference to the music above it. Such cases are comparatively rare with composers of the first rank, though common enough with imperfectly trained musicians

524. It is a matter of great importance for the composer, whether writing for one voice alone or for different voices in combination, to consider carefully the question of their compass. It is impossible to define this accurately within a note or two, because there is so much difference in individuals; but a general approximation may be given, which will be sufficiently near to serve as a guide for the student. It will be known to every one that the male voice is in pitch about an octave lower than the female voice of the same kind. To understand what is meant by these words, it must be remembered that there are three classes of voice—high, medium, and low, the female voices being called respectively Soprano (or Treble), Mezzo-Soprano, and Contralto, and the corresponding male voices, Tenor, Baritone, and Bass. To these must be added the Male Alto, an artificial voice, seldom to be met with except in this country.

525. The average compass of the six kinds of voices just enumerated is about the following—

It must be distinctly understood that the compass here given is only approximate. For instance, it is not uncommon, especially with young people, to find soprano voices easily able to reach the upper C, or even (though less frequently,) D; while, on the other hand, some contraltos can sing down to F, and many basses can touch E, or even D below the staff. But in writing for the voice it is not advisable to reckon upon an exceptional compass.

526. The student must not suppose that, even within the limits above assigned, it is a matter of indifference for what part of the voice he writes, just as, in writing for the piano, he might use any part of the key-board that he chose. Each voice contains what are known as different "registers," the sounds obtained from these varying in quality, and being produced by different methods. The question of voice-production is one into which we have no room to enter here; the student will obtain the needful information in any good treatise on singing; we must confine ourselves to the practical results. The lower notes of the voice are mostly the weakest; this is especially the case with the soprano and tenor. Though in the table given above we have indicated C as the lowest note of the tenor voice, it will not be advisable in general to write much below the E on the first space, the tone of the notes below this being generally thin and ineffective. On the higher part of the voice, on the other hand, the notes are powerful, and sometimes even piercing; but it is important to remember that they are produced with more effort, and that the voice soon becomes fatigued if too many high notes are introduced in succession.

527. The great composers are not always sufficiently careful in the matter of writing effectively for the voice. We give an example from Schumann of a tenor solo passage written for a part of the compass so low that hardly one singer in ten can produce a good tone.

SCHUMANN: 'Das Paradies und die Peri.'

528. Too free employment of the upper notes is even more to be deprecated. Not only, as already said, are they fatiguing to the singer, but they are almost necessarily produced with a feeling of effort which is very unpleasant to listen to. In this matter Beethoven was the greatest offender. In the finale of the choral symphony the soprano voices have to sing the upper A for thirteen bars, while in his great mass in D the voices are still more thoughtlessly treated. The worst example in Beethoven, however, is to be found in one of his least known works—the incidental music to 'King Stephen.' In the final chorus he has written a passage for the trebles which is as cruel as it is all but impracticable.

BEETHOVEN : 'King Stephen.'

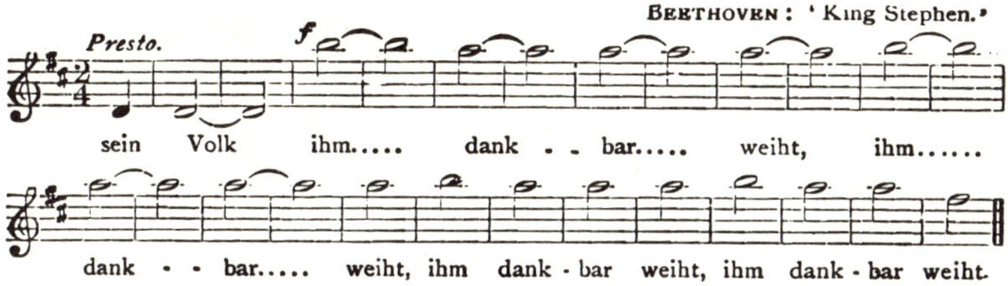

This is written, it must be remembered, not for an exceptional solo voice, but for a *chorus*. One wonders, in reading it, whether it was ever really sung as written; if it was, the effect in performance must have been absolutely painful.

529. It must not be supposed that the use of these higher notes is prohibited; far from it. They are often most effective, especially in dramatic music; but they should be employed with moderation and judgment. It will be well here to recommend the student to be careful, when writing high notes, as to the vowels on which they are to be sung. It is much more difficult to produce them on a syllable such as "me," which requires the mouth to be nearly closed, than on a broad open vowel, such as "far."

530. A very important caution to be given to the student is not to write *unvocally*—that is, uncomfortably for the singer. It is not easy to define exactly in so many words what is meant by this, though an experienced composer knows well enough. The student will best understand it by a few examples. Music may be unvocal because of difficulties either in the intervals, or in the rhythmic subdivisions of the time—the former being the more common. It must be remembered that the voice is not a mechanical instrument, like the piano. On the latter the player has only to know what is the next note to strike, and he has mostly no difficulty in striking it. But with the voice it is different. Unless a singer has a clear conception in his mind of the relation of the note which he is about to sing to that which he has just sung, it will often be impossible for him to sing in tune, and he may even fail to hit the right note at all. This is especially the case with choral music, which is mostly written for singers less perfectly trained than solo-singers. Hence music in which the tonality is vague, doubtful, or constantly varying, is always difficult to sing. For this reason, augmented intervals (seconds, fourths, fifths, or sixths) and most chromatic intervals should be introduced with great discretion. The more certain the singer is of his key, the more correct will be his intonation.

531. As an illustration of this kind of unvocal writing, we give a well-known passage from the finale of Beethoven's Choral Symphony.

BEETHOVEN: 9th Symphony.

This extract, which is without harmony, being accompanied simply in the unison and octave, is preceded by a cadence in the key of D major. The difficulty here arises from the undefined tonality. The bass passage suggests G minor rather than any other key; but the entry of the tenor is not in that key, and what has just been heard in the bass gives the tenor no help in finding the first note, E natural, which is a diminished fifth below the last note of the bass. The entry of the treble on B flat, after the F sharp in the alto, is also very difficult. Of course the passage *can* be sung, but it is none the less most uncomfortably written for the voices.

532. The other kind of difficulty to which we have referred is rhythmic, and is less frequently met with than that of which we have just spoken. Accents displaced by means of syncopation, and what are known as "cross accents" (*Musical Form*, § 287,) are a fruitful source of trouble to singers, especially to chorus singers. In solo music syncopation is not infrequent, as in the familiar passage of the air, "With verdure clad," in Haydn's 'Creation,' beginning

though even a soloist would find such a passage troublesome were the syncopation long continued; but for a chorus it would be almost impracticable. Even more troublesome to sing is a figure employed by Beethoven in the fugue which ends the 'Credo' of his great Mass in D.

BEETHOVEN: Mass in D.

Considered from a musical point of view, the work from which we are quoting is one of the grandest in the whole range of art; but neither this, nor the fact that Beethoven was the greatest composer of the present century should blind us to his shortcomings as a writer for voices; and there is no doubt that the reason why the Mass in D is hardly ever heard is that it presents such enormous difficulties to the singers. Even the greatest genius may sometimes go astray.

533. As an example of cross accents we give a fine passage by Brahms—

Brahms: 'Schicksalslied.

This is not quoted as being unvocal; but it is difficult for a chorus because of the sudden contradiction of the triple-time accent which has been established in the preceding part of the movement. Such passages require great care and judgment for their introduction.

534. Before proceeding to speak of the more important vocal forms, it will be well to say a few words about vocal music without words. Of this there are two kinds. That most commonly met with is found in what are known as *Solfeggi*, or *Vocalises*—exercises written for training the voice, and therefore corresponding in their aim to the Etudes spoken of in Chapter IV. of this volume. Such *Vocalises* are intended to be sung on an open vowel sound, such as *ah*, and the form is quite at the discretion of the composer; that most frequently adopted being the small binary form.

535. The other sort of vocal music without words is that known by the French name of *bouche fermée*. This is simply humming, with the mouth closed, and is sometimes employed as a choral accompaniment to a solo, as at the beginning of the 'Gloria' of Gounod's Cecilian Mass.

Larghette. Gounod: Cecilian Mass.

Another very effective example of the use of this device will be seen in the song "C'est la corvette," in the second act of Auber's 'Haydée,' in which the refrain is similarly accompanied. It is less often used in solo music, though an instance will be found in Solveig's first song in Grieg's music to 'Peer Gynt.' Unless for very special effects, we advise students to abstain from its employment, as it has a tendency to approach dangerously near to clap-trap.

536. Coming now to the forms of vocal music properly so called, we speak first of that written for a single voice, and commence with that which, if we may so speak, is intermediate between song and speech. This is what is known as Recitative. Marx in his great treatise on Composition, to which we have so often referred, defines Recitative as "speech raised to musical precision" (or "definiteness," *German*, 'Bestimmtheit'). Of this there are two varieties,—free Recitative, and Recitative *a tempo.* The former is simply musical declamation, in which the object of the composer should be to express as accurately as possible the sense of the text by the inflexions of the music, just as a good reader would deliver it; while the performer is left absolutely free in *tempo*, so as to be able to declaim it with more expression. Such recitative as this was formerly accompanied mostly only by harpsichord or piano with chords spread in *arpeggio*, and was then known as *recitativo secco* (literally "*dry*" recitative), or, in English as "plain" or "simple" recitative. But where the sentiment of the words required it, in opera or oratorio, the orchestra was used instead of the harpsichord, not merely to accompany with chords, sustained or detached, but to heighten the emotional effect by instrumental passages interspersed between the vocal phrases. Such was called *accompanied recitative.* As examples of the *recitativo secco* may be named "Behold a virgin shall conceive" and "Then shall the eyes of the blind be opened" in the 'Messiah,' while "Thy rebuke hath broken his heart," from the same work, is an example of the accompanied recitative. It should be added that the former is now almost, if not entirely, obsolete.

537. The other variety of recitative is the *recitativo a tempo.* In this the vocal portion is declamatory, rather than melodious, just as is the case with the simple recitative; but the accompaniment consists, not of plain chords, but of some rhythmic figure or figures, so that it is impossible for the singer to vary the time at his discretion. Referring again to the 'Messiah' for illustrations, we see examples in the recitatives relating the Nativity. The first and third of these ("There were shepherds," and "And the angel said unto them,") are *recitativo secco;* while the second ("And lo! the angel of the Lord,") and the fourth ("And suddenly there was with the angel,") are *recitativo a tempo.* In

"Comfort ye" we see the first part *a tempo*, and the latter part ("The voice of him that crieth in the wilderness") free in time, but accompanied by the orchestra. In "For behold darkness," which is *a tempo* throughout, the middle portion, at the words "But the Lord shall arise upon thee," is in a more definite melodic form than that of ordinary recitative, and approaches nearer to the character of a song. Such a passage is called Arioso, though Handel has not given it that name. Bach frequently introduces an *arioso* at the end (sometimes in the middle,) of his recitatives.

538. We have selected all our illustrations from the 'Messiah,' because that work is in everybody's hands; but the student who would learn how to write recitative effectively must examine many models. In Handel's works the recitatives in 'Samson' are particularly worthy of his attention, while he will find a remarkably fine, though little known specimen in the opening recitative, "Vain, fluctuating state of human empire!" in 'Belshazzar.' The magnificent recitatives in Bach's 'Passion Music,' and in his Church Cantatas should be also examined. Those of Gluck's operas deserve careful study, being admirable in the truthfulness of their expression, and those of Mozart are also excellent models. Beethoven wrote very little recitative; but those in 'Fidelio,' and the "Ah! perfido, spergiuro!" deserve close examination. Spohr and Mendelssohn in their oratorios are also very successful in their treatment of this form, which is, from its very nature, so indefinite that it can only be acquired by the study of the best examples.

539. Occasionally in modern music recitative has been written for chorus, instead of for a solo voice. This is known as *Choral Recitative.* Perhaps the earliest instance of its employment is in the chorus "He sent a thick darkness" in Handel's 'Israel in Egypt,' of which all the last part, though not so called, is really recitative in its form and style. Mendelssohn has used it twice in 'Elijah' ("The deeps afford no water," and "Go, return upon thy way"), and we also find it in his music to 'Antigone' and 'Œdipus at Colonos.'

540. Music written for a single voice varies widely both in form and dimensions, ranging from the simplest 'Volkslied,' or popular air, to the most elaborate *scena.* The form and style of the music will to a great extent depend upon the text. The simplest form is that which may be described as the *Strophic Song*—that is, a song of which the words consist of several strophes, or stanzas, the music being the same for all. Most national airs, Volkslieder, &c., are of this kind, as are also a large number of the smaller songs of the great composers (Schubert, Mendelssohn, Schumann, &c.). The musical form of such pieces is always the simple binary, sometimes containing only two

sentences, sometimes three or four. Several examples of songs of this kind are given or referred to in Chapter IX. of *Musical Form* (§§ 318–320, 328). The majority of ballads* is also in the same form.

541. A larger form of song, containing much more variety in its outlines, is that which is known in Germany as a "durch-componirtes Lied"—literally a "through-composed song." We have no exact equivalent for this term, probably because the form itself is comparatively seldom employed by English composers. Here the form depends very largely upon the words. This will be best seen by examining a collection of songs containing both forms. We select Schubert's 'Die schöne Müllerin,' as being well known and easily accessible. The cycle contains in all twenty songs; several of these (Nos. 1, 7, 8, 9, 13, 14, 16, and 20,) are strophic, having the same music for each stanza; No. 10 (Thränenregen,) is also strophic, but the music of the last stanza differs from that of the preceding. No. 3 ('Halt'), though composed throughout, is a large binary form; Nos. 5, 11, 12, 17 and 19 are ternary, Nos. 12 and 17 having long codas. In 'Der Neugierige' (No. 6,) and 'Trockne Blumen' (No. 18,) we see a kind of double binary form—the first two stanzas set to the same music, and the remaining ones to a different melody, the mode changing in the latter from minor, for the first part, to major for the second. The remaining numbers of the series are in more or less irregular forms, and cannot be exactly classified. In such cases unity is often preserved (as in 'Wohin') by the persistence of one figure of accompaniment. The question whether any particular poem should be set strophically or not is one which must be left entirely to the judgment of the composer.

542. Many songs are written in the simple ternary form, on a larger scale than those above referred to from the 'Schöne Müllerin.' Such are all those written in the old *da capo* form, so common in the middle of the last century. The application of the ternary form to vocal music was spoken of in *Musical Form* §§ 392–398, and we refer our readers to what was there said.

543. The older Rondo form can also be used for vocal music. An exceedingly beautiful example of this will be seen in the bass song "Schlummert ein, ihr matten Augen," in Bach's Cantata "Ich habe genug." To save space, we give in our quotations only the

* The word "ballad" is here used in the sense commonly given to it in this country; the German 'Ballade' is a different form altogether, and is either a poem set for one voice, and composed throughout, as in Schubert's 'Erl King' or Schumann's 'Belsatzar,' or sometimes a species of cantata for chorus and orchestra, with or without solo voices. Mendelssohn's 'First Walpurgis Night' is a Ballade of this kind.

voice part and the bass, which Bach has figured so fully that students will readily see the harmony. After an orchestral prelude of nine bars in which the chief subject of the song is announced, the voice begins as follows—

BACH: Cantata, "Ich habe genug."

The continuation of this melody leads at bar 27 to the close oi the principal subject in the tonic key, after which the opening symphony is repeated. The first episode commences at bar 37,

and ends at bar 48, with a full cadence in G minor. Note, in passing, that the first principal modulation is to the *dominant* side of the original tonic. The chief subject is then repeated, with a slight alteration in the first bars, and followed by one bar of interlude for orchestra, leading to the second episode—

This episode is mostly in the keys of F minor and C minor, but it ends with a full cadence in A flat, after which the first 36 bars of the song are repeated *da capo*. It will be seen that there is here a perfectly regular rondo form, with two episodes in different keys, and that the whole movement follows exactly the form described in Chapter VI. of this volume.

544. In the vocal compositions of Mozart several good examples of the older rondo form are to be found. We refer students to the air "L'amerò, saro costante" in 'Il Rè Pastore,' and to the two Concert Arias "Io ti lascio" and "Mia speranza adorata" as fine specimens. The songs "Non più di fiori" in 'La Clemenza di Tito,' and "Non mi dir" in 'Don Giovanni,' are also in rondo form, though both are less regular in their construction than the movements we have just named. We cannot recall any instance of the modern rondo (Rondo-Sonata) form being employed in vocal music.

545. Though less common than the older rondo form, the sonata form is sometimes to be found in songs, especially in the operas of Mozart. Our space will not allow us to give illustrations; students will find examples which deserve careful analysis in the airs "Zeffiretti lusinghieri" and "Se colà ne fati è scritto" in 'Idomeneo' and in the allegro of the song "Ach, ich liebte" in the first act of 'Die Entführung aus dem Serail.' All these movements are in regular sonata form; the modified sonata forms are much more frequently met with.

546. Hitherto we have spoken only of single vocal movements; but we often find songs and other compositions in which there is more than one movement. Some of the examples to be found in Schubert's songs, *e.g.* 'Der Wanderer,' contain several changes of tempo; and such are even more common in dramatic music than in that intended for the concert room. A form frequently found in opera is that known as the Scena. This is a development from the older Italian cantata, of which many specimens are

to be seen in the works of Carissimi, Scarlatti, and Handel. These cantatas consisted of two or more airs, generally (though not invariably,) connected by recitatives. The form of the separate movements was entirely at the discretion of the composer. The modern Scena always begins with a recitative, which is mostly followed by two movements, the first in slow, and the second in quick tempo. These movements will be in one of the various forms that we have described in this chapter; but it is not at all unusual to find more than two movements following the first recitative. The form of the Scena as a whole depends almost entirely upon the text to which it is set. Among the finest examples in dramatic music may be named Marx's scena "Durch die Wälder," in the first act of 'Der Freischutz,' that for Agathe "Wie nahte mir der Schlummer," in the second act of the same opera, and the well-known "Ocean, thou mighty monster" in 'Oberon.' Beethoven's 'Fidelio' also contains two magnificent examples of this form—the "Abscheulicher" in the first act, and "Gott! welch' Dunkel hier" in the second.

547. The term 'Scena' is sometimes applied only to the opening recitative, when followed by other movements as described above, the whole piece being thus designated 'Scena ed Aria.' Inasmuch, however, as that which follows the recitative is by no means invariably in song form throughout, but frequently (as in the examples from the 'Freischutz' above referred to,) contains more recitative passages, it seems better to give the name 'Scena' to the entire composition, rather than to restrict it to the first portion.

548. The Scena is also to be found in music written for the concert-room, though not so frequently as in opera. Beethoven's "Ah perfido" is an example of this, as also is Mendelssohn's "Infelice!"—this piece, it should be remarked, being entitled 'Concert Aria.' Mozart has also left us a large number of concert pieces of this kind, some of which, however, were written to be introduced, according to the custom of the time, into operas by other composers.

549. In writing the accompaniments to a vocal solo, whether such be for the piano or the orchestra, no account need be taken of the difference in pitch between the male and female voice. Thus, a tenor solo can be accompanied like one for soprano, and the bass like the alto. But when in part-music male and female voices are used together, the difference of an octave in their pitch must be carefully attended to.

550. Pieces written for more than one solo voice (duets, trios, &c.,) have in general the same forms as those written for one voice only. But it is possible also with these to employ imitation, more or less strict; and we sometimes find entire movements written in canon. The quartett in the first act of 'Fidelio' is a well-known instance of this, and another excellent example will

be seen in the trio from Cherubini's 'Faniska' given in § 330 of *Double Counterpoint.* Still more common, especially in duets, are incidental passages of imitation, as in the duet "O death, where is thy sting?" in the 'Messiah.' Numerous examples of this kind will be found in Handel's Chamber Duets, in those of Clari, Steffani, and other Italian composers, and in Marcello's Psalms. The employment of such imitative devices does not affect the form of the movements, which will for the most part, be either binary or ternary.

551. A species of composition for solo voices which is peculiar to England is the GLEE. The name has nothing to do with merriment, for serious glees are quite as common as lively ones; it is derived from the Anglo-Saxon word *gligg*, which signifies 'music.' A glee is for at least three voices, frequently for four, and sometimes for five, and should not be sung by more than one voice to a part. It may be either for mixed voices, that is, for male and female voices together, or, perhaps more commonly, for male voices alone. In the latter case the upper part (or, if there are five voices, occasionally the two upper parts,) are given to the alto voice.*

552. The form of the glee varies so much that it is impossible to generalize concerning it. In the shorter specimens, such as Stevens's "The cloud-capt towers," Spofforth's "Hail, smiling morn," or Paxton's "Breathe soft, ye winds," the time is unchanged throughout; but more elaborate examples (*e.g.* Webbe's "Discord, dire sister," and "When winds breathe soft,") often contain several movements in different *tempi.* As the form selected by the composer largely depends upon the words which he is setting, such glees more nearly resemble the fantasia than any of the instrumental forms described in the earlier chapters of this volume. Here it may be said once for all that in vocal music, excepting in the smaller varieties, the forms are almost always more indefinite and more difficult to analyze than in instrumental, because of the disturbing element introduced by the text which has to be set, and which can never be left out of consideration by the composer.

553. Nearly akin to the glee is the PART SONG. The chief differences between the two are that, whereas the glee is written for solo voices the part-song is for chorus, and that the latter is generally more homophonic than the former. The part-song also is frequently strophic in its construction, as in Mendelssohn's

* The male alto voice, referred to in § 523, which is so frequently employed in glees and in English church music, is an artificial, or "falsetto" voice, the compass of which is from 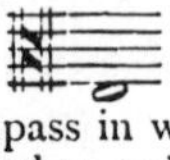 to  The composer should be careful not to exceed this compass in writing glees or church music, as in many of our cathedrals and churches only male altos are to be found. Even within this compass the extreme notes should be used sparingly.

"O forest, deep and gloomy," and in many other specimens by the same composer. Excellent examples of the part-song will be seen in the works of Weber, Schubert, and Mendelssohn, and, of English writers, in the compositions of Henry Smart, Sullivan, J. L. Hatton, and others too numerous to mention.

554. A form now nearly obsolete, but which formerly was one of the most important in vocal music, was the MADRIGAL. The origin of the name is involved in deep obscurity, but the nature of the composition can be clearly seen from the numerous existing specimens by Flemish, Italian, and English composers. The Madrigal is much older than either the Glee or the Part-Song, and differs essentially from both in its construction. The more ancient examples, being anterior in date to the introduction of modern tonality, are mostly written in the older church modes. But an even more important difference is seen in the fact that, whereas the Glee and Part-Song are chiefly homophonic, the Madrigal is essentially polyphonic in style, abounding in passages of imitation, canon, &c. Hence it results that, while in the more modern forms the rhythmic construction is generally very clear, and the cadential formulæ frequent, continuity is one of the chief features of the madrigal form, as it is also of the fugue. It is not meant by this that no full cadences are to be met with in madrigals, but only that such are less frequent than in glees or part-songs, and that, as with fugues, they often furnish the starting point for a new departure. Among the best models for the student who wishes to write in this old form are the madrigals of Luca Marenzio, Palestrina, and Orlando di Lasso among the Italians, and those of Gibbons, Wilbye, and Weelkes among English composers.

555. Very similar to the Madrigal was the older form of the MOTETT. This was almost always written to sacred words, while the Madrigal was mostly a secular composition, though 'Madrigali spirituali' were published by Palestrina and Felice Anerio. The motett was generally, though not invariably, polyphonic in construction, and was at first written for voices alone. The term was subsequently applied somewhat differently. The motetts of Sebastian Bach were intended to be sung with organ accompaniment,* and in one instance, that of the motett "Der Geist hilft uns'rer Schwachheit auf," orchestral parts exist in the composer's own handwriting. A special feature of the motett is that the instrumental accompaniment doubled the voices, and was only *obbligato* in most exceptional cases. With more modern motetts, however, free orchestral accompaniments are sometimes to be found, as in Haydn's fine motett "Insanæ et vanæ curæ," while Mendelssohn's 'Three Motetts for Female Voices,' Op. 39,

* This is clearly shown by Spitta, in his great work on Bach, and there can be little doubt that the performance of these great works by an unaccompanied choir is not in conformity with the composer's intentions.

have an organ accompaniment which is in many places independent of the voices. It will be seen that so many different kinds of composition are met with under the same name that the 'Motett' is almost as vague in its meaning as the instrumental terms Toccata and Capriccio.

556. Closely approximating to the Motett are the ANTHEMS of the old English church composers. Here, again, we find such great differences in the form of various specimens as to render it quite impossible to generalize. In some cases, as for instance in Farrant's "Lord, for thy tender mercies' sake," the music is mostly homophonic, and very simple, while many anthems abound in passages of imitation, and regular fugues are often to be found. In cathedrals and in many of the larger churches the choir is divided, half of the singers sitting on the south and half on the north of the aisle, the former being known as the 'Decani,' or dean's side—that is, the side on which the dean's stall is placed—and the latter as the 'Cantoris,' or precentor's side. In many anthems antiphonal effects are obtained by the alternate employment of the two halves of the Choir. Anthems are further divided into 'Full' and 'Verse'; the former being those written for chorus throughout, and the latter containing passages for one or more solo voices, such being called "verse" passages.

557. Though the anthem is generally accompanied by the organ alone, numerous examples are to be found of the employment of the orchestra also. Many of the anthems of Purcell, Blow, and other early English composers, have instrumental accompaniments, as also have the anthems which Handel wrote for the Duke of Chandos, for the coronation of George II., for the Funeral of Queen Caroline, &c. These anthems are in several movements, and resemble large sacred cantatas, containing not only choruses, but airs, duets, &c.; the form of the separate movements being largely influenced, as in all vocal music, by the text.

558. The CHURCH CANTATA, a form largely cultivated in Germany in the last century, took in the Lutheran service nearly the same place as the anthem in the Anglican. Nearly two hundred specimens of this class of composition exist from the pen of J. S. Bach, all being with orchestral accompaniment. Some are for solo voices, and consist of two or three songs, divided by recitatives, the last movement being generally (though by no means invariably,) a choral for the full choir, accompanied by instruments in unison with the voices. The larger number of the cantatas are written for chorus with solos, and these mostly begin with a chorus, sometimes founded upon a choral; this is followed by various airs, divided, as in the solo cantatas by recitatives, and a choral, sometimes with florid orchestral interludes and accompaniments, at other times accompanied in unison, mostly

concludes the work. In nineteen instances Bach commences his cantatas with an orchestral introduction, and twice he introduces an instrumental movement in the middle of the work.

559. The CHURCH SERVICE is the name given to the musical setting of the Canticles and the Communion Service in the Book of Common Prayer. The Morning Service consists of the 'Te Deum,' (more rarely the 'Benedicite opera omnia,') and either the 'Benedictus' or the 'Jubilate'; the Communion Service generally contains settings of the 'Kyrie,' the Nicene Creed, 'Sanctus' and 'Gloria in Excelsis,' frequently also of the 'Benedictus' and 'Agnus Dei'; while the Evening Service includes either the 'Magnificat' and 'Nunc Dimittis,' or less frequently the 'Cantate Domino' and 'Deus misereatur.' The form and style of these pieces varies greatly according to the purpose for which they are intended. If written for an ordinary parochial choir, or for congregational use, they should be simple and easy of performance; if written for a cathedral, a greater degree of elaboration is allowable, and indeed advisable. It is quite impossible to give any precise rules; the student will best learn how to write by studying the numerous existing specimens by distinguished composers, ancient and modern. But it may be said that a plain, diatonic and dignified style is far more suited to the service of the church than the sentimental writing, with cloying chromatic harmony, which is to be seen in some of the modern examples of so-called sacred music.

560. Both in church services and in anthems, fugal writing is not infrequently to be found; and a word may be appropriately said here as to the treatment of choral fugue. The whole structure of fugue has been treated in detail in previous volumes of this series; what is now to be said relates to the choice of subjects for vocal fugues. Though in the works of Bach and Handel, and occasionally also with more modern composers, choral fugues are to be found written upon florid subjects, with 'divisions,' as they are called, of semiquavers, it is generally advisable to select subjects of a more stately character, moving with one, or at most two, notes to a syllable. Such a subject as the following,

HANDEL: 'Alexander Balus.

interesting though it be from a musical point of view, seems to our modern ideas more fitted for a solfeggio than for a choral fugue, and the same thing may, with all deference, be said of the subjects of several of the fugues in Bach's Church Cantatas, which are certainly more instrumental than vocal in their character.

561. As particularly good examples of subjects for choral fugues, we give the following, by the great masters.

(a) BACH: Cantata, "Ich hatte viel Bekümmerniss.

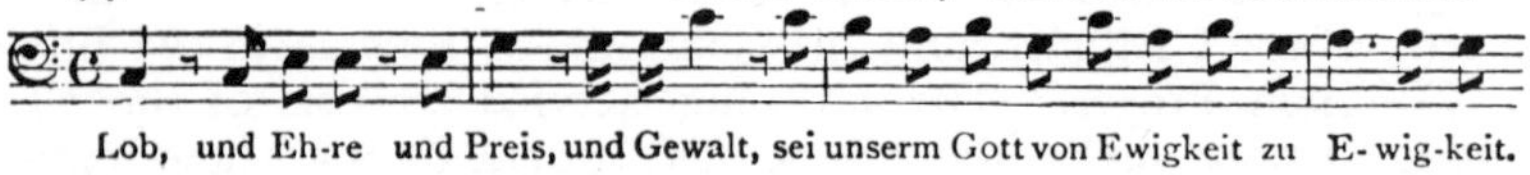

(b) HANDEL: 'Belshazzar.'

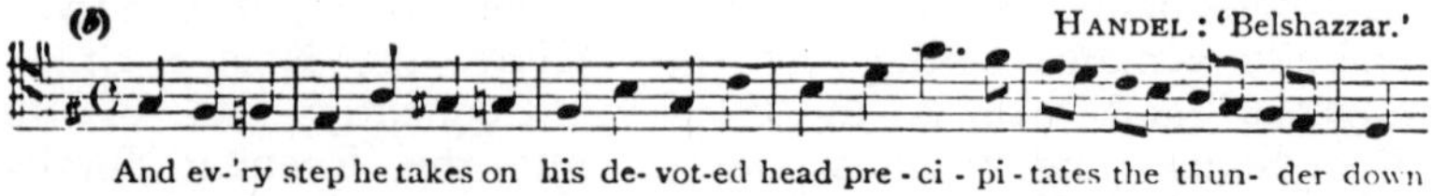

(c) GRAUN: Passion Oratorio.

(d) HAYDN: 3rd Mass.

(e) MOZART: Vespers.

(f) CHERUBINI: 1st Mass.

(g) MENDELSSOHN: 114th Psalm.

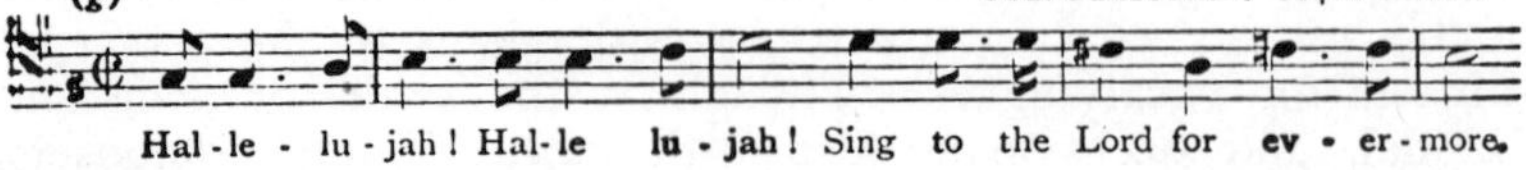

(h) BRAHMS: Ein deutsches Requiem.

These subjects have been chosen as being very various in style; but, in spite of their differences in character, they all resemble one another in these respects, that each has easily recognizable melodic features, and the declamation of the words is broad and clear in every case. A well-selected subject is, if possible, of even more importance in a vocal than in an instrumental fugue.

562. We spoke in § 559 of the Church Service. This is a species of composition peculiar to English music; its equivalent in Roman Catholic countries is the MASS. This is a setting of the Communion Service of the Roman Church, and consists of five parts, the 'Kyrie eleison,' 'Gloria in excelsis,' 'Credo,

'Sanctus' and 'Benedictus,' and 'Agnus Dei.' To these is sometimes added the 'Offertorium' and 'Graduale,' which correspond nearly to our anthems. In shorter masses ('Missa Brevis,') each section is generally complete in one movement; but in those written for the festival services of the church the music is much more extended, the 'Gloria' and 'Credo' being each frequently divided into three, four, and occasionally even more movements In such cases, the final clauses of the 'Gloria' ("Cum sancto spiritu"), the 'Credo' ("Et vitam venturi") and the 'Sanctus' ("Osanna in excelsis,") are generally treated fugally. As models for the student, we recommend especially the masses of Cherubini and Schubert, and the mass in C of Beethoven. Haydn's and Mozart's masses may also be studied with advantage, from the point of view of their construction; but it must be remembered that musical taste has much changed since these works were written, and that in Haydn's masses especially we meet with much that, however delightful as music, seems altogether unsuited to the character of the words. It is not with any intention of disparaging Haydn that we say that such lively movements as the 'Kyrie' in his first and second masses are absurdly inappropriate as a musical illustration of such words as "Lord, have mercy upon us! Christ, have mercy upon us!"

563. Of the largest forms of vocal composition—the Cantata, Oratorio, and Opera,—only a few words can be said here. As with so many of the other works of which we have spoken in this chapter, it is impossible to generalize concerning their forms, because these depend largely, one might almost say entirely, upon the libretti. Further, it would be necessary to write a lengthy history of both oratorio and opera, and this would be beyond the scope of the present volume. While the principal instrumental forms, such as the Sonata and Rondo, may be said to have been practically fixed by Beethoven, and his immediate successors, the opera and oratorio are still in the process of development; and there is as much difference between one of Handel's operas and, let us say, Gounod's 'Faust' or Wagner's 'Lohengrin' as there is between a sonata of Scarlatti and one of Beethoven. The same thing, though to a less extent, is true of oratorio. Compare, for instance, Handel's 'Messiah' with Gounod's 'Redemption,' or his 'Jephtha' or 'Judas Maccabæus' with Parry's 'Judith,' and it will be felt at once that the former breathe the spirit of the eighteenth, and the latter of the nineteenth century. For this reason it is impossible to give any rules for the composition of such large works. The student who has thoroughly mastered the various forms treated in this volume should have little difficulty, assuming him to be naturally gifted, in applying them to the different movements contained in the oratorio or opera. But it is most important that he should be well acquainted with the chief masterpieces of both

schools. In oratorio he should know those of Handel, Haydn, Mendelssohn, and Spohr, besides the more recent works produced in this country (the special home of oratorio,) by Sterndale Bennett, Sullivan, Mackenzie, and Parry.

564. The study of operatic literature offers a still wider field for investigation. The student should have at least a fair acquaintance with the great operas of Gluck ('Armide,' 'Alceste,' 'Orphée' and the two 'Iphigenias'), Mozart, and Cherubini ('Les deux Journées,' 'Medée,' 'Faniska' and 'Lodoiska'). He should of course be familiar with Beethoven's 'Fidelio,' Weber's 'Freischütz,' 'Euryanthe' and 'Oberon,' and the principal works of Wagner. Nor should the French school, as illustrated by Boieldieu, Auber, Meyerbeer and Hérold, be neglected; while in Italian opera, the best specimens of Donizetti, Bellini, Rossini, and Verdi should be studied. This appears to be what Americans call "a large order"; but everyone who aspires to distinction as a composer must study the masterpieces of his art, not for the purpose of slavish imitation, but because by this means only can a complete knowledge of the various forms be acquired. Not long since a candidate for a musical degree at one of our Universities was examined as to his knowledge of the works of the great masters, and he replied that "he never studied them, for fear of destroying his own originality." The man failed, and rightly so; for, as we have continually insisted throughout the whole of this series, more is to be learned from the example of the greatest composers than is possible in any other way.

565. We have dealt in this chapter with the forms of vocal music,—as regards the larger forms, in a necessarily incomplete manner. This, as has been incidentally said, is the inevitable result of the disturbing influence exercised over the form by the words. Beyond general outlines it is impossible for us to go. Even the instrumental forms, though far more definite than the larger vocal forms, cannot be thoroughly mastered from such a text-book as this. The student must analyze for himself, must carefully note what has been done by his predecessors, and, unless he is sure of being able to improve on their procedure, should go and do likewise. And this analytical process is even more necessary with vocal music. All that we can do is to put him on the right track for his own investigations, and to wish him God speed!

ANALYTICAL INDEX.

**** The numbers refer to the paragraphs, not the pages.*

Abridged sonata form (*see* Modified Sonata Forms, I.).
Absolute music, 519.
Abstract music, 4.
Accompaniments to Vocal music, 549.
Air with variations (*see* Variation Forms, I.).
Allemande (*see* Dance Forms, I.).
Alto voice, male, compass of (*see* note to page 286).
Ancient suite (*see* Dance Forms, II.).
Anthem (*see* Vocal Forms, I.).
Applied form defined, 6.
Arioso (*see* Vocal Forms, X.).
Arpeggios and broken chords, treatment of, in pianoforte writing, 35-40.

BAGATELLES of Beethoven referred to and analyzed, 103; Binary and Ternary form in, 103.
Ballad Form, 540.
Baritone voice, compass of, 525.
Bass voice, compass of, 525.
Bolero (*see* Dance Forms, III.).
BOUCHE FERMÉE, meaning of, 535; examples in chorus by Gounod, and Auber, 535; example in solo voice by Grieg, 535.
Bourrée (*see* Dance Forms, IV.).
BRIDGE PASSAGE—and Link, difference between, 217; defined, 195, 217, 233; in Modern rondo form—examples, 390, 396, 398-403; in Older rondo form—examples, 195, 198, 199, 202-204; in Sonata form—examples, 217, 218, 220, 233-238; length of, 237, 238; material of, 237; modulation in, 233, 237.
Broken chords and arpeggios, treatment of, in pianoforte writing, 35-40.

CADENZA, defined, 381; examples referred to, 381.

Canonic variations (*see* Variation Forms, II.).
Cantata, 563.
Cantoris, meaning of, 556.
Caprice (*see* Indefinite Forms, I.).
Cassation and Divertimento (*see* Cyclic Forms, V.).
Chaconne (*see* Variation Forms, III.).
Choral recitative (*see* Vocal Forms, X.).
Church cantata (*see* Vocal Forms, III.).
Church service (*see* Vocal Forms, IV.).
Classical form, origin of, 446.
Clearness of tonality, importance of, in composition, 135, 530.
CODA in Abridged sonata form—examples, 351, 354, 358; in Dance forms—examples, 81, 83; in Modern rondo form—examples, 396, 399, 402, 407; in Older rondo form—examples, 197, 199, 201, 203, 204; in Sonata forms—examples, 339-342; in Variation forms—examples, 153, 162, 176.
CODETTA in Modern rondo form, 392, 399; in Older rondo form, 204; in Sonata form, 266, 274.
Composition pedals and knobs (*see* Organ).
Compound common time defined—example of, 50.
Compound stops (*see* Organ II.).
Concerto (*see* Modified Sonata Forms, II.).
Concerto as a Cyclic form (*see* Cyclic Forms, VI.).
Contralto voice, compass of, 525
Contrapuntal development, 292 (*see* Sonata Form, II.).
Courante (*see* Dance Forms, V.).
CYCLIC FORMS:—Classical form, 446; defined, 442; Modern cyclic forms developed from the Ancient suite, 446; process of evolution, 443; Typical

cyclic form, the *Three*-movement form, 444; its variations, the *Two*-movement form, the *Four*-movement form, and those forms containing *More than four* movements, 444; Unity of character in, 445; different methods of obtaining unity, 470-472; used for Sonatas, Trios, Quartetts, and other chamber music, 446; used in the Orchestra for Symphonies and Serenades, 446.

I. TWO MOVEMENT FORM. A contraction of the Typical three movement form, 462; contrast in form of the two movements desirable, 463; examples by Haydn, Clementi, Dussek, Mozart, Beethoven, Mendelssohn, referred to, 462; seldom found except in Sonatas, 463.

II. THREE MOVEMENT FORM. An introduction sometimes precedes the first movement, 448; *Keys* of the different movements, 448; *Order* of the movements—*Regular*, 448;—*Irregular*, 460, 461; the Typical form, 447; used mostly in chamber music for two or at most three instruments, 447. *The First movement*—an allegro in Regular sonata form, 448; an Introduction sometimes precedes the first movement, 448; *Irregular* movements: an Andante; Variation form, 460, 461. *The Second movement*—a Slow movement: Andante, Larghetto, Largo, or Adagio, in a different key to the first movement, 448. *Choice of key*—(*a*) for a Cyclic work in a Major key—in nearly related key, 450-452; in key in the second degree of relationship, 453; in unrelated key, 454; (*b*) for a Cyclic work in a Minor key, 455, 456. *Form of:* Full sonata, Abridged sonata, Older rondo, Rondo-sonata, Variation, simple Ternary, 457. *Irregular* movements: second movement exceptionally in the same key as the first—examples by Clementi, Mozart, Schubert, referred to, 449; second movement sometimes in quick *tempo* instead of slow, 458; examples by Haydn and Beethoven referred to, 458. *The Third movement*—a quick movement, 448. *Form of:* Complete sonata, Variation, Older rondo, Rondo-sonata, or simple Ternary, 448. *Key:* the same as the first movement, or at all events with the same tonic, 448; *Irregular* movements, 460, 461.

III. FOUR MOVEMENT FORM. An extension of the typical three movement form, 464; *Form* of the four movements, 465; *Keys* of the four movements, 465; *Order* of the two middle movements optional, 466; two middle movements usually a slow movement and a Minuet and Trio, or scherzo, 465; *Irregular* movements, 468, 469.

IV. IN MORE THAN FOUR MOVEMENTS, rarely met with, 473; examples by Raff, Schumann, Goldmark, referred to, 473; *Forms* of the various movements, 473.

V. CASSATION AND DIVERTIMENTO. Choice and order of the movements left to the composer, 477; examples by Beethoven and Schubert referred to, 477; how they differ from the Serenade, 477.

VI. CONCERTO, defined, 478; usually in three movements, 479; examples by Brahms, Scharwenka, and Tschaikowsky, 479; *Irregular* movements, 480; examples by Max Bruch, 480; Saint-Saëns, 481, 482; Liszt, Metamorphosis of themes, 483.

VII. MODERN SUITE. The *Old* and *Modern* suite, difference between, 474; wide application of the word "*Suite*," 474; examples by Bizet and Hamerik, 474.

VIII. SERENADE. A work for Full orchestra, 476; derivation of the name, 476; example by Mozart referred to, 476; *Form* of the various movements, 476; *Keys*, 476; sometimes containing as many as *eight* movements, 476.

IX. STRING QUARTETT. The invention of Haydn, 475; with *five* movements—examples, 475.

X. SYMPHONIC POEM, defined, 484; Metamorphosis of themes, 484; example by Liszt—the Themes, analyzed, 484.

Damper pedal (*see* Pianoforte—Pedals).

DANCE FORMS:—Dances form and dance music, difference between, 44; directions for writing in, 100; Form in, 48; Modulation in, 48; regular and irregular rhythm, 44; varieties of, 45.

I. ALLEMANDE, described, 49; *first* of the four indispensable movements of the Ancient suite, 49; its special characteristics, 49; *example* by Bach analyzed; rhythmic construction, 49-51.

II. ANCIENT SUITE. Additional dances sometimes introduced, 47; described, 46; each movement in the same key, 46; Form of each movement, 48; its indispensable movements, 47; Modulations, 48; Old and Modern suites, 99; Rhythmic construction, 48.

III. BOLERO, described, 90; its origin, 90; its special characteristics, 90; example by Weber, 91.

IV. BOURRÉE, described, 70; difference between Bourrée and Gavotte, 70; its special characteristics, 70; often followed by a second one, 70; the second Bourrée is sometimes written on a tonic pedal, in which case it is called a *Musette*, 70.

V. COURANTE, described, 52; *second* of the four indispensable movements of the Ancient suite, 52; its special characteristics, 53; two distinct varieties in $\frac{3}{2}$ and $\frac{3}{4}$ time, 52. (*a*) *The Courante in $\frac{3}{2}$ time*—cross accents, 53; described, 53; example by Bach, 53; example by Couperin, 54. (*b*) *The Courante in $\frac{3}{4}$ time*—described, 55; example by Bach, 55; mostly simpler in construction, 55.

VI. GAVOTTE, described, 64; its special characteristics, 64. (*a*) *Its earlier and simplest form*, 64; example by Couperin, 64. (*b*) *Its later development*—example by Handel, 66; often followed by a second Gavotte, 67; the second Gavotte is sometimes written on a tonic pedal, in which case it is called a *Musette*, 67.

VII. GIGUE. Fourth of the four indispensable movements of the Ancient suite, 60; described, 60; its rhythmic construction, 60; its special characteristics, 60. (*a*) *The gigue for dancing*—example by Handel analyzed—regularity of cadence, 60. (*b*) *The gigue as a dance form*—example by Bach analyzed, 61, 62; irregular rhythmic construction, 61, 62; treatment in the free Fugal style, 61; the time in, 63.

VIII. MARCH, described, 93; in theatrical and operatic music, 95; march forms, 94-96; rate of speed, 97; simple Binary or Ternary form mostly used, 97; example by Beethoven, 98.

IX. MARCHE AUX FLAMBEAUX, described, 89; its form, 89; its rhythmic construction, 89; the finest models by Meyerbeer, 89.

X. MAZURKA, described, 84; employment of rhythmic figure, 84; its origin, 84; its rhythmic construction, 85; its special characteristics, 84; examples by Chopin, 84, 85; their form, 85.

XI. MINUET. (*a*) *The old Minuet*—described, 71; often followed by a second one which, if written in three-part harmony, was described as a *Trio*; rhythmic construction, 71; example by Bach, 71; when followed by a trio, the form of the whole becomes *Ternary*, 72; when followed by more than one trio, the whole becomes *Rondo* form, 72. (*b*) *The modern Minuet*—described, 73; how it differs from the older form, 73; rhythmic construction, 73; examples referred to, 73.

XII. MODERN SUITE, described, 99; *Old* and *Modern* suites, 99; use of the word Suite, 99.

XIII. PASSEPIED, described, 68; its rhythmic construction, 68; its special characteristics, 68; example by Bach, 68; often followed by a second one in three-part harmony, and called a "*Trio*," 69; example by Bach, 69.

XIV. POLONAISE or POLACCA, described, 86; its form, 86; its origin, 86; its special characteristics, 86, 88; the *Older* form, example by Bach, 87; the *Modern* form, example by Schubert, 88; rhythmic figure of accompaniment, 88.

XV. RIGAUDON, described, 70; almost, if not quite, identical with the Bourrée, 70.

XVI. SARABANDE. Third of the four indispensable movements of the Ancient suite, 56; described, 56; its rhythmic construction, 56; its special characteristics, 56; sometimes followed by a variation known as a "*Double*"—examples by Bach, 57, 58; example by Handel, 59.

XVII. SCHERZO. A development of the Minuet, 74; innovations introduced by Beethoven, 75; Scherzos with two trios, 76; Ternary form abandoned, 77; examples referred to by Beethoven, 74-77.

XVIII. TARANTELLA, described, 92; its origin, 92; example by Auber, 92. *The Saltarello*—described, 92; example by Mendelssohn referred to, 92.

XIX. WALTZ, described, 78; its origin, 78; Mozart's waltzes; their form—the Coda, 78; example by Mozart, 78; Beethoven's waltzes, 79; Schubert's waltzes, 79, 80; examples by Schubert, 79, 80; modulations in, 80; employment of the Link, 80; irregular rhythmic formations *exceptional*, 81. *Valse de salon*—Chopin's waltzes, 82; their form, 82. *Waltzes for dancing*—how written, 83; the Coda, 83.

Decani, meaning of, 556.

Development, meaning of, 276; means of (*see* Sonata Form, II.).

Divertimento and Cassation (*see* Cyclic Forms, V.).

Double, defined; example by Bach, 58.

Double exposition, meaning of, 371.

Double variations (*see* Variation Forms, IV. and VIII.).

Doubling of dissonant notes in Pianoforte writing, 32.

EPISODE, in the *Older* rondo form (*see* Rondo Form, I.); in the *Modern* rondo form (*see* Rondo Form, II.); in Sonata form, sometimes found in place of the "Free" fantasia, 296, 297 (*see* Sonata Form, II.).

Étude (*see* Instrumental Forms, the smaller, I.).

Evolution of music, 1-3.

Exposition—of a Fugue, 128; of a Sonata (*see* Sonata Form, I.); Double, 371.

Fantasia (*see* Indefinite Forms, II.).

First movement form (*see* Sonata Form).

First subject in Older rondo form (*see* Rondo Form, I.); in Modern rondo form (*see* Rondo Form, II.); in Sonata form (*see* Sonata Form, I.).

Flue stops (*see* Organ, II.).

Form, applied, defined, 6.

Form in music influenced by the nature of the instruments for which it is written, 5.

Form in pianoforte music of small dimensions is mostly found to be simple Binary or simple Ternary, 102, 106.

Form, modern rondo (*see* Rondo Form, II.).

Form, older rondo (*see* Rondo Form, I.).

Form, sonata (*see* Sonata Form).

Forms, dance (*see* Dance Forms).

Forms, indefinite (*see* Indefinite Forms).

Forms, mixed (*see* Mixed Forms).

Forms, modified sonata (*see* Modified Sonata Forms).

Forms, organ (*see* Organ Music)

Forms, smaller instrumental (*see* Instrumental Forms, the smaller).

Forms, variation (*see* Variation Forms).

Forms, vocal (*see* Vocal Forms).

Foundation stops (*see* Organ, II.).

Four-movement form (*see* Cyclic Forms, III.).

Free fantasia (*see* Sonata Form, II.).

Fugal form in the Overture (*see* Modified Sonata Form, III.).

Fugue (*see* Instrumental Forms, III.).

Full, meaning of the word when found in Anthems, etc.), 556.

Gavotte (*see* Dance Forms, VI.).

Gigue (*see* Dance Forms, VII.).

Glee (*see* Vocal Forms, V.).

Ground bass (*see* Variation Forms, V.).

Harmonies, position of, in Pianoforte writing, 31.

How to write for the voice (*see* Vocal Music).

Incidental variation defined, 136.

INDEFINITE FORMS:—

I. CAPRICCIO or *CAPRICE*, defined, 432; freedom of, 432;

examples referred to by Bach, Handel, August E. Müller, Weber, Mendelssohn, Stephen Heller, 433.

II. FANTASIA, defined, 436; most indefinite and varied of all forms, 436; the Old and Modern forms, 436. (*a*) *Fantasias with several connected movements*, 436; examples referred to by Hummel and Beethoven, 436. (*b*) *Fantasias in one movement*, 437; examples referred to by Mozart and Mendelssohn, 437; unity obtained by the recurrence of the first subject at the end, 438; examples referred to by Mozart and Schubert, 438. (*c*) *Fantasias with detached movements*—examples referred to by Schumann and Mendelssohn, 439. (*d*) *Sonata quasi fantasia*—two examples referred to by Beethoven, 440; example referred to by Mendelssohn, 440; example by Raff analyzed; Metamorphosis of themes, 440. (*e*) *Operatic fantasias and transcriptions*—defined, 441; examples referred to by Thalberg, Liszt, Heller, and Raff, 441.

III. INTERMEZZO, described, 434. (*a*) *As a middle section of a movement*—example by Schumann, 434. (*b*) *As a middle movement of a Cyclic work*—examples referred to by Mendelssohn and Schumann, 435. (*c*) *As an Independent piece*—examples referred to by Schumann, 435.

IV. INTRODUCTION, defined, 428; ends mostly with half cadence in the key of the following movement, 428; material of the introduction, 428; met with chiefly at the commencement of a work in Cyclic form, 428; mostly in slow time, 428; examples referred to by Beethoven, 428; sometimes met with before Variations and Rondos when these form separate pieces, 429; examples referred to by Beethoven, Chopin, Hummel, 429.

V. TOCCATA, defined, 430; derivation of the word, 430; loose application of the name, 430; examples referred to by Bach, 430; Beethoven, 431; Schumann, 431.

INSTRUMENTAL FORMS (SMALLER), are usually in either simple Binary or simple Ternary form, 101. *Pieces written for children*—examples by Schumann, Mendelssohn, and Heller, 102. *Bagatelles*—Beethoven's "7 Bagatellen," referred to and analyzed, 103. *Leider ohne Worte*—by Mendelssohn, first book, referred to and analyzed, 104. *Phantasiestücke*—by Schumann, referred to and analyzed, 105.

I. ÉTUDE, may be written in any form, 111; simple Binary and simple Ternary most common, 111; examples by Czerny of the most elementary kind of Étude—no complete form, 107; example by Cramer analyzed, 108; its rhythmic construction, 108; example by Steibelt analyzed, 109; example by Henselt, 110; the Studies of Chopin, Henselt, Heller, and Clementi, 111.

II. PRELUDE, defined, 113; meaning of the word, 113; various application of the name, 112. (*a*) *Its simplest form*—example by Bach, 113; example by Handel, 114; example by Bach, its harmonic and rhythmic construction, 115; example by Bach, its harmonic and rhythmic construction, 116. (*b*) *In the larger Binary form*—examples referred to by Bach, 117. (*c*) *Organ preludes of Bach*—the preludes founded on chorales; examples referred to, 118; the Larger organ preludes, 119; example by Bach analyzed, 120-123; its rhythmic construction, 121-123; employment of the larger Binary form, 120. (*d*) *The largest forms*, 124; examples referred to by Bach, 124; use of Fugato, 125; the Preludes of Beethoven, Mendelssohn, and Chopin, 126.

III. FUGUE. Fugue form a modification of simple Ternary, 130-133; Exposition and Counter-exposition, 128; the Subject and Answer, 128; the Episode, 129; Modulations, 129; Middle entries, 129; Return to key of tonic, 129.

Instrumental and vocal music—difference between, 7.

Instruments, musical, two classes of, 8.

Intermezzo (*see* Indefinite Forms, III.).

Introduction (*see* Indefinite Forms, IV.).

Irregular rondos (*see* Rondo Forms, I. and II.).

Keys for Episodes in Older rondo form, 184; in Modern rondo form, 391.
Keys for movements of Ancient suite, 46; Modern suite, 474, 99.
Keys for Second subjects in Sonata form, 240-247.
Keys for various movements of Cyclic forms, 448-456.

Lieder ohne Worte—Mendelssohn's first book analyzed, 104.
Link and Bridge Passage, difference between, 217.

Madrigal (*see* Vocal Forms, VI.).
Manuals of the organ (*see* Organ, I.).
March (*see* Dance Forms, VIII.).
Marche aux flambeaux (*see* Dance Forms, IX.).
Mass (*see* Vocal Forms, VII.).
Mazurka (*see* Dance Forms, X.).
Means of development, 306 (*see* Sonata Form, II.).
Metamorphosis of themes, examples, 482, 484, 485.
Mezzo-soprano voice, compass of, 525.
Minuet, the Old and Modern (*see* Dance Forms, XI.).
Minuets, in Ternary form—in Rondo form (*see* Dance Forms, XI.).
MIXED FORMS:—Available combinations very numerous, 413; defined, 412. (*a*) Irregular combination of the Older and Modern rondo forms, 414, 415; example by Weber analyzed. (*b*) Combination of the Variation and Older rondo forms; example by Weber analyzed, 416. (*c*) Combination of the Sonata and Rondo forms, 417, 418; example by Mozart analyzed, 417, 418; recapitulation commences with Second subject, 418. (*d*) Sonata movement, with Episode in place of "Free fantasia," example by Beethoven analyzed 419. (*e*) Combination of Ternary with Irregular sonata form; example by Beethoven, 420. (*f*) Combination of Ternary and Older rondo form, example by Beethoven, 421. (*g*) Combination of Sonata and Rondo forms, example by Beethoven, 422. (*h*) A very irregular form, 423; example by Schubert, 423, 424. (*i*) A unique example of irregular form by Schubert, 425, 426.
Modern cyclic forms developed from the Ancient suite, 446.
Modern rondo form (*see* Rondo Form, II.).
Modern sonata form (*see* Sonata Form).
Modern suites (*see* Dance Forms, XII., and Cyclic Forms, VII.).
MODIFIED SONATA FORMS:—defined, 345.
I. ABRIDGED SONATA FORM. A binary form, 347; defined, 346; exposition never repeated, 359; how it differs from the Old sonata form, 347; its employment in cyclic works, 348; no development, 346; ornamentation of subjects in recapitulation, 353. (*a*) *Example of slow movement* by Beethoven analyzed, 348-353; exposition immediately followed by the recapitulation, 346, 350; second subject not divisible into sections, 352; the ornamentation of subjects in the recapitulation, 353; the Coda, 351. (*b*) *Example of slow movement* by Beethoven analyzed, employment of the link, 354; the Coda, 354. (*c*) *Example of slow movement* by Mozart, no bridge passage, 356. (*d*) *Example of quick movement* by Mendelssohn analyzed, 357, 358; a long Coda, 358. *II. CONCERTO.* Defined, 370; form of the Modern concerto fixed by Mozart and adopted by Beethoven, Weber, and Spohr, 370; modern meaning of the word, 370; old meaning of the word, 370. (*a*) *The Double exposition*, 371; difference between the two expositions, 372, 373; first exposition for orchestra alone, 371; second exposition for Solo instrument, 371; examples referred to by Mozart and Beethoven, 373; the practice of Mozart, 374, 375; the practice of Beethoven, 376; the Solo instrument—its entry, 379. (*b*), (*c*) *Development and recapitulation*—The cadenza—defined, 381; introduced on second inversion of tonic chord, 381; or, sometimes on a dominant seventh chord, 381. *The Modern concerto form* innovation by Mendelssohn, 382; the double exposition dispensed with, 382; effect of this on the form—

adoption of this form by Schumann and Brahms, 382.
III. OVERTURE. Derivation of the word, 361; defined, 361; its old form, 361. *Various forms used for*—Abridged sonata form, 362; Modern sonata form, 362; Old sonata form, 362, 363; the Fugal, 363, 367; the Overtures of Mozart and Beethoven, examples referred to, 363-365; the Overtures of Weber, Spohr, and Mendelssohn, examples referred to, 367, 368. *Modern opera overture*, 369; various methods of writing, 369; (i) *in Regular form*, examples referred to by Weber, 369; (ii) *in Irregular form*, examples referred to by Hérold and Rossini, 369.
IV. SONATINA. Defined, 383, 384; derivation of the word, 383; examples by Kuhlau analyzed, 384; sonata form sometimes abandoned, 386; vague use of the name, 383, 385, 386.
Modulation in composition, 135.
Motett (*see* Vocal Forms, VIII.).
Musette (*see* Dance Forms, IV. and VI.).
Music, vocal, different kinds of, 9.
Music, evolution of, 1-3.
Musical instruments, two classes of, 8.
Mutation stops (*see* Organ, II.).

Older rondo form (*see* Rondo Form, I.).
Old sonata form (*see* Sonata Form).
Opera, 563.
Opera overtures, 369.
Operatic fantasias and transcriptions (*see* Indefinite Forms, II. (*e*)).
Oratorio, 563.
ORGAN (THE):—Composition pedals and knobs, 505; defined, 487; varieties of organ tone, 503.
I. THE MANUALS. Their compass, 487, 488; the Great, Swell, Choir, Solo, and Echo organs, 487.
II. THE STOPS OR REGISTERS. *Compound stops*—defined, 493; Sesquialtera, Cornet, Mixture, Furniture, 493; object of these stops, 493; voicing, 493. Defined, 488; difference in "pitch" of the various stops, 489, 490; difference in *pitch* depends upon the length of the pipe, 489, 490, 495; difference in *quality* upon the shape of the pipe, 495; *Double* stops—16-feet stops, 491; 8-feet stops—the unison stops, 489; 8-feet stops and 8-feet tone, 489; *Flue stops* defined, 494; *Foundation* stops defined, 491. *Mutation stops*, defined, 492; the Twelfth, 492; the Quint or double twelfth, 492. *Octave* stops, defined, 490; open pipes and stopped pipes, defined, 489, 491; *Reed stops*, defined, 494; 16-feet stops and 16-feet "tone," 491; unison stops the 8-feet stops, 489.
III. THE PEDAL ORGAN. Its compass, 496; double stops—32-feet, 496; 16-feet stops the unison stops, 496.
ORGAN MUSIC:—*How to write*—Composition pedals and knobs, 505; Expression, crescendo, and diminuendo, 501; Manuals, combination of, 499; how to indicate, 498; Pedal passages, heel and toe, 497; pedal points, organ point, 502; pedal solos, 507; pedals not to be used continuously, 506; phrasing, tempo rubato, 501; Polyphonic writing, 508; sustaining power of the organ, 500; three staves mostly used in organ music, occasionally four are used, 498. *Variety of organ tone*—how to indicate, 503, 504; how to vary, 504; use of the *Doubles*, 504.
ORGAN MUSIC, FORMS IN:—
THE ORGAN SONATA. Bach's organ sonatas, 510; in simple Binary or simple Ternary form, example, 510; Mendelssohn's Organ sonatas, 511, 512; "Sonata form" in, 511, 512; variety in the movements as contrasted with Pianoforte sonatas, 513; Rheinberger's Organ sonatas, 513; Organ symphonies of C.-M. Widor, 514; smaller forms of organ music, 515; duets, 516; clap-trap, 517.
Organ preludes (*see* Instrumental Forms, II.).
Organ Sonata (*see* Organ Music).
Overture (*see* Modified Sonata Forms, III.).

Part-song (*see* Vocal Forms, IX.).
Passacaglia (*see* Variation Forms, VII.).
Passepied (*see* Dance Forms, XIII.).
Pedal organ (*see* Organ, III.).
Pedal point, defined, 502.

Phantasiestücke of Schumann referred to and analyzed, 105.

PIANOFORTE (THE):—Its inherent defects, 15; most useful of instruments to the composer, 14; uniformity of tone-quality, 16.

THE PEDALS. (*a*) *The Damper pedal*, 21; increases the volume of tone—the reason, 24; its mechanism explained, 22, 23; its principal uses, 27; examples by Schumann, 27; Kullak, 28; Heller, 28; sympathetic resonance, 25, 26; use of, to obtain wider positions of harmony, 29. (*b*) *The Una corda pedal*, 30; its mechanism explained, 30; its use, 30; examples referred to, 30.

Pianoforte pieces of small dimensions mostly written in simple Binary or simple Ternary form, 106.

PIANOFORTE WRITING:—Broken chords and arpeggios, treatment of, 35; composing at the piano, 42; consecutive Fifths, 37, 38; consecutive Octaves, 32; dissonances in arpeggios should be resolved in the same octave in which they are taken, 39; doubling of dissonant notes, 32; doubling of leading note, 32; interlacing of hands, 18; examples by Liszt, 19; passages in only two or three parts—the number of parts, 33, 34; Polyphonic writing, 33; position of the harmonies in, 31; relaxation of the strict laws of part-writing in, 36-38; repetition of melody notes as accompaniment, 28; sustained melodies *best* in medium part of the instrument, examples referred to, 20; example by Beethoven of sustained melody at high pitch, 20; technique of the instrument to be considered, 41; treatment of isolated low notes in the bass, 40; variation in the number of parts, 32.

Polonaise, or polacca (*see* Dance Forms, XIV.).

Polyphonic writing in organ music, 508; in pianoforte music, 33.

Prelude (*see* Instrumental Forms [the smaller], II.).

Quint (*see* Mutation Stops, Organ, II.).

Recapitulation (*see* Sonata Form, III.).

Recitative (*see* Vocal Forms, X.).

Relaxation of the strict laws of part-writing in Pianoforte writing, 36-38.

Rigaudon (*see* Dance Forms, XV.).

RONDO FORM, an extension of Ternary form, 187, 188; defined, 179; found in both instrumental and vocal music, 179; meaning and derivation of the word "Rondo," 179; "Rondeau" and "Couplets," 179; rondo originally a dance, described, 179; Rondo and Sonata form—difference between, 216; two varieties—the Older and Modern rondo form, 180.

I. THE OLDER RONDO FORM. (*a*) *The old form*—example by Bach referred to and analyzed, 185, 186; example by Couperin—*the Principal subject*, 182; *the Episodes*, 182; their number, 183; keys, 184; the final episode, necessity for contrast, 184. (*b*) *The more modern form*, 187; an essential characteristic of Rondo form, 188; change of time for one of the episodes allowable, 205; defined, 187, 188; developed from the simple Ternary form, 187, 188; double variations sometimes in Rondo form, 211; episodes almost invariably in some different key to principal subject, 190; *Irregular rondos*—example by Beethoven, 210; keys for the episodes, 190, 191; Minuet or Scherzo with two Trios in rondo form, 189, 190; some pieces incorrectly described as rondos—examples referred to, 212; *Three episodes* sometimes found—examples referred to, 206; variation of principal subject on repetition, 197; example by Haydn analyzed, 192-195; example by Dussek referred to and analyzed, 196, 197; example by Mozart referred to and analyzed, 199, 200; examples by Beethoven referred to and analyzed, 201-204; examples by Weber, Schubert, and Schumann referred to, 205; examples by Mozart referred to and analyzed, 207-209.

II. THE MODERN RONDO FORM. (Rondo-sonata form)—A modification of the "Sonata-form," 387; defined, 388, 396; always met with either as an independent piece or as the Finale of a Cyclic form. 411;

thematic development sometimes takes the place of the episode, 403. (*a*) *The Exposition*, always ends in the tonic key, 393; first subject invariably repeated at the end of the exposition, 393; the whole of the exposition never repeated, 393. *The First subject*—its length, 388; its rhythmic form, 388; its song-like character—examples, 389; is followed by a *Bridge passage*, 390. *The Second subject*—difference between second subject and episode, 391; followed by *Codetta*, 392; generally shorter than in sonata-form, 392; how it ends, 392; key of, 390. *Repetition of first subject*, 393; exposition ends in tonic key, 393. (*b*) *The Episode*—change of tempo sometimes found—example referred to by Beethoven, 394; end of episode contrived to lead to the recapitulation, 395; in a different key from first and second subjects, 394; keys usually chosen for —practice of Beethoven, Schubert, and Mozart, 394; thematic development sometimes takes the place of episode, 403. (*c*) *The Recapitulation* –first subject sometimes ornamented, 395; the *Coda*, 395. (*d*) *Examples analyzed*—by Beethoven, 397-399; by Beethoven — thematic developments, 400-402. (*e*) *Rondos without episode* —examples by Beethoven referred to and analyzed, 403; example by Schubert analyzed, 404-408. (*f*) *Irregular rondos*—example by Beethoven analyzed, 409, 410.

Rondo-sonata form (*see* Rondo-form, II.).

Saltarello (*see* Dance Forms, XVIII.).

Sarabande (*see* Dance Forms, XVI.).

Scena (*see* Vocal Forms, XI.).

Scherzo (*see* Dance Forms, XVII.).

SECOND SUBJECT—in modern rondo form (*see* Rondo Form, II.);—in sonata form (*see* Sonata Form, I.).

Serenade (*see* Cyclic Forms, VIII.).

Smaller instrumental forms (*see* Instrumental Forms).

SONATA FORM—and Modern rondo-form, difference between, 390, 393; and Older rondo form, difference between, 216; best models—Haydn, Mozart, Beethoven, and Mendelssohn, 344; derivation and original meaning of the word "Sonata"—its modern sense, 214; first movement form, 215; infinite variety of sonata form, 344; used not only in sonatas, but in Trios, Quartetts, Quintetts, and Symphonies, and also with modifications in Concertos and Overtures, 215. *The old Sonata form*—defined, 217; difference between Sonata form and a Rondo, 216; example by Scarlatti analyzed, 217-220; later examples of the old form referred to by Clementi, Haydn, Mozart, Schubert, 222; this form now entirely obsolete, 222.

THE MODERN SONATA FORM. Difference between the *Old* and *Modern* form, 224; its introduction due to C. P. E. Bach and Haydn, 223; the modern form is a modified Ternary, 224; the older form is a large Binary, 224; the three divisions of a Sonata form are: (i) the *Exposition*, (ii) the *Development*, (iii) the *Recapitulation* 225; unity of style, how obtained, 261.

I. THE EXPOSITION. Defined 225, 268-274; its three parts are: (*a* the First subject, (*b*) the Bridge pas sage, (*c*) the Second subject, 225 repetition of, *not* obligatory, 267. (*a*) *The First subject*—examples ending with full cadence in tonic key, 225-227; examples by Beethoven, 225; by Haydn, 226; by Schumann, 227; ending with half cadence in tonic key, examples by Mozart, 228; by Beethoven, 229; by Beethoven, 230, 231; how to determine the limits of the First subject, 233; *Introduction* consisting of a few bars sometimes precedes the first subject, 232; long first subjects, examples referred to by Beethoven, 231. (*b*) *The Bridge passage*, defined, 233, 270; example by Mozart analyzed, 234-236; frequently begins with repetition of the commencement of the first subject, 235; how to know where it begins, 233; immediately follows the first subject, 233; its course of modulation, 237; length of, 237, 238; material of, 237; usually ends on the dominant harmony of the key of the second subject, 236. (*c*) *The Second subject*—change of mode in, examples referred to by Beethoven, 257 ; change of tonic in, examples referred to by Beethoven, 258, 259 ; defined, 239, 271 ; examples of, by Haydn, 250, 251 ; by Beethoven, 253 ; by Mendelssohn, 255 ; by Beethoven, 259 ; how to determine the limits of the second subject, 265, 266 ; in remote key, examples referred to by Beethoven and Schubert, 262 ; in two keys, examples by Mendelssohn, Clementi, and Dussek, 255 ; incidental modulation in, 260. *Keys for*, (i) in Major movements, 240-243 ; (ii) in Minor movements, 240, 244-247 ; length of, 239, 248, 271 ; material of, example by Haydn, 250, 251 ; modulation in, 253, 255, 256 ; Sections of, 248, 249 ; their key, 253 ; subdominant key not advisable for—why, 247 ; unity of style, how obtained, 261 ; use of flat keys for, 247. *The Codetta*, example by Beethoven, 266 ; repetition of exposition *not* obligatory, 267.

II. THE DEVELOPMENT. A key once quitted should not be again introduced, except transitionally, 305 ; *Contrapuntal* development, examples referred to by Haydn, Beethoven, and Mozart, 292 ; *Course of modulation*, 304, 305 ; examples by Beethoven, 281 ; by Haydn, 285 ; defined, 276 ; free fantasia, consisting *partly* of episode, 296 ; consisting *entirely* of episode, 297 ; how it ends, 308 ; freedom of the form in the second and third parts of a movement in sonata form, 275 ; general principles for the construction of the "Free fantasia," 301-306 ; how it differs from the second part of a genuine Ternary form, 277 ; how to end the free fantasia, 308 ; examples by Haydn, 309, 310 ; by Beethoven, 311, 312 ; by Mozart, 312 ; *Incidental episode*, example by Beethoven, 294 ; independent episodes, example by Beethoven, 295 ; introduction of episode, 293, 307 ; keys of the first and second subjects best avoided in the free fantasia, 302 ; the reason for this, 303 ; material used for development, example by Beethoven, 279-281 ; example by Haydn, 282-285 ; means of development, 306 ; not to remain too long in any one new key—why, 304 ; return to the tonic key, how to manage, 304 ; slow introduction to a sonata sometimes made use of in the "free fantasia," examples by Beethoven referred to, 298-300 ; example by Clementi analyzed, 299 ; subdominant key, effect of, 304 ; *Thematic* development, 286 ; example by Haydn analyzed, 282, 283 ; example by Beethoven analyzed, 287-290 ; working of small fragments of themes, 291.

III. THE RECAPITULATION. Defined, 313 ; immediately follows the "free fantasia, 315. (*a*) *Regular recapitulations—First subject :* sometimes reappears with ornamentation, example by Beethoven referred to, 315 ; sometimes accompanied with a new counterpoint, 315 ; example by Haydn, 315 ; examples referred to by Mendelssohn and Beethoven, 315. *Bridge passage*—generally modified, 316 ; occasionally unaltered, example referred to by Haydn, 316 ; sometimes omitted altogether, examples by Beethoven and Weber, 317. *Second subject :* keys for, in movements in Major keys, examples by Beethoven, 318, 319 ; when in more than one key, 320, 321 ; keys for, in movements in Minor keys, 322-326 ; when in two keys, 326. (*b*) *Irregular recapitulations*, 327. *First subject :* abridged : examples by Schubert, Mendelssohn, Clementi, and Dussek, 330 ; beginning in a different key to that in which it ends, examples referred to by Weber, 332 ; extended, example by Beethoven, 331 ; *not* in the tonic key—the object of this, examples by Clementi, Schubert, and Hummel, 328 ; omitted altogether, examples referred to by Clementi and Dussek, 330. *Second subject :* alteration of second subject more frequently met with than that of the first subject, examples referred to by Haydn and Dussek, 333 ; examples referred to by Beethoven and Dussek, 334 ; examples referred to by Haydn and Mozart, 335 ;

exceptional key for, example referred to by Beethoven, 336; occasionally recapitulation of a minor movement in tonic major, 337; example referred to by Spohr and Weber, 337; preceding the first subject, 329; examples referred to by Mozart, Haydn, Spohr, and Dvořàk, 329. *Very irregular recapitulation*, 338; examples referred to by Hummel and Schumann, 338. (*c*) *The Coda*, 339; alteration of *tempo* in, 343; examples referred to by Beethoven and Schubert, 343; entirely *new themes* introduced in, examples by Schumann and Mendelssohn, 341, 342; follows the recapitulation, 339; generally found in the works of modern composers, 339, 343; of variable length, 339; themes not previously treated sometimes developed in, 339; example by Beethoven, 340.

Sonata forms, modified (*see* Modified Sonata Form).

Sonata, organ (*see* Organ Music).

Sonatina (*see* Modified Sonata Forms, IV.).

Songs (*see* Vocal Forms, XII.).

Soprano voice, compass of, 525.

Strophic song (*see* Vocal Forms, XII.).

Stops or registers of the organ (*see* Organ, II.).

String Quartett (*see* Cyclic Forms, IX.).

Suite, ancient (*see* Dance Forms, II.).

Suite, modern (*see* Dance Forms, XII., and Cyclic Forms, VII.).

Symphonic poem (*see* Cyclic Forms, X.).

Symphony form or sonata form, 215.

Tarantella (*see* Dance Forms, XVIII.).

Tempo rubato, 501.

Tenor voice, compass of, 525.

TERNARY FORM APPLIED TO:—Fugue, 130-133; Sonata, 224; the Older rondo form, 187, 188; the Modern rondo form, 396.

Thematic development (*see* Sonata Form, II.).

Three-movement form (*see* Cyclic Forms. II.).

Toccata (*see* Indefinite Forms, V.).

Transcription (*see* Indefinite Forms, II. *e*)

Trio, original meaning of the word, as applied in Minuet and Trio, Scherzo and Trio, 69.

Two-movement form (*see* Cyclic Forms, I.).

Typical cyclic form and its variations, 444 and 447.

Una corda pedal (*see* Pianoforte—Pedals).

Unity of character in the different movements of cyclic works, 445, 470-472.

Valse de salon (*see* Dance Forms, XIX.).

VARIATION FORMS, as an independent form, 136; change of mode in, 161; change of time in, 153; Coda, 153, 162, 176; diversity of these forms, 177; incidental variations, 136; Introduction — examples referred to by Beethoven and Chopin, 172; length of the sentences, 176, IV. *Means of varying a theme*—(*a*) Ornamentation of the melody, 174, I.; (*b*) Changing the harmony, 174, II.; (*c*) Changing the tempo and rhythmic figuration, 175, III.; *older* and *newer* style in, 148; *strict* and *free* variations, 147; the theme, its form, etc., 137, 156, 173; variation defined, 137; variety of key and time, 157.

I. AIR WITH VARIATIONS, as an Independent piece, 143; as a movement of a Cyclic work, 143; cadences in, 145; change of key, 152, 157, 161; change of mode, 152, 161; change of time, 153, 157; choice of the theme, 173; cadences in, 145; its character, 145; its form, 144; its length, 144; Coda, 153, 162, 166; defined, 143; final variation and coda, 166; "*Formal*" and "*Characteristic*" variations, 147; long themes—examples referred to by Mozart and Beethoven, 146; *Older* and *Newer* styles of, 148; rhythm of the variations, 166; strict and free variations defined, 147; variations of Mozart—example analyzed, 150-153; example referred to, 154; variations of Beethoven, 155; example analyzed, 156-162; variations of Schubert, Weber, and Mendelssohn, 164; variations of Schumann, Brahms, and Raff, 165; variety of cadence, 145.

II. CANONIC VARIATIONS, examples referred to by Bach and Beethoven, 167.

III. CHACONNE, defined, 139; example by Handel, 139; examples by

Bach, 140; *Modern* example by Beethoven, 142.
IV. DOUBLE VARIATIONS, defined, 168; example analyzed by Beethoven, 168.
V. GROUND BASS, defined, 138; example by Purcell, 138.
VI. IN VOCAL MUSIC. Examples referred to by Auber and Beethoven, 171.
VII. PASSACAGLIA, defined, 139; derivation of the word, 139; example by Bach, 141.
VIII. VARIATION ON TWO THEMES, defined, 169; example by Haydn referred to and analyzed, 169; examples by Haydn and Beethoven referred to, 170.

Variation in number of parts in pianoforte writing, 32.

Verse—meaning of the word when found in Anthems, etc., 556.

VOCAL FORMS :—
I. ANTHEM, both Homophonic and Polyphonic, 556; decani and cantoris, meaning of, 556; form largely influenced by the text, 557; full,—verse, meaning of, 556; orchestral accompaniment occasionally employed, 557; organ accompaniment mostly used, 557; variety of form in, 556, 557.
II. CANTATA, ORATORIO, OPERA. Indefiniteness of the larger vocal forms, 565; works to study in oratorio and opera, 563.
III. CHURCH CANTATA. Numerous examples by Bach, 558; of German origin, 558; orchestral accompaniments in, 558; written for solo and chorus, 558.
IV. CHURCH SERVICE, defined, 559; Fugal writing—choice of subjects, examples, 559.
V. GLEE, defined, 551; its form—examples referred to by Spofforth, Stevens, Paxton, Webbe, 552.
VI. MADRIGAL. A form now nearly obsolete, 554; continuity one of its chief features, 554; mostly written to secular words, 555; Polyphonic in style, 554; the best models, 555.
VII. MASS, defined, 562; examples referred to by Cherubini, Schubert, Mozart, Beethoven, Haydn, 562.
VIII. MOTETT. A special feature—the accompaniment doubling the voices, 555; examples by Haydn and Mendelssohn, 555; mostly written to sacred words, 555; similar in style to the Madrigal, 555; sometimes written with free orchestral accompaniment, 555.
IX. PART-SONG, defined, 553; difference between Glee and Part-song, 553; Homophonic in character, 553; examples referred to, 553.
X. RECITATIVE. Accompanied recitative—example, 536; Arioso, defined, 537; Choral recitative, defined, 539; examples referred to by Handel and Mendelssohn, 539; defined, 536; Plain recitative, 536; Recitative *a tempo* defined, 536, 537; Recitativo secco, 536, 537; two varieties, 536.
XI. SCENA, as an independent form, 548; defined, 546; in Opera, 546; the *Modern* form, 546; examples referred to, 546; the *Old* form, 546; examples referred to, 546.
XII. SONGS. *Binary form* in—examples referred to, 540; form dependent on the words, 541; *Older rondo form* in, 543; examples referred to by Bach, 543; by Mozart, 544: *Sonata form* in—examples referred to by Mozart, 545; Strophic song, defined, 540; *Ternary form* in, 542; Through-composed song, "durchcomponirtes Lied," 541.

VOCAL MUSIC :—Accent in the poetry to be carefully noted, 520; compass and quality of voices to be carefully considered, 524. *Duets, Trios, Quartetts*, 550; different kinds of, 9; example of ineffective writing for tenor by Schuman, 527; faulty setting of words to music—example by John Davy, 520, 522; by Balfe, 522; by Handel, 523; hints on writing for the voice, 527-533; rhythmic difficulties — cross accents—examples, syncopation—examples, 532; setting words to music, 520; unvocal writing, 530; use of the upper notes of the voice, 526-529; bad example by Beethoven, 528; vague tonality—use of augmented and chromatic intervals, 530; writing

accompaniments, 549. *Vocal music without words.* Bouche fermée—examples by Auber, Gounod, Grieg, 535; solfeggi and vocalises, 534.
Vocal music—Variation forms in (*see* Variation Form, VI.).
VOICE (THE):—Compass of, the soprano, mezzo-soprano, contralto, tenor, baritone, bass, 525; the Male alto, *page* 286 (note); the different registers, 526.
Voice—Unvocal writing, 530.

Waltz (*see* Dance Forms, XIX.).
Writing accompaniments to Vocal Music, 549.

MUSICAL ILLUSTRATIONS.

AUBER, "Masaniello," 92.

BACH, Cantata, "Ich habe genug," 543; Cantata, "Ich hatte viel Bekümmerniss," 561; Choral, "Wo soll ich fliehenhin," 507; 'Französische Ouverture,' 68, 69; Organ Fugue in D major, 497; Organ Fugue in G minor, 508; Organ Prelude in F minor, 120; Organ Sonata, No. 2, in C minor, 510; Passacaglia, in C minor (Organ), 141; Prelude to Fugue in A minor, 113; Prelude and Fughetta in G, 223; Suite in B minor, 87; Suites Anglaises, No. 3, 61; Suites Anglaises, No. 4, 53; Suites Anglaises, No. 6, 57, 58; Suites Françaises, No. 3, 71; Suites Françaises, No. 5, 50, 55; Wohltemperirtes Clavier, Prelude 1, 115; Wohltemperirtes Clavier, Prelude 6, 116.

BEETHOVEN, Andante in F, 201; Bagatelle, Op. 119, No. 11, 20; 'Egmont,' 98; 'King Stephen,' 528; Mass in D, 532; Rondo in C, Op. 51, No. 1, 202; Six Variations, Op. 34, 156-162; Sonata, Op. 2, No. 1, 419; Sonata, Op. 7, 36, 279, 280, 340, 389; Sonata, Op. 10, No. 1, 349, 350; Sonata, Op. 10, No. 2, 225, 331; Sonata, Op. 10, No. 3, 259, 260, 266; Sonata, Op. 14, No. 1, 296, 398, 399, Sonata, Op. 22, 400-402; Sonata, Op. 27, No. 1, 403; Sonata, Op. 31, No. 1, 38, 389; Sonata, Op. 53, 204, 229, 291; Sonata, Op. 54, 421, 431; Sonata, Op. 101, 292; Sonata, Op. 106, 31; Sonata, Op. 109, 168; Sonata Pathétique, 35, 298; Symphony, Second, 311; Third, 253, 295; Fourth, 294; Eighth, 230; Ninth, 531; Pastoral, 287, 288-290; Thirty-two Variations, 142.

BRAHMS, "Ein deutsches Requiem," 561; 'Schicksalslied,' 533.

CHERUBINI, First Mass, 561.

CHOPIN, Mazurka, Op. 6, No. 3, 85 Mazurka, Op. 7, No. 3, 84.

CLEMENTI, Sonata, Op. 34, No. 2, 299.

COUPERIN, Pièces de Clavecin, Ordre 18, 181; Pièces de Clavecin, Book I. 54, 64.

CRAMER, Studies, No. 4, 108.

CZERNY, 101 Exercises, No. 1, 107; No 38, 107.

DAVY, JOHN, 'The Pilot,' 520-522.

DUSSEK, Sonata, Op. 10, No. 2, 334.

GOUNOD, Cecilian Mass, 535.

GRAUN, Passion Oratorio, 561

HANDEL, 'Alexander Balus,' 560; 'Belshazzar,' 561; 'Ottone,' 66; 'Solomon,' 523; Suites de Pièces, No. 1, 114; Suites de Pièces, Book II., 139; 'Terpsichore,' 59, 60.

HAYDN, 'Creation,' 532; Quartett, Op. 50, No. 2, 292; Quartett, Op. 54, No. 3, 309; Quartett, Op. 64, No. 5, 226; Quartett, Op. 74, No. 1, 250, 251; Quartett, Op. 74, No. 2, 292; Quartett, Op. 76, No. 1, 315; Quartett, Op. 77, No. 1, 333; Sonata in D, No. 7, 192; Sonata in E flat, 32; Symphony in D, 310; Symphony in G, 282, 283; Third Mass, 561.

HELLER, S., Études, Op. 45, 28.

HENSELT, Étude, Op. 2, No. 3, 110.

KESSLER, J. C., Étude in C sharp minor, 40.

KUHLAU, Sonatina, Op. 55, No. 2, 384.

KULLAK, "Les Fleurs Animees," No. 5, 28.

LISZT, Transcription of Beethoven's Symphony in C minor 19; "Les Preludes," 484, 485.

MENDELSSOHN, First Organ Sonata, 498, 499; 114th Psalm, 561; Presto Agitato, 357, 358; Sonata, Op. 58, 29, 342; Symphony, Fourth, 295; Trio in C minor, Op. 66, 255.

MOZART, Concerto in C, 375; Concerto in E flat, No. 9, 379; Concerto in G, No. 17, 375; Concerto in C minor, No. 24, 374; Fantasia in C minor, 437; Horn Quintett, 335; Piano Quartett in G minor, 312; Rondo in D, 212; Rondo in B flat, 212; Sonata in B flat, 389; Sonata in C major, 207; Sonata in D, 292, 297, 329; Sonata in D, No. 17, 417; Sonata in E flat, 389; Sonata in F, No. 12, 355, 356; Sonata in F, 237; Symphony in G minor, 228, 234, 322; Trio in E flat, 208; Variations on "Je suis Lindor," 150-153; Vespers, 561; Waltz, 78.

PURCELL, 'Dido and Æneas,' 138.

RAFF, Fantasie-Sonate, Op. 168, 440.

SAINT-SAËNS, Third Concerto, 482.

SCARLATTI, Sonata in G, 217.

SCHUBERT, Impromptu, Op. 142, No. 1, 423; Polonaise, Op. 75, No. 1, 88; Quartett in E flat, Op. 125, No. 1, 472; Rondo, Op. 107, 404-407; Sonata in A, 389; 12 Deutsch Tänze, No. 2, 79; 20 Waltzer, No. 10, 80; Unfinished Symphony, 238

SCHUMANN, 'Das Paradies und die Peri,' 527; Etudes Symphoniques, Op. 13, 27; First Symphony, 227, 341; Humoreske, Op. 20, 17, 18; Symphony in C major, 470.

STEIBELT, Op. 78, No. 68, 109.

WEBER, 'Preciosa,' 91; Sonata in D minor, Op 49, 414-416; Variations on "Vien quà, Dorina Bella," Op. 7, 37.